Approaches to
Training and
Development

Approaches to Training and Development

Third Edition

Dugan Laird

**Third Edition Revised and Updated
by Sharon S. Naquin and
Elwood F. Holton III**

New Perspectives in Organizational Learning,
Performance, and Change

PERSEUS
PUBLISHING

A Member of the Perseus Books Group

Many of the designations used by manufacturers and sellers to distinguish their products are claimed as trademarks. Where those designations appear in this book, and where Perseus Publishing was aware of a trademark claim, the designations have been printed in initial capital letters.

Library of Congress Control Number: 2003103395
ISBN 0-7382-0698-9

Perseus Publishing is a member of the Perseus Books Group.
Find us on the World Wide Web at http://www.perseuspublishing.com.

Perseus Publishing books are available at special discounts for bulk purchases in the U.S. by corporations, institutions, and other organizations. For more information, please contact the Special Markets Department at the Perseus Books Group, 11 Cambridge Center, Cambridge, MA 02142, or call (800) 255-1514 or (617) 252-5298, or e-mail j.mccrary@perseusbooks.com.

Set in 10.5-point Minion by the Perseus Books Group

First printing, June 2003

1 2 3 4 5 6 7 8 9 10—06 05 04 03

Publisher's Note

Organizations are living systems, in a constant state of dynamic evolution. *New Perspectives in Organizational Learning, Performance, and Change* is designed to showcase the most current theory and practice in human resource and organizational development, exploring all aspects of the field—from performance management to adult learning to corporate culture. Integrating cutting-edge research and innovative management practice, this library of titles will serve as an essential resource for human resource professionals, educators, students, and managers in all types of organizations.

The series editorial board includes leading academics and practitioners whose insights are shaping the theory and application of human resource development and organizational design.

Series Editor
Jerry W. Gilley, Colorado State University

Editorial Board

Reid Bates, Louisiana State University

Gloria A. Regalbuto Bentley,
Ohio Principals' Leadership Academy

Laura L. Bierema, University of Georgia

Nathaniel W. Boughton,
Performance Consulting Group

Jamie L. Callahan,
Texas A&M University

Neal Chalofsky,
George Washington University

Patrick Combs, WAITT Radio

Joseph Davidson, Deloitte & Touche

Peter J. Dean, University of Pennsylvania

Ann Maycunich Gilley,
Trilogy Consulting Group

Tim Hatcher, University of Louisville

Barbara Hinton,
University of Arkansas

Erik Hoekstra,
The Harbor Group

Susan A. Lynham,
Texas A&M University

Robert Lingren,
PriceWaterhouseCoopers

Pat McLagan, theRitestuff, Inc.

Hallie Preskill,
University of New Mexico

Nora Ruder, Foremost Insurance

Darlene Russ-Eft,
American Institutes of Research

Darren Short, Perspectives, UK

Douglas Smith,
Florida International University

John Stuart Walton,
London Guildhall University

L. Michael Wykes, Steelcase

Contents

Illustrations

Boxes

Charts

Tables

Why This Book?

Reflections on a Revision

The second edition of this book opened with this statement:

> Revising an old manuscript, I have discovered, can be either exhilarating or grue-some. At its worst, the process must be like giving artificial respiration to the very, very dead. At its best, it's like attending commencement exercises for a favorite offspring—and discovering to your glee and surprise that the youngster has a great deal of sense and is part of an expanding and maturing university. Fortunately, revising *Approaches to Training and Development* has been one of those happy, "commencement" kinds of experience.

In his opening note to the second edition of this book, Dugan Laird eloquently captured the agony and the ecstasy of creating a new edition. However, our task was even larger as we approached this third edition. First, because seventeen years had passed since the last revision, the potential existed for lots of revising. Second, and more important, we had been entrusted with a classic. Despite its age, many still consider this book a "must read" for someone new in training and development. It is an awesome responsibility to be handed a classic and to be entrusted with preserving what made the book so successful while making revisions so that another generation finds it timely.

We were pleasantly surprised to find that much of what Dugan had to say seventeen years ago is still quite appropriate. As an HRD (human resource development) thinker, he was well ahead of his time. Much of his advice, which may have seemed more radical in 1985, is mainstream thinking now. For example, his performance-oriented approach to training is more important today than ever.

In addition, this book is targeted at readers who need to become well grounded in the basic *how-tos* of our field. Thus, the core of what Dugan offers as best practices still fits today. We have worked hard to preserve the timeless wisdom of a skilled practitioner while infusing some new thinking that expands on his foundation.

In 1985, Dugan also said, "First of all, training and development is alive and well and growing. In fact, it has grown to be a part of a much larger arena than envisioned when this book first appeared in 1978."

We suspect he would be quite happy to know that the trend continues to this day. Not since World War II has HRD/T&D (training and development) enjoyed the status, demand, and prestige that it does today. In fact, the old pattern that training would be the first budget cut in lean times is no longer true today. HRD/T&D is stronger, more vibrant, and growing faster as a profession than ever before.

Interestingly, the academic research community in HRD has grown quite significantly since the last edition of this book. The volume of research produced by HRD professors is enormously greater than it was in 1985. Much of what Laird offered at that time has been supported and strengthened by new research. So, although we have changed about 50 percent of the book, the core of Laird's advice and voice remains.

An especially challenging part of this revision was Laird's writing style. He had a unique, engaging, and sometimes irreverent voice that is impossible to duplicate. We worked hard to preserve as much of his voice as possible because so many found it enjoyable to read. To do that, we decided that it would be okay for readers to "hear" different voices in the book; that is, making the book speak in one voice would have meant stripping the book of Laird's personality and substituting our own. That just didn't make sense. Instead, we let you hear his voice and ours, trusting that you will enjoy the interplay between them.

Human Resource Development (HRD) and Training and Development (T&D)

Dugan Laird faced the same dilemma in 1985 that we did in 2002: "In fact, HRD is a beguiling concept; it tempts one to re-title the book to cover that larger spectrum. But the book really deals with the training and development function, so the title remains the same—as does the abbreviation T&D—for the people we are and the things we do."

As professors of human resource development at Louisiana State University, we were *very* tempted to change the label used in the book to HRD. This book has always been about more than just training, as evidenced by chapters on what to do when training isn't the answer as well as information on organization development. Yet, we have opted to continue to use the "T&D" label. As Dugan concluded in 1985, the book is predominantly about training. We join him in rejoicing that training is part of the wider umbrella of HRD. We also know that training and development remains a very large part of HRD practice. Thus, we take pride in continuing to focus this book primarily on the training and development function, which is responsible for the individual learning in organizations.

Philosophy of This Book

We didn't change the basic philosophy Laird brought to the book:

> This book pictures what T&D really is and how it operates, answers typical questions about what we do and why and how—offering answers that are more thoughtful than one can improvise in the heat of a workshop or while pressured to leave for the airport. We have tried to be complete enough to be lucid, brief enough to be digestible, solid enough to be believable—but heretical enough to be provocative. Above all, we hope that this book will be a useful needle, jolting readers into creative action, yet sedating them against that inevitable pain which always accompanies caring about growth in others or in organizations.

This is a book about the *practice* of training and development. Although we hope to provoke you to best practices, we are realistic in believing that nobody lives in a world of only best practices. Thus, the practical "survival skills" are still mixed with the pushes to advance your practice. To Laird's thirty-three years of experience we add our thirty-seven collective years. This is the book we wish had been available to us when we started our careers.

How to Read This Book

This book contains many basic ideas that will answer the questions newcomers honestly ask—and old-timers often ought to be asking. So, one might read from cover to cover.

But there are two problems with that. First, the book reflects many approaches—too many to incorporate into a single training system. Therefore, small training departments will need to sort out the useful parts. Then, too, the book uses what Laird called a "spiral system" of organization. It zooms around concepts, defining and describing them the first time they naturally come up in the conversation. It zeroes in on these concepts later, developing them in detail when they're central to the analysis. We hope this technique proves useful, and that the repetition will be balanced by clarity and unity.

The book might also be read by checking chapter titles, then reading only the parts that seem interesting or relevant or momentarily useful.

That brings us to another method: to keep the book on the shelf and read it when problems arise. That strikes us as a smart thing to do with any book—provided, of course, that you've underlined the things you liked, added some items of your own to the lists and charts, and written words of protest beside ideas that didn't digest very well the first time you read them!

Well, these are just a few ideas about making the book useful. Here's hoping that if you've spent the money to own a copy, you'll find some added, personal ways to put the book to work for you and your staff.

ELWOOD F. HOLTON
SHARON S. NAQUIN
Baton Rouge, Louisiana

The Need for Training and Development Departments

How Organizations Perform

Organizations are systems designed to achieve a goal or perform a particular function such as delivering a completed product to a customer. To illustrate our point, we will use a cafeteria analogy to describe the systematic nature of organizational processes. Although the organization as a whole is a system, it is also comprised of built-in subsystems and subprocesses. The subsystems and subprocesses are designed to achieve the subgoals that are necessary to produce the overall output. For instance, the process of delivering the receipt to the customer is a subprocess of the overall goal of the cafeteria.

To continue with our analogy, imagine yourself in line at a cafeteria. You come to the coffee urn and turn the spigot. Out comes some coffee. Presumably, when the liquid went into the machine, it was water—not coffee. When the coffee grounds were put into the machine, they weren't in consumable, drinkable form. The water and the coffee are the material "inputs" to the system called a coffee machine; the "output" is drinkable coffee. But someone had to add the water and the coffee grounds. This person is also an input. Furthermore, the machine will work properly only if these materials are added in the proper amount, in the proper place, and in the proper sequence. There is a technology for the machine and for making the coffee. That technology is a third vital "input" to the system. And after the machine is turned on, it takes a little time for the water to heat and the coffee to percolate; therefore, time is also an "input." So we have identified four necessary inputs to every system: material, people, technology, and time.

When you reach the end of the line, a cash register "outputs" an itemized bill for your meal—but it can do so only if the cashier "inputs" the prices.

Later, when you decide you'd like another cup of coffee with dessert, you tell an attendant, who then brings that second cup to your table. The attendant provides an "output" in the same sense as the coffee machine or the cashier, but this output is different: It's a service rather than a product.

The organizational processes are another component of the organizational systems. Processes represent the series of planned steps involved as an organization progresses toward its final output. The work performed within the system and subsystems transforms the inputs into outputs.

In that cafeteria, in rooms you can't see, some people create recipes and menus; others add up the bills to see how business is going and make sure that all funds are accounted for. These are the people who select the outputs, procure the materials, select the people, and establish the standards. These are the systems and subsystems of the overall processes of the cafeteria. Employees involved are called "managers" and have titles such as President, or Chief Executive Officer (CEO), or General Manager; there will be subsystems with managers for Sales, Manufacturing, Research and Development; there may even be someone called Training and Development Manager.

By definition, every system must have an output. The cafeteria must produce food; its coffee machine must make coffee; its cashier must collect money; the CEO must see that the cafeteria shows a profit. In the same way, the Sales Manager must produce advertisements and campaigns; these, in turn, produce customers. What does the Training and Development Department produce?

Preparing Employees to Perform

Understandably, some organizations' systems and subsystems may be larger and more complicated than others. For instance, the systems and processes used in an industrial manufacturing plant are undoubtedly more intricate than those of the cafeteria described above. Despite the variance in complexity and size, all systems have three basic components: inputs, process, and outputs.

The ability to recognize the systems and subsystems of an organization is an important element in all training and development activities. Training and development exists to promote individual and organizational excellence by providing opportunities to develop workplace skills. The design and implementation of effecting training interventions cannot be accomplished without first identifying the various processes operating within the system. But who is responsible for that task?

The Human Resource Development (HRD) or Training and Development Department (or somebody called the "trainer") is a familiar subgroup in most organizations. Why? Because the people of any organization are like the water put into the coffee machine: For their output to be acceptable, they must change from what they were when they reported for work. At that time, they neither knew what a proper output looked like nor were they familiar with the technology by which to achieve it. They must be prepared—trained—to do their jobs. That's the big reason for a Training Department!

One way of looking at it is to envision training as the subsystem that acquaints the people with the material and the technology. It helps them learn how to use the material in an approved fashion that allows the organization to reach its desired output.

Because growth and change are inherent in organizations, they create a plethora of training needs. The term "learning organization" has become a popular buzzword to describe the way organizations must cope with their dynamic nature. A learning organization is based upon the principle of continuous learning, or a systematic method designed to increase learning within an organization, thereby enabling a more effective response to organizational change. Learning organizations emphasize the importance of learning at the individual, team, and organizational levels, thereby increasing the likelihood of further developing a competent and competitive workforce. Peter Senge defines the term as an organization that is "continually expanding its capacity to create its future." Doing so requires that individuals improve existing skills as well as learn new skills. Collectively, these newly acquired or refined skills can accomplish shared organizational goals. And, by anticipating future changes and working toward the knowledge and skills necessary to meet the demands resulting from these changes, the organization can systematically expand its capacity.

Able people may grow to a point where they are ready for responsibilities beyond their initial assignments. When this happens, the organization can profitably help them develop new, larger capabilities. In turn, performance improvements—individual and organizational—result. That's why it's called a "Training and *Development* Department."

Furthermore, the organization itself may grow and develop. The cafeteria may acquire other cafeterias, or open an "exotic" cafe that specializes in foreign cuisine. It might set up a catering service that delivers food to industrial or institutional clients. It might even select totally different outputs by founding an Institute of Haute Cuisine or buying an existing firm that is unrelated to food. After all, ours is the era of the creative conglomerate.

The point is this: Training and development has become concerned not only with helping individuals to fill their positions adequately but also with helping entire organizations and subdepartments to grow and develop. Thus the sign on the door has changed from "Training and Development" to titles reflecting missions such as "Employee Development," "Organization Development," or "Human Resource Development."

This trend makes it wise for us to look a bit more closely at the interrelationship of the four inputs: people, technology, materials, and time.

Training and development, though primarily concerned with people, is also concerned with technology and processes, or the precise way an organization does business. That technology might be the way a flight attendant greets a passenger on an airliner, or the way an egg is fried; it might be the recipe that makes one soft drink distinctly different from all other soft drinks. It might be the design that makes one automobile more attractive or more efficient than its competitors. It might include the procedures for mixing and bottling the drink, or for assembling the automobile. The point is this: To accomplish the desired final output, an organization requires work. That work is divided among positions; and positions are divided into tasks—and tasks are assigned to people.

And there we have our second input: people! To perform their assigned tasks properly, all workers need to master and apply the unique technology governing their tasks. So here's where training enters the picture.

Civilization has not yet found the way to conceive and run an employee-free organization. Nor has it found a magic technology-and-skill potion that can be injected into people. Training is concerned with the meeting of two inputs to organizational effectiveness: people and technology. Since organizations can rarely find people who are, at the time of employment, total masters of the unique requirements for specific jobs, organizations need a subsystem called "training" to help new employees master the technology of their tasks. Training changes uninformed employees into informed employees; training changes unskilled or semiskilled workers into employees who can perform their assigned tasks in the way the organization wants them done; employees become workers who do things "the right way."

This "right way" is called a standard—and one major function of training is to produce people who do their work "at standard." In fact, one simple way to envision how training contributes is to look at the steps by which people control their positions:

Step 1. Define the right (or standard) way for performing all the tasks needed by the organization.

Step 2. Secure people to perform these tasks.

Step 3. Find out how much of the task they can already perform. (What is their "inventory" of the necessary technology?)

Step 4. Train them to meet skill gaps—the difference in what they cannot already do and the standard for performing the task.

Step 5. Test them to make certain they can perform their assigned tasks to minimum standards.

Step 6. Give them the resources necessary to perform their tasks.

From that six-step process, we can also identify the two remaining inputs: time and material. People can't be miracle workers who create something from nothing. So we give them materials such as fabric from which they can cut dresses; parts they can assemble into machines; parts of a broken machine they can analyze and repair. In all these situations, management usually makes some statement about quality; it specifies what the finished product must look like. By stating how many units should be repaired in an hour, or how many dresses sewn in a day, management also sets quantity standards. The job of the training department is to "output" people who can meet those standards, both in quality and quantity.

This description may imply that all training takes place after people are hired but *before* they are assigned to their jobs. That's obviously not true. Just look at the rosters of training programs and you'll see the names of lots of old-timers. What are they doing there?

One legitimate reason for including old-timers in training programs is that the organization has undergone a major change. Equipment changes, processes change, policies change, and procedures change. Thus, veteran employees and new employees alike need training initiatives and benefit from them. When change occurs, an organization will have incumbent workers who no longer know how to do their jobs the new, right way. When people do not know how to do their jobs the right way, there is a training need. People do not usually know how to do the "next job" properly. Thus transfers, or the promotions implied in some career-planning designs, imply potential education needs. Some organizations have training departments that help prepare for the future.

But sometimes we find people in training programs even when the technology hasn't changed, or even when they aren't preparing for new responsibilities.

When Employees Can Do Their Jobs Properly, But Don't, What Then?

That raises the question, "What about employees who have been doing their present jobs properly—but no longer do so?" It's certainly true that these people are not meeting the established standards of performance—but will training do them any good? The answer is: not really.

You see, they already know how to do their work; they've shown that in their previous satisfactory performance. Thus the reason for their present non-performance can't possibly be that they don't know how. And training is a remedy for people who do not know how—not for people who do know how but for one reason or another are no longer doing it.

These other problems are performance problems—but they are not truly training problems; therefore, training is not an appropriate solution. Of course, good training departments don't ignore these other performance problems. The smart training and development manager never says, "Sorry, we can't help you!" when managers report old-timers who no longer perform properly.

Learning vs. Performance

Now we must answer this question: Is performance "bad" and learning "good?" Since 1995, there has been an intense debate in U.S. research literature around the "learning" versus the "performance" paradigms of HRD. That debate has often positioned performance as inherently bad.

Underlying these core beliefs and the continuing debate are certain assumptions that are not clearly articulated. Let's define certain perspectives of performance and learning that seem to be embedded in the learning vs. performance debate. Learning and education have been the subject of philosophical work dating back to ancient times. Many of the early works on adult education were philosophical statements about the purposes of adult learning. Thus, education and learning have grown as disciplines with strong philosophical roots, traditions, and explications.

Performance, on the other hand, has largely been a practice-based phenomenon with little philosophical consideration. Indeed, it is difficult to even think of philosophical sources on performance.

Performance

Three basic views of performance pervade our thinking:

Performance As a Natural Outcome of Human Activity. In this view, performance is seen as a natural part of human existence. Human beings are seen as engaging in wide varieties of purposeful activities with performance as a natural outcome. Furthermore, the accomplishment of certain outcomes in these purposeful activities is a basic human need. That is, few people are content to go through life without engaging in purposeful activities during which they achieve desired outcomes. Said differently, few people are content if they are not performing.

Many of these activities occur in work settings, where we traditionally think performance belongs; but they may also occur in leisure settings. For example, a person may play softball for leisure but also be quite interested in winning games. Or a person might be heavily involved in church activities such as membership drives or outreach programs and exert great effort to make them successful. In both of these examples, performance is a desired aspect of freely chosen behavior.

This view embraces performance as a valued part of human existence. Thus, for HRD or T&D to embrace performance it must also embrace the enhancement of human existence. This is the perspective that performance-based HRD advocates, though it has rarely been articulated as such. Performance-based HRD does not see a conflict between advancing performance and enhancing human potential. Rather, they are seen as perfectly complementary.

Performance As Necessary for Economic Activity. This perspective of performance is a more utilitarian view whereby performance is an instrumental activity that enhances individuals and society because it supports economic gain. More value-neutral than other perspectives, this view sees performance as neither good nor bad inherently, but rather as a means to other ends. It is largely a work-based view of performance. Performance is seen as necessary for individuals to earn livelihoods and be productive members of society. Performance at the individual level leads to enhanced work and careers; performance at the organization level leads to stronger economic entities capable of providing good jobs.

Performance-based HRD originated from this perspective as it attempted to link learning to individual and organizational performance outcomes to enhance the utility of learning. Although this objective is worthy by itself, it lacks the intrinsic "goodness" of the first perspective. As the performance paradigm has matured, it has evolved into the first perspective.

Performance As an Instrument of Organizational Oppression. From this perspective, organizations see performance as a means of control and dehumanization. Through performance, organizations coerce and demand behaviors from individuals in return for compensation. Performance is viewed as threatening to humans and potentially abusive. As such, it is largely a necessary evil that denies human potential.

The underlying presumption of this perspective is that performance is antithetical to human potential. It seems to be most closely aligned with critical theorists who wish human resource development to challenge organizational power structures that seek to control performance outcomes.

Learning

As stated earlier, education and learning have undergone extensive philosophical discussion. For purposes of this discussion, we will look at three analogous views.

Learning As a Humanistic Endeavor. The primary purpose of learning is seen as enhancing human potential from this perspective. Most closely aligned with humanistic psychology and existentialist philosophy, humans are seen as growing, developing entities. Learning is seen as a key element in helping individuals become more self-actualized and is inherently good for the person.

Most scholars of human resource development view learning from this perspective. They believe deeply in the power of learning to enhance human potential. It is important to note that performance-based HRD also sees learning in this way. Learning and performance are seen not as antithetical but as complementary.

Learning As a Value-Neutral Transfer of Information. Learning in this view has instrumental value in that it transfers information that individuals need and desire. Learning is seen as a means to solve the problems of everyday living. Instructional designers and many organizational trainers approach learning from this perspective in that their primary task is to transfer information effectively. A large part of training practice is grounded in this perspective, which sees learning as largely value-neutral, but instrumental.

Learning As a Tool for Social Oppression. That learning can also be a tool for oppression outside of organizational settings is largely overlooked by HRD scholars in the United States. For example, communism uses learning to control people; cults use learning to brainwash people; some religions use learning to restrict the world views of people; and education has used learning to distort history by eliminating black and female perspectives. Thus, learning can also be a tool for oppression and control.

Key Conclusions Regarding Performance/Learning

Several key conclusions can be drawn from the above discussion:

1. Neither learning nor performance is inherently good or bad. Both can be instruments of oppression or means to elevate human potential.

2. Learning and performance may simultaneously be good and supportive of human potential and need not be antithetical.
3. Debates about performance reflect diverse perspectives about performance. Specifically, critics of performance-based HRD incorrectly portray learning as inherently "good" and performance as inherently "bad." It is equally possible for performance to be "good" and learning to be "bad."
4. Finally, performance-based HRD adopts the perspective that *both* learning and performance approaches are inherently good for the individual because both are natural.

Training

The function once known as "training" has had to expand its own technology, strategies, and methodologies. It has had to locate and adopt nontraining solutions for all those performance problems that are not caused by not knowing how. Later on, we can look at these "other problems and other solutions" in detail. For now, let's just summarize our answer to the question, "Why have a training department?" this way:

Organizations get outputs because people perform tasks to a desired standard. Before people can perform their tasks properly, they must master the special technology used by the organization. This means acquiring knowledge and skills. Sometimes this acquisition is needed when the employee is new to the organization; sometimes it is needed as a result of some organizational change such as new technology; sometimes it is necessary if an individual is to change places within the organization—either by lateral transfer or by promotion.

Training is the acquisition of the technology which permits employees to perform to standard. Thus training may be defined as an experience, a discipline, or a regimen that causes people to acquire new, predetermined behaviors. Whenever employees need *new* behaviors, then we need a training department. But as we have already noted, training departments do more than merely fill the gaps in peoples' repertoires for carrying out assigned tasks; training specialists are also now involved in career development: developing people for "the next job," for retirement, and for their roles in society outside the employing organization.

That brings us to the word "education," a timely concept in our era when "lifelong learning" is a current or imminent reality. Not all training specialists distinguish among "training," "education," and "development." They use the three words interchangeably to describe what they do for their organizations.

But for those who distinguish, as does Leonard Nadler (1970) in his *Developing Human Resources,* training is what we've described: "Those activities which are designed to improve human performance on the job the employee is presently doing or is being hired to do" (40). Education is those human resource development activities which "are designed to improve the overall competence of the employee in a specified direction and beyond the job now held" (60). To Nadler, development is concerned with preparing the employees so they can "move with the organization as it develops, changes, and grows" (88).

Education and Development

Most writers of human resource development and adult education history focus on the development of worker and employee education and ignore a vital part of HRD; namely, management education and development (hereafter referred to as MED). MED has developed largely as a separate field of adult education spurred by unique and independent forces. It is only in modern times that mainstream human resource development and MED have converged.

The history of MED is also the history of a relatively young profession of management. One thing that is clear when studying the history of MED is that the field has many different components. It is also clear that it is difficult to divorce the higher education component from the more traditional HRD components since there are important interactions between them. MED has developed into a concept of lifelong learning for managers, and since management is regarded as a profession requiring professional preparation, the higher education component is part of the lifelong process. The system of MED providers includes higher education, university-based MED, corporate-based training programs, association activity, and private training.

As a final introductory note, it is also useful to define the term "management education and development" because it is subject to greatly varied use. We use the term broadly to include any educational or developmental activity specifically designed to foster the professional growth and capability of persons being prepared for or already in management and executive roles in organizations. Several aspects of this definition deserve highlighting. First, it includes formal educational activities and on-the-job types of programs. MED is more than just classroom activity, and all aspects of it must be included. As will be seen, the concept of MED has changed significantly through the years, but it included primarily more informal activities, though systematically planned and designed, in the early years.

Second, it includes only those activities designed to prepare employees for managerial and executive roles. There is a distinction between training for management roles and training for managers, although the two training types have some overlap. Many managers and executives might participate in training that is skill-oriented rather than managerial-oriented. For example, a manager might take classes to improve his or her computer skills. Obviously, such classes cannot be considered as training in management development.

Finally, it includes MED programs designed for all levels of management, including what is often called executive development, but excludes supervisory development. Supervisory development is generally considered to be targeted at employees supervising hourly, or nonprofessional-level, employees.

Let's apply these definitions to familiar activities. We can quickly identify some "leadership" and "presupervisory" and "personal development" programs as educational activities. People who have been identified as "promotable" often attend such workshops to enhance their capacity for leadership—to receive special orientation in organization goals, policies, or procedures. Assessment centers and career-planning systems often reveal lapses in people's capabilities for future assignments. Education is needed. In these cases, the word is apt, paralleling the Latin origin of "educing," going out from something that is already there. The identified capabilities are used as a basis for an expanded repertoire of skills in the individual. Why increase this repertoire or inventory? So these individuals can make larger contributions to the organization in their next positions for which they are presumably bound. Such activities are legitimately called "education."

The development activity can often take the form of university enrollments for top executives. They can thus acquire new horizons, new technologies, new viewpoints. They can lead the entire organization to newly *developed* goals, postures, and environments. This is perceived as a way to maintain growth and development for the entire organization, not just for the individual. Yet that's misleading, since the sponsors of such "developmental" activities feel that the organization will grow to meet the future precisely because the individual leaders will grow in their insights about the future in their capacity to bring change when the future has become the reality of the present.

Training and development also encompasses organizational development (OD) efforts. OD is a change program where change is observed as it happens. It involves launching and managing change in the organizational society. OD is very definitely within the purview of the training and development department.

However, in OD training and development specialists focus on the organization first—and on the interrelationships of people and units within the organization, on structures and communications—not on the growth of the individual. To be sure, individuals will change—and, hopefully, in larger, "growthful" directions. Thus cause and effect are inextricably linked: People develop because an organization develops; the organization develops because people grow to new dimensions!

Why have such an OD program? Quite possibly because too many resources (human and material, time and technological) are being invested or squandered in ways that do not produce the desired output. Or perhaps they produce the desired output—but at too great a cost in time, material, or human values. Organization development may question the real "success" of organizations that meet their goals in ways that make the human resources feel miserable or unfulfilled, and, in the process, miserable about the condition of their work lives. They agree with Hamlet: "Something is rotten in the state of Denmark"!

How can things become that rotten? There are lots of reasons. For instance, such a thorough reappraisal of an organization may be necessary because individuals or subgroups have consistently invested their talent, energy, and resources to achieve personal or departmental goals rather than the objectives established for the entire organization. Such reappraisals might be needed simply because communications go sour—key messages are never sent, or they become distorted, or they are lost. Perhaps feelings are never shared; they are "all bottled up" and only the content of doing business is shared. Everything is tasks, tasks, and more tasks!

Organization development programs use the human beings within the organization as resources in a problem-solving effort that might reassign or reorganize the subgroups, restructure the communications channels or media, and reshape individual responsibilities, behavioral modes, or communicative style. It might even examine every facet of the interhuman and systemic structure in an effort to find a better way—a way that would permit the human energy to produce desired outputs cooperatively to reach organizational goals in ways that prove satisfying and fulfilling to all participant members of the organization.

Summary

Training departments seek to be ever more relevant to organization goals, to solve performance problems throughout the entire organization—and to do so in a variety of ways. Thus they are concerned with things other than just training. They seek other solutions to other types of human performance problems.

In 1983, the American Society for Training and Development (ASTD), under the leadership of Patricia A. McLagan, completed its *Models for Excel-*

lence, a competency study. It listed fifteen distinct roles and thirty-one specific competencies required for total performance by a training and development professional. Three additional competencies were added in a follow-up study. A look at those roles and competencies reveals the breadth and depth of a thorough answer to our question, "Why have a Training and Development Department?"

The roles include needs analyst, program designer, task analyst, theoretician, instructional writer, media specialist, instructor, group facilitator, individual development counselor, transfer agent, program administrator, evaluator, marketer, strategist, and manager of training and development.

The competencies vary from the understanding of adult learning to computer competence, from questioning skills to presentation skills, from futuring skills to library skills, and from cost-benefit analysis skills to group process skills (McLagan 1983, 4, 6).

Despite the new, larger charter of the training departments all around us, this book will call the person who leads the development of an organization's "human inputs" the T&D manager. Staff members who assist the growth of people will be known as T&D specialists. "T&D," of course, means training and development.

There are lots of organizations in which one person is the entire operation, the director who decides what training will happen and when and where and how. Such a person designs the visuals and creates the lesson plan, leads the learning experiences and handles the follow-up. This happens again and again in the single office, the single shop, the local plant, or the branch office. This is a true T&D manager/specialist, all rolled into one!

Then there are other organizations so large and so complex that the T&D department, like all the other departments, is specialized. There are the decisionmakers with lofty titles; there are the media specialists who put lettering onto visual aids; there are instructional technologists, and there are instructors; there are programmers who put learning systems onto computers for "assisted instruction."

This book will try to examine principles and practices for all these situations. It will examine ideas that have been used with common effectiveness in T&D departments from the most Spartan to the most sophisticated. No matter how big or how small the T&D operation, they all have in common that one important goal: to keep the human resources performing at or above the established standards.

Why have a T&D department? Because to achieve desired results, organizations need to appoint employees responsible for:

- Training people to do their present tasks properly
- Educating certain employees so they can assume greater responsibilities in the future
- Developing people and entire organizations for the foreseeable and unforeseeable future
- Training to facilitate both individual and organizational performance

Why? Because someone needs to be responsible for human growth if the status quo is to be maintained satisfactorily—and if the future is to be met. Because someone must help people make tomorrow a successful "today."

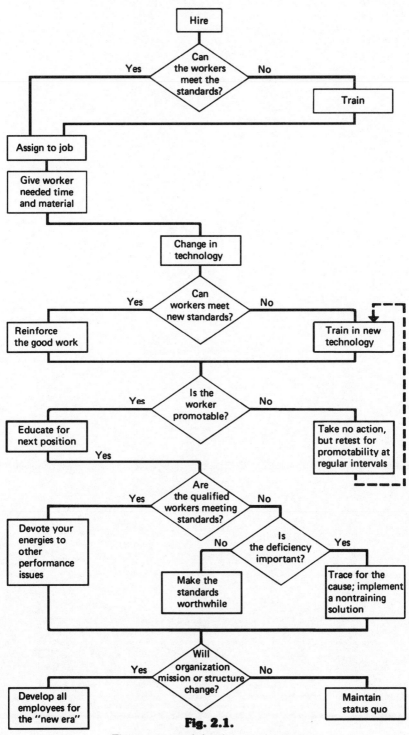

Fig. 2.1.
The training and development process.

Function and Role of
T&D Managers

Competencies Needed

Without a doubt, the training and development function encompasses several facets and requires T&D professionals to wear multiple hats. They must be managers/administrators, consultants, designers of learning experiences, and instructors.

A broad range of skills is required for the T&D specialist to perform the multiple functions associated with the role. A 1989 revision to the classic 1983 American Society for Training and Development (ASTD) study, *Models for Excellence,* identifies thirty-five competencies that are still applicable today. This long list of competencies involves a wide range:

1. Adult Learning Understanding
2. Career Development Knowledge
3. Computer Competence
4. Electronic System Skills
5. Industry Understanding
6. Facilities Skill
7. Organization Behavior Understanding
8. Objectives Preparation Skills
9. Subject Matter Understanding
10. Training and Development Theories and Techniques Understanding
11. Research Skill
12. Performance Observation Skill
13. Business Understanding

14. Cost-Benefit Analysis Skill
15. Delegation Skill
16. Organization Development Theories and Techniques Understanding
17. Organization Understanding
18. Project Management Skill
19. Records Management Skill
20. Coaching Skill
21. Feedback Skill
22. Negotiation Skill
23. Group Process Skill
24. Presentation Skill
25. Questioning Skill
26. Relationship Building Skill
27. Writing Skill
28. Data Reduction Skill
29. Information Search Skill
30. Model Building Skill
31. Intellectual Versatility
32. Observing Skill
33. Futuring Skill
34. Self-Knowledge
35. Competency Identification Skill

When T&D managers work alone as the training department for the organization, they must indeed be expert in all four areas. When they head a larger staff, they must provide for and manage all four functions—management, consulting, design, and instruction.

Let's look at each of the four roles in greater detail.

As Managers/Administrators

As manager/administrator of the training function, the T&D manager must perform typical managerial duties. This means planning, organizing, directing, and controlling the ongoing function. Thus T&D managers set policy for developing the human resources of the organization. They then see that the policy is carried out through systems and programs, possibly through a T&D staff, and assuredly with the active involvement of line management—and presumably with the support and commitment of upper management.

What Are the Policy Decisions the T&D Manager Must Make?

First, someone must decide what the training needs are and what training initiatives will be provided. Of course, these training needs must support the organization's mission and goals. That means there must be a definition of what training is, and a set of criteria on which validated training needs will be prioritized. Often, when the training needs are greater than the available resources, a decision must be made about where the resources will actually be expended. This decision is simplified and expedited when there is a policy statement about which criteria have priority—the dollar impact, the costs of providing the training, ROI (return on investment), the number of people to be trained, pressure from competition, the political clout of the requester, or government mandate? A policy clarifying such priorities needs organizational sanction, but usually originates with the T&D manager.

It may be painful to refuse requests for help, but that is less likely to happen if the T&D manager is a good planner who sees performance-related problems before they arise; when one must say no, it is less painful if a clear-cut policy is available to explain why.

Naturally then, this T&D manager must have ready access to organizational goals, problems, and strategies. To know what new products, programs, technologies, or approaches the organization is contemplating is to be a proactive rather than a belated solver of human performance problems. To be proactive is to prevent human performance problems rather than be a mere "firefighter" who handles problems after they have already become full-blown crises.

At other times the T&D manager will become aware of performance problems that remain unseen by an operating management because it is somehow "blinded" to the failure of its own staff to meet desired performance standards. Does the T&D manager take the initiative in revealing such problems? Or does the organization have to wait until the potential client grows painfully aware of the situation? Someone must make a policy statement to answer that question—and that "someone" is the T&D manager.

Someone must also set scheduling policy: setting the dates and locations for programs, determining the length of the training day, deciding whether enrollments should involve trainees from many departments and locations or from homogeneous groups. Someone must ask, "In what programs does the synergism of exchanging departmental technology and values exceed the faster mastery and potential team building possible when the rosters include learners from the same discipline or location?" Scheduling raises this question: "Should the shop be shut down for every participant to achieve the expected learning outcomes?" The answers to such questions are sometimes hard to find and even harder to "sell." Someone must find them and someone must sell them— and that someone is the T&D manager.

How will participants be selected for training? On what priority? How is their immediate manager or supervisor expected to brief them on the reasons they are being trained? How will that manager/supervisor review the learning objectives with them before the training? Who will tell them the quality and quantity standards they are expected to achieve when they return to work after the training? The content of these vital messages, the mechanisms for sending them and the policies governing them must be established and communicated by someone. That someone is the T&D manager.

The word "communicated" is critically important. T&D managers are not only responsible for setting policy but also for communicating that policy to all other parts of the management structure. How can the T&D department expect compliance if clients do not know the criteria for determining training needs, for enrollments, or for achievements? How can the line managers make effective use of their investment in training processes if they are not given guidelines?

A written statement of training policy is a vitally important document for several reasons:

- First, it serves as a day-to-day reference in making those innumerable "subdecisions" that arise for managers in both the T&D and client departments.
- Next, it provides a useful checkpoint for renewing and redirecting the training activity from time to time.
- It can be a useful planning document.
- It becomes a valid checklist when the T&D manager evaluates the contributions and performance of his or her department.
- Above all, a written statement of T&D policy helps all members of the T&D department function in ticklish moments! Perhaps the issue of "Why?" or "Why not?" or "What shall we do?" hangs heavy over a discussion with a line client. The written policy can explain, clarify, and solidify organizational values. Even if it doesn't provide the precise detailed answers needed at the moment, it can give guidance and suggest actions.

A word about "ticklish moments": They can be very valuable "teachable moments." We need to learn from mistakes and from crises. The ticklish moments requiring a formal policy statement for guidance are cues to ask ourselves why the crisis occurred and whether it was a useful crisis. This is also a time to ask whether we need an amended or expanded policy statement. If the same "tickle" comes up again and again, it is a catalyst to improved statements—and improved *policy*—in the future!

If there's a definite policy, why are there ticklish moments? Possibly because the T&D manager involved too few line clients when first creating the policy. This raises another policy issue decided by the T&D manager: Which clients? How often should they be consulted when policy is being reformulated?

As administrators, T&D managers not only set policy but also manage an ongoing function. This happens whether they have a staff or whether they are the entire department in just one person. But if we define management as "getting work done through other people," then T&D managers are just like all other managers. They must plan, delegate, motivate, mentor, coach, monitor, control, and evaluate. Their T&D department is, after all, simply one of the suborganizations within the larger organization it serves.

This means that T&D managers establish budgets and monitor costs. In doing this, they may control decisions about learning methods and media. For example, it may be necessary to use a printed book as the medium for programmed instruction because budgets won't permit the expense or development time for computer-based training (CBT).

T&D budgets must provide facilities where learning can take place and where it can be designed, as well as places to meet with clients to discuss performance problems, possible programs, learning objectives, evaluation criteria, and procedures for adopting any activity resulting from the consultation. To plan these places properly, T&D managers must know something about methods and media. Managing the ongoing function in most organizations implies that T&D managers select and manage some staff, but also have course designers, instructors, consultants, media specialists, and clerical support. To give that staff a sense of belonging, security, and recognition, T&D managers must provide environments that accommodate activities ranging from confrontation to quiet meditation.

To build staff, T&D managers need skill in selecting personnel. They want a balance of temperament, experience, and special expertise.

If T&D managers preach the gospel of the ever-developing employee to clients (and they'd *better* preach it!), it's vital that they practice this gospel on their own staff. It's imperative to give periodic upgrading so that all T&D specialists can acquire new skill and expertise. Growth should be the norm of the T&D department! This means that time and dollars must be budgeted so that staff can attend conferences, workshops, seminars, and developmental activities within the department.

And then there's evaluation. Someone must see that evaluation mechanisms are built into all phases of the change program. This means that there must be measurement before the evaluation. This means that programs will be tested and revised before final implementation. It means that completed programs will be evaluated. But on what criteria? Will they be evaluated on cost effectiveness? On perceptions? On the achievement of learning goals? On changes in employees' on-the-job performance? On changes in operating indices? Some of the above? All of the above? Someone must decide—and make a statement on the decision.

Administratively, the T&D manager must do lots of planning and organizing, must translate the abstractions of policy into workable day-to-day decisions of control and implementation. Those decisions must improve people-performance at all levels, and in all departments.

As Consultants to the Organization

In their role as consultants to the organization, T&D managers help managers of "client" departments solve human performance problems. That isn't always easy.

For one thing, when people have problems, the real nature of the problems is often hard to identify. It is absorbed inside the people who aren't performing properly. For another thing, the manager whose department is distressed doesn't always find it easy to admit that a problem exists. Such admissions can be very threatening. Thus the consultative skills of the T&D manager involve knowing what questions to ask, when to ask them, and how to create an environment in which facts—including the facts of feelings—become the basis of decisions. This implies that the clients' feelings must be expressed and facilitated, must be a part of the consultant's probe and part of the decision. That is correct. After all, feelings are a part of the reality of the whole performance problem being probed.

If the problem is properly identified, the T&D manager may need to bow out of the problem-solving process. Why? Well, the problem may not stem from human behavior at all. To precisely the degree that T&D managers have high credibility, they will be asked to solve all kinds of problems. But if sales have slumped because products are no longer competitive, or if manufacturing levels are low because one plant was lost in a flood, the T&D manager is not the person best qualified to help solve the problem. T&D managers are useful in solving human performance problems. When they go beyond that, they are exceeding their expertise and their charter.

This does not mean that T&D managers bow out of problems when training is not the solution—only when the problem doesn't stem from human performance. Most organizations expect a full range of human performance improvement services from the T&D department.

Performance problems—all of them!—are the legitimate and obligatory concern of the T&D manager, but not all human performance problems can be solved by training.

We have already noted that when people know how to do their jobs, but aren't doing them, then training is not a useful solution. After all, there is no sense in sending workers to class to learn what they already know! If they aren't doing what they know how to do, then there must be some cause. T&D managers help management discover that cause—and for working with managers to identify, design, develop, and implement effective solutions.

Managers in client departments are frequently inclined to think that training is what their people need. The T&D manager is responsible for helping them see the fallacy in that viewpoint; the T&D manager is ultimately responsible for distinguishing training from nontraining needs. As they watch T&D managers make this analysis, line managers can grow in their insight about how training contributes toward people's contribution to organization goals.

If training won't work, what will? Consider motivation as well as ability. One possibility to explore is changing the consequences for satisfactory performance. Many times employees cease to do their work the "right way" because there is no positive consequence for doing so. Sometimes, doing the job properly is actually punished by the system. In one company, salespeople who exceeded quotas (in other words, the overachievers!) actually had their territory divided among new salespersons. Customer service representatives who take the time to do thorough jobs may be abused verbally by irritated customers—or even by supervisors who "chew" them for keeping people waiting!

All the training in the world won't produce behavior that perfectly fits the realities of the workplace. Discovering these inconsistencies between goals and rewards is the common task of the T&D specialist and the manager who has the problem in the performance of subordinates. It is one facet of the consulting function of the T&D department.

Another consideration is the establishment of proper feedback systems. To the degree that workers receive continuous quantitative feedback about their achievements, they will tend to maintain acceptable performance levels. This is very different from management's saying, "Well done, thou good and faithful servant!" Admittedly, that is a desirable behavior by managers and supervisors—but the feedback that consistently motivates and maintains performance is likely to be a simple numerical tally by the workers themselves.

If workers have specific checkpoints about the quality, and are allowed to count their accomplishments, the quality can be monitored along with the quantity. Thus feedback becomes a motivator, a monitor, and a controller all at once. Installing effective feedback mechanisms has become part of the technology of the T&D staff, an important tool in solving performance problems. It is yet another "solution" the T&D manager may offer to managers of employees who aren't performing their tasks properly.

At other times, jobs don't get done because they are basically "undoable." That can happen when jobs are too complex or too simple. The trend toward specialization and work simplification has proved to be a mixed blessing. On the positive side, it has eliminated some tasks that were superhuman in their expectations. Some work was so complex, varied, or exacting that one person alone could not be expected to master the entire technology—much less to apply it hourly! Other work was so taxing to the body that no physique could bear the strain. Some tasks required discriminations so fine that neither the eye nor the mind of the worker could perform them correctly or continuously. Work simplification has helped eliminate such excesses, but it has brought with it a trend toward specialization that has also endangered some jobs. It has so oversimplified them that they've become stupid and degrading to the performer. Modern business, industry, and bureaucracy are infested with such jobs. They deprive the worker of a sense of variety, dignity, and accomplishment.

Thus we hear terms such as "job design," "job enrichment," and "job engineering" as important solutions to human performance problems. Effectively designed or "engineered" jobs not only get the work done but also get it done in quantities and varieties that match the humanity of the employee. T&D managers perform more effectively if they can spot problems caused by jobs that are impossibly complex or simple and if they can help management reengineer positions so that workers find the work at least bearable—and, hopefully, challenging and fulfilling.

But there are other performance problems when the incumbents know how to perform the job (so that training isn't required or useful) and when the consequences are appropriate and feedback is provided and the job is well designed. Still, tasks aren't being completed properly in the necessary quantities and the organization's, or unit's, goals are not being met. How can that happen?

It often happens because the organization, or organizational unit, is itself confused about goals and objectives. The entire unit may need to be redirected and renewed. If personal tensions are high and trust levels are low; if decisions are slow or absent; if there is more energy expended on personal and subgroup goals than on the mission of the entire organization, then organization development (OD) seems appropriate. T&D managers who substitute training or feedback systems as a remedy in such situations inevitably end up with egg on their faces. They have, in effect, prescribed an aspirin as a cure for cancer!

Thus the consultant role of the T&D manager is not merely to find places where training is an appropriate remedy. Rather, it is to find all the performance problems, to analyze each, and to recommend an appropriate solution. That solution may be any one, or a combination of training, contingency management, feedback systems, job engineering, or organization development. After the recommendation, the T&D manager is responsible for providing, assisting in carrying out, and evaluating whatever solution is adopted.

As consultants, therefore, T&D managers need to know how to ask questions—and what questions to ask.

Several types of questions immediately come to mind. When consultants want to uncover the feelings surrounding (and sometimes obscuring) a given situation, they want to use open-ended questions. Open-ended questions can't be answered with a yes or no, nor can they be answered with specific data such as "seventeen years" or "the first-line supervisor is responsible for that." Open questions are "How do you feel about it?" or "What do you think about this?" or "How would you describe that?" or "What is your analysis of the situation?"

When feelings are out in the open, the consultant is ready to ask some directive questions. These might be "How long has the problem been evident?" "Who has responsibility for?" "What is the published performance standard?" "Who sets that standard?" "What actual baselines are you now getting?"

Of course, some questions should be avoided—loaded questions such as "Don't you think that?" or "Wouldn't you agree that?" Indeed, any question that starts with "But . . ." is probably a loaded question—one that will put the client on the defensive and obscure the real feelings and the real facts. With such unproductive loaded questions, the client ends up feeling more entrapped than consulted.

Once clients have revealed their feelings, and stated the facts as they see them, the consultant can summarize with reflective questions that achieve the desired basis for action. Reflective questions tend to sound something like "You feel, then, that?" "Is this how you see the situation?" These reflections provide two things: a double check that the consultant understands the problem from the client's viewpoint, and a probable expansion of the area of agreement. In their reflective summaries, T&D specialists, wearing their consultants hats, are careful to reflect back only what they did in fact hear from the client—and to include the feelings as well as the facts.

It is not easy to summarize the consultant activity of the T&D manager because it involves at least eleven of the fifteen roles identified in the ASTD competency study. Besides being Manager of Training and Development, this manager will probably also be Evaluator, Group Facilitator, Instructor,

Marketer, Individual Development Counselor, Needs Analyst, Program Administrator, Strategist, Theoretician, and Transfer Agent (McLagan 1983, 4). The role requires skill in

- getting at real facts about performance problems;
- uncovering and responding to feelings, which must also be listed among the facts of the problem;
- matching appropriate, effective solutions to specific problems rather than invariably recommending a pet remedy such as training or OD or a pet method such as role-plays; and
- locating specialists who have skill in training, feedback, contingency management, job engineering, and organization development.

Effective T&D managers are no longer solutions looking for a problem! They are true consultants for the performance problems in the organizations they serve.

As Designers of Learning Experiences

In T&D for small shops, the entire staff works to create lesson plans, produce learning materials, and write role-playing scenarios, case studies, and simulations.

When the T&D department has a fairly large staff, the director may be only an observer or advisor in the selection of learning and teaching methods. But even then that manager must know enough to effectively counsel the staff members who do make the decisions and must also possess a wide knowledge of learning methods and some idea of when each is likely to be productive. There is such explosive expansion in the knowledge about how people learn that many T&D managers find they must hurry just to fall slightly behind the times!

One of the fundamental tasks of the design process is conducting a needs assessment—determining which skills or competencies are required and which skills the employees are deficient in. The skill gaps that the needs assessment identifies become the focus of the learning experience—the springboard for the instructional design.

Most modern organizations need a sizable number of instructional methods. Why? One of the primary reasons is that learning styles vary—as do teaching styles. What may be effective for one scenario may be totally ineffective in another. The objectives are so varied that a limited inventory of learning approaches is invalid. Then, too, the physical distribution of the trainee population may require that some programs be administered to individuals, others to large groups. For individuals, programmed instruction or auto-instructional and highly mediated programs are useful. Certain objectives may be achieved only in the group mode. Examples would include interpersonal skills, team building, and the manipulation of sophisticated heavy equipment. Team-building skills don't come very easily in programs where the learner interacts only with the printed page, a computer, a teaching machine, or even just one instructor. Handling a heavy piece of machinery can't be mastered from the printed page.

Some training is more effective when the learners are sharply removed from the workplace, able to introspect, analyze, and synthesize without the pressures or interruptions that go along with the office or the shop. Other learning outcomes are just plain impossible to achieve away from the real-world environment. If overcoming distractions is one of the learning objectives, what better place to face distractions than the busy office or the noisy shop? Such learning experiences should not be scheduled at Valhalla on the Hudson or Cozy Nook in the Poconos or Ocean Beach by the Pacific.

There are three distinct domains of behavior in which trainees must be asked to grow:

1. *Cognitive* or mental skills may actually be best acquired through reading, lectures, or demonstrations. But the word "demonstration" implies some step-by-step process or skill, which the learner must acquire and then perform back on the job—and we can pretty well rule out reading or lecture as the total learning experience!

2. *Psychomotor skills* involve using the arms, the legs, the torso. For the mind to direct reliable performance by these parts of the body, some practice or drill seems mandatory. Psychomotor growth often relies heavily on On the Job Training (OJT), in which instructors "tell and show" the task one step at a time, learners "doing and reviewing" that step as soon as possible.

3. In the *affective domain,* learners are expected to grow in the realm of emotions or feelings. Such new awareness or control of emotional energy can hardly result from a lecture or reading assignment, no matter how inspiring. (Not that inspiration is impossible; it's just never been an effective method of producing lasting on-the-job changes in affective behavior.) New research in personality and dispositions, the use of music and metaphor, controlled environments and right brain/left brain dominance studies offer new excitement in creating affective growth. (They also offer still more evidence that T&D managers always have something new to learn!)

Professional designers of learning experiences know when to use which method, how to effect necessary compromises between the most desirable method and the one the budget can afford—or the environment accept. They provide for try-out when skill is demanded, for participation when current emotional or intellectual biases would block acceptance of new ideas or new technology. They can arrange furniture so that it is conducive to proper communication and to an environment that properly stimulates and controls the things trainees say and do. Even if T&D managers don't get directly involved in such designs, they need to counsel their staff members who do get involved.

Effective leadership from the chief T&D manager is critical. There is the ever-present pitfall of faddism in training methodology. There is no absolutely foolproof certain theory about how adults learn; there is a great deal of exciting experimentation with new methods. Therefore, a brilliant success with one method can cause T&D specialists to become addicted to that method. They soon ardently advocate using it for all learning objectives in all learning environments—even when it is terribly inappropriate. But it is important to match the methodology to the learning variables. The effective T&D manager is able to counsel staff members in the proper selection to the proper match of learning objectives, trainee population, and organizational environment.

To counsel wisely, T&D managers also need to be well informed about current learning theory. But learning theory concepts aren't easily acquired. For one reason, the knowledge explosion has hit the field of learning theory just as it has hit other fields of human inquiry. Perhaps a bit more. Yet for consistent training policy and for effective adaptation into individual training programs, the T&D manager needs a grasp of all these concepts. Conscientious T&D specialists develop a personal theory of how people learn, and they expand it as new research and theories become available.

As designers or as managers of the design process, T&D managers need knowledge, experience, and a value system of learning/teaching methods. Nowadays, methodology will probably reflect a unique blend of several theories about how people (adults in particular) learn and change their on-the-job performance.

Regardless of what the training content is or the methodology used, the training will not "stick" unless the designer addresses the issue of transfer of training. Transfer refers to how well the learners apply the newly acquired knowledge to their work. Conditions before and after the training (pre and post training conditions in T&D jargon) greatly affect transfer results, and T&D managers must address these issues.

As Instructors

Often, the instructor is the ultimate "delivery agent" of the learning system. Instructors therefore manage the critical dynamic process: acquisition of new behaviors by the learner.

This implies skill in bringing to life all the content and all the methods called for in the "lesson plan." It implies skill in two-way communication. It implies flexibility, spontaneity, empathy, compassion—almost everything except feeding the multitudes with "but five loaves and two fishes."

The truth is that in recent years our perception of the effective instructor has changed sharply. We are less and less concerned with platform skills; we are more and more concerned with skills in facilitating learning in others. This means that instructor-training workshops don't stress oratorical skills or count the "ers" and "uhs" or practice gestures. Rather, the emphasis is on questioning and listening, on putting feedback and positive reinforcement into the learning experience. Involvement, rather than favorable impression, becomes the focus.

Instruction is both a science and an art—and the T&D function must provide people who have mastered instructional skills sufficiently to ensure that behavior change does indeed take place in the learners assigned to them.

Recent years have placed heavy emphasis on the importance of ensuring that learners do something other than listen and watch while in class. Indeed, this is the central question: "Do they ever actually learn anything at all by merely listening and watching?" The answer: "No—at least not much that carries over with them into improved on-the-job performance." So recent instructor-training programs (and most instructional design) have moved toward participatory types of learning experience. The word "experience" is not accidental; it implies that learners must experience something during the learning if their performance is to be significantly and permanently altered after the training ends.

So it is that B.F. Skinner (1974) points out in *About Behaviorism* that students must engage in behavior to learn new behaviors. That arch-advocate of facilitative learning, Carl Rogers (1969), points out in *Freedom to Learn* that learners must participate in order for significant learning to occur.

Malcolm Knowles (1977), whose life study is andragogy, the science of adult learning, insists that adults learn best when they can invest their own valued experience in the learning effort.

All these theories point toward participative learning designs—but with what degree of stress, responsibility, aversive consequences, and control? Teachers who conduct organizational learning experiences face just those questions—and must make decisions. It's up to the T&D manager to provide them with effective counseling when such decisions stare them in the face.

Summary

That's the four-faceted nature of the T&D manager's position: administrator, consultant, designer, and instructor. It's a big job—and a changing job. As organizations face new problems, the T&D manager, or the staff of T&D specialists, must be ready to face new situations and to offer new solutions. Fortunately, the technology of adult learning and of organizational behavior is expanding as rapidly as relevant experience is acquired by T&D departments.

How do the four roles function to make continuous, integrated contributions to the organization? A graphic answer would probably look something like Figures 3.1 and 3.2. Figure 3.1 shows the T&D manager's key responsibilities; Figure 3.2 lists the critical skills.

ADMINISTRATOR	CONSULTANT	DESIGNER	INSTRUCTOR
Sets policy:	Analyzes performance problems	Selects methods	Delivers learning design
Scope of services:		Selects media	Analyzes and responds to individual learner needs
Training	Recommends solutions:	Synthesizes methods and media into an integrated program	Adapts design to meet learner needs
Education	Training		
Development	Education	Provides outlines and materials to implement the program	Provides ongoing feedback and evaluation to facilitate learning
Feedback systems	Development		
Contingency management	Feedback systems	Evaluates tryout	Counsels learners
Job engineering	Contingency management	Redesigns programs as tryout data indicate	Provides feedback to designers about strengths and weaknesses of designs
Organization development	Job engineering		
Scope of useful methods	Organization development		
Scheduling	Establishes program goals (with client-managers)		
Participant selection			
Participation norms	Evaluates programs		
Evaluation criteria	Assists with programs		
Communicates policy	Counsels designers		
Sets program objectives			
Establishes budget			
Monitors expenditures			
Sets facilities standards			
Provides facilities			
Selects staff			
Manages staff			
Develops staff			
Evaluates T&D effort			

←——————— Counsels client-managers ——————→

Fig. 3.1.

The T&D officer's key areas of responsibility.

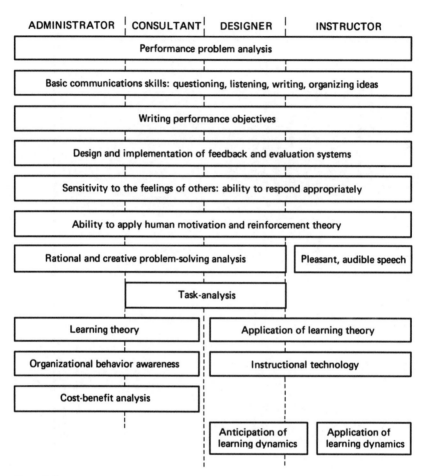

Fig. 3.2.

The critical skills needed by the T&D officer.

The T&D Department and the Organizational Structure

Trends in Organizational Placement

Organizations are increasingly recognizing that the key to their success is largely contingent upon the capabilities of their employees—their human capital. Organizational performance is understandably dependent upon individual performance. As society moves toward increased emphasis on human rights, so organizations are moving toward sharper focus on developing the human potential. Thus it is only natural that the traditional concept of "Training and Development" has expanded to include concern for Human Resource Development (HRD)—a much broader concept than the old notion of T&D. Swanson and Holton (2001, 4) define HRD as the process for developing and unleashing human expertise through organizational development and personnel training and development for the purpose of improving performance. Clearly the roles and responsibilities of the T&D manager are important ones in addressing performance issues.

What is unclear, however, is where this position should be located on the organizational chart. The shift toward becoming learning organizations makes the placement of the training department an important variable in organizational success. Does it fit best as a line position or as a staff position? Let's explore the differences.

Line and Staff Considerations

The line/staff dichotomy has blurred, and this distinction has grown rather unpopular with organization theorists. Yet the division still exists as a practical reality in most organizations, and we must regard it as a real issue in placing the T&D function.

Assume for just a moment that your organization has never had a specialized training and development department. It has just decided to create such a group, and has asked for your opinion: "Where should we locate this new department on our organization chart? Who should be responsible for what part of the T&D activity?"

This is where a policy statement would come in handy; however, there is no such statement. It's up to you to decide. On what basis do you make your decision? Two basic issues come to mind:

1. Is training and development a line function or a staff function?
2. How do you guarantee sufficient authority for your T&D manager to meet the responsibilities implied in the title?

It's a cliché to say that training is a line responsibility. Yet in actual practice, training has often been placed on the "staff" side of most organizations. Just look at the organization charts. To whom does the T&D manager report? Such placement often brings an immediate stigma: "They're just staff people, you know!"

In *Developing Human Resources*, Nadler (1970) says that although training is a line responsibility, education is not. Any kind of employee development is, by its very nature, a support function. In itself, it doesn't result in products such as automobiles or clothing; it doesn't in itself cause customers to buy, or users to be satisfied with a service. T&D supports and enables those results. Yet, if T&D is to be relevant to the main outputs of the organization, it must have proximity to the line operation. It must "speak their language" and share the line (or production) values. There is a constant give-and-take between the T&D specialists and their line clients.

If we examine the processes of a typical training program, we can see the precise nature of this interchange. To do so clarifies the reasons why T&D people and line people must work harmoniously in a common activity having inherent differences in viewpoints, values, and expertise.

Often training activity starts when a line manager says to the T&D manager, "I have a training problem." Astute T&D managers overcome their instinctive reaction: "You *may* have a training problem—but at the moment we don't know that for sure. Besides, *I'm* the one who decides when we have training problems. After all, my expertise is to determine when training will work and when it won't."

Of course, such arrogance is unpardonable. Yet there are times when the T&D manager must realize that line managers sometimes expect training to be a panacea for all their people problems. Thus nearly all T&D managers must eventually deny a highly motivated customer the very product the customer is so anxious to buy.

At such times professional T&D managers use effective consultative questions. They respond to the manager who mistakenly wants training with words more like these: "I'm glad you came to talk it over. What, exactly, are your employees doing that they shouldn't be doing?" And then, "What aren't your employees doing that they should be doing?"

In this way the proper mental processes are launched. Let's examine the ensuing steps to see what responsibilities and what resources both elements (line and staff) can offer to effective performance problem solving.

TABLE 4.1   Contributions of Line and Staff to Solving Performance Problems

Phase A: Analysis	Line Contributions and Responsibilities	Staff Contributions and Responsibilities
1. Discover a problem	The line may initiate the analysis with a request for help. By monitoring management reports and operating indices or through surveys, the T&D manager may initiate the analysis. In any event the client manager must eventually agree that there is a painful situation. The line has thus taken a very necessary first step: "ownership" of the problem.	Monitoring the operation, or data gathered in periodic surveys and interviews, may permit the initiative to originate in the T&D department. Must use special tact and skill in presenting the "bad news" to a client who isn't yet aware of a performance problem—or who is generally insensitive to performance problems. May find it difficult to persuade the client that training is not the best solution.
2. Performance standards	Must "sign off" that the standards are correct and reasonable. If standards don't already exist, participates as the final authority in their documentation.	Can be party to the analysis of existing printed standard. If no standards exist, can facilitate their creation and documentation by suggesting quantities (units, percentages, dollars, milestones, or time lapse) and vocabulary to describe actions and processes.
3. Identify the deficiency	Must ultimately admit that a problem exists ... that it "has a hurt," but may find this admission more painful than the performance problem itself.	Able to offer larger and more objective perspective ... a fresh viewpoint. Skills in consultative questioning help clients admit and define the exact nature and scope of the performance problem. May suggest the verbs, which define observable actions, and the adverbs to identify satisfactory performance. Should insist on measurement of the scope of the problem. This is establishing baselines. Doing so will tell how serious the problem really is and how widespread.

(continued on next page)

TABLE 4.1 *(continued)*

Phase A: Analysis	Line Contributions and Responsibilities	Staff Contributions and Responsibilities
4. Cost the deficiency	May resist this step, saying it's impossible to put a price on the task. Can, when persuaded to do so, lead analysis to hard data about costs of units, time, and products—as well as to hidden costs.	Knows the technology of putting price tags on the units of performance. Knows the formula for estimating training costs, and can thus make an accurate cost-benefit analysis.
5. Identify causes of the deficiency	May have dangerous and misleading preconceptions. May tend to "jump to cause" to get quick remedy or to escape culpability. May urge quick solution. Is not truly interested in causes.	Should prevent jumping to conclusions by offering several possible causes. Must avoid preconceptions by client and self. May be seen as an enemy of progress by insisting on long-range solution, lacking energy for "quick fix" of symptoms. May need to accept both quick and long-range solutions.
6. Design and select solutions	May jump to first option, as "I told you all along that a little training would fix everything!" Has no real basis for performance analysis and may feel threatened by such new solutions as contingency management, feedback, or feedback mechanisms. May need help in seeing why evaluation criteria need to be established so soon.	Must be "the pro" at this stage; is the only party with the expertise. Requires patience in deterring client from jumping to first possible solution. May be in awkward spot—a training specialist refusing to prescribe own product. May need to accept some short-range solution as a way to get to the long-range solution. Should insist that evaluation criteria be established at this point.

Phase B: Solving the Problem	Line Contributions and Responsibilities	Staff Contributions and Responsibilities
7. Decide to go ahead with the best solution	Lacks perspective; can't put this problem into proper perspective for the entire organization. Must be the one to say yes if T&D department offers its resources for continuing the activity.	Has perspective to assign proper priority to this problem and to this project. Can only recommend; does not "own" the problem. Can assist client with identifying and prioritizing key variables in decision.

(continued on next page)

TABLE 4.1 *(continued)*

Phase B: Solving the Problem	Line Contributions and Responsibilities	Staff Contributions and Responsibilities
8. Establish behavioral (performance objectives)	Not trained in this technology. Can check validity only. Can supply the numbers and quantities. Has first-hand knowledge of the current inventories of the workers who will become the trainees. If necessary to eliminate some objectives, can make the decision.	Owns this technology and is thus responsible. Knows that if standards have been well defined much of this work is already complete. Can check reasonableness, observability, and measurability of the expected behavioral outcomes. Can query for variable conditions, which might require flexibility in applying standards.
9. Design the program	Has neither skill nor reason for participating here. May be able to offer answers to questions about suitability of some methods in the physical and social environment where training will occur.	Must do this step. Can check to see that all methods suit physical and social climate where training will happen. (Should adapt, not drop, a method just because it's new to the society where training will happen.) Should insist on establishing the evaluation mechanism at this time.
10. Select trainers	Not trained in what to look for; tends to pick the person who does the work best. Can prevent selection of local trainers who would cost the program its credibility. Can recommend local trainers who would have instant credibility with learners. May have regular trainers on own staff. Will hopefully accept some responsibility for conducting the training.	Should explore possibility of using trainers from client organization to give full credibility to the program and the behaviors it teaches. Should look for instructional and communicative skills when picking trainers from client organization. Should encourage active role for management in all sessions.
11. Upgrade trainers	Has little energy or expertise for this task, but must comprehend its importance. Can learn, at this phase, the value of having qualified instructors as permanent resources within the department.	A must! Unless client has staff of qualified instructors, local trainers must learn how to teach. If qualified instructors are available, they must learn course content. If "outside" trainers are used, they must learn course content, climate, and norms for the client organization and probable inventory of student population. Some standard program for upgrading line trainers should be part of the permanent resources of the T&D department!

(continued on next page)

TABLE 4.1 *(continued)*

Phase B: Solving the Problem	Line Contributions and Responsibilities	Staff Contributions and Responsibilities
12. Select trainees	Must be accountable for this activity. Must get help in communicating the enrollment so it's not seen as punitive—yet so it is seen as an accountability to learn to do the job as taught in the program ... and to apply this on the job afterwards. Needs to reallocate or reschedule workload to accommodate the training.	Must refuse to do this. Can assist by seeing that only those who perform the task are enrolled. Can assist (insist?) in seeing that trainees know what is expected of them in the training and later when they apply the learnings on the job. Should stress reasons for the enrollment and accountability for meeting the learning objectives and applying the learnings on the job.
13. Conduct the training	Not often skilled in how to teach—so will need help in carrying out assigned roles in presenting the program. Can be an effective way to educate good workers for positions of greater responsibility. If training is done by those in client organization, it gains credibility. Active participation (at a minimum, attendance) by all line managers gives credibility and urgency to the training. Make excellent members of "teaching teams" composed of trainers from both the line-client and the T&D department.	If staff instructors do the teaching, they may lack awareness of the norms and "no-nos" in the client climate. Can lack credibility since they don't work for management in the client organization. However, if the climate is extremely suspicious, the mantle of the "objective outsider" can be converted to an asset. Can offer sensitivity and insights about the learning dynamics—things to which client trainers are sometimes blind.

Phase C: Evaluation	Line Contributions and Responsibilities	Staff Contributions and Responsibilities
14. Measurement	Has access to the date sources which establish pre/post baselines. Unskilled in designing the measurement instruments. May have to be convinced of the vital importance of this activity.	Must insist that this be done during and after the training. Provides feedback at all phases of training so measurement of group and individual trainees contributes to the learning itself.

(continued on next page)

TABLE 4.1 *(continued)*

Phase C: Evaluation	Line Contributions and Responsibilities	Staff Contributions and Responsibilities
15. Evaluation	Must "sign off" on how well the program solved the problem.	Can help identify and quantify symptoms of success and failure.
	Not trained in analysis or interpreting symptomatic data. Will need help from the T&D specialist.	Can design instruments for the measurement—but must do so as early as steps 3, 8, and 9.
	Can provide confirmation of the evidence revealed by the measurement.	Can manage statistical processes needed to make sound judgments about the effectiveness of the program. (May need to check a tendency to let the evaluation become an exercise in statistics rather than a realistic appraisal of how conditions have or haven't changed for the client with the problem.)
	Can confirm (and must be party to) conclusions drawn from the data about the effectiveness of the program.	
	Can identify remaining problems and/or new performance deficiencies.	Can retrain or reprocess the existing new levels and/or new problems to see if training will help. If not, help find other solutions.

Cooperative Effort

It might be interesting to examine all the entries in the preceding table to see how many actions involve cooperation and collaboration between the T&D manager and the client manager. Few are totally assignable to one side of that line/staff boundary. There is an incredible amount of give-and-take, of mutual effort required to solve performance problems.

And the reason always boils down to this: The line knows its own operation best (including its problems and resources), and the staff sees larger perspectives as it brings its special technology to the solution of performance problems.

It is common for the T&D function to be headquartered in a staff location and thus have "functional" responsibility for training line employees. When such arrangements are installed, a staff of "professionals" inhabits the central T&D department, and "on-the-job trainers" answer to local management within the line operation.

One danger of this system is that the line trainers may become second-class citizens. They do the routine work, teaching from outlines prepared by the "supertrainers" from the central staff. Indeed, staff instructors are often better paid; they have organizational rather than local visibility; they attend outside seminars and grow in professionalism. Because the local trainers are all too often given little upgrading, their instructional skills deteriorate.

Yet the so-called second-class trainers are often perceived as doing the real training work in the real world of the organization. They're out there "on the firing line" and they know "where the real action is." Staff trainers are called such things as "ivory-tower theoreticians." They are often accused of being "too academic."

As long as the rivalry between line and staff trainers can stay affectionate and collaborative, it presents little real danger to an organization. Furthermore, there are definite ways to overcome the dangers that do exist.

One excellent method is to use teaching teams composed of T&D specialists and line instructors. In small organizations, as with a one-person T&D department, the T&D line-manager team offers both local credibility and instructional expertise. The cross-pollination from such teams is obvious: Line trainers are exposed to the technology and larger perspective of staff specialists; T&D specialists have first-hand data and experience in operating shops and offices (see Figure 4.1).

Unfortunately, team teaching is expensive: two leaders instead of one. Nor is it always appropriate to the methods needed for the learning. But even if teams cannot be used all the time, they can be used *some* of the time. Team-design efforts are equally useful. Involvement by both line and staff personnel enhances the quality of the program—and can contribute to the education of all who participate.

Other collaborative efforts can be designed. The nature of the operation, the philosophy about line/staff prerogatives, the position in the marketplace, the marketing strategy—all these influence decisions about what tasks are assigned to staff and what tasks to line elements. But in any arrangement, as many collaborative interfaces as possible between T&D staff, client-management, and line instructors are highly desirable. Central arrangements may prevent inventing the wheel all over again—but they also create some square wheels unless such collaboration exists!

Placement Purely As a Staff Function

If you look at the organizations around you, you'll find that most T&D managers occupy a staff position. As we've noted, that may bring an automatic "curse" unless collaborative activities are devised to overcome the staff stigma.

All apart from the stigma, there may be communication channel problems when T&D activities are centered in a staff location.

But the fact is, it often exists, and one question remains: When T&D is a staff function, to whom does the T&D manager report?

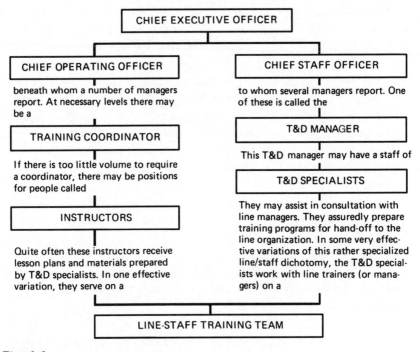

Fig. 4.1.

A productive, traditional system.

A traditional answer (probably by far the most common answer) is to put the T&D manager in the Human Resource Department. No matter what you call them (Vice President of Human Resources, Human Resources Development Director, Training Director, or Director of Employee Development), they report in as peers of Industrial Relations, Employee Relations, and Employee Communications.

With the kind of thinking that envisions the employee roster as a major organizational resource, and with the insight that that roster consists of *individuals* who offer unique contributions, there is a diminished rationale for placing T&D within the Human Resources (HR) department.

Indeed, in some significant ways, the Human Resource Management (HRM) function and the T&D function are counterthrusts: HRM tries to get the right people into the right cubbyholes; T&D, or HRD, on the other hand, not only wants to insure that their capability matches the cubbyhole, but that it grows so that they can fill other cubbyholes. T&D is even concerned with cubbyholes that haven't yet been designed or imagined! Perhaps this disparity of philosophy and purpose explains the recent departure of the T&D function from the HRM department in so many organizations.

When T&D leaves HRM, where does it relocate? Well, if it stays on the "staff side," it tends to answer to the Vice President of Administrative Services, the Director of Support Services, or whatever title applies to the highest-ranking staff officer in the organization. It is significant that the T&D position reports to the top of the staff hierarchy. The position power resulting from this placement cannot be ignored. After all, when T&D is a staff function, its representatives visit the "line territory" much as missionaries visit the frontier. This missionary status is especially noticeable when T&D specialists are consulting, designing, or instructing. As missionaries performing those tasks, they should represent the deities who rank high in their own heavens.

Placement As a Line Function

If the T&D function can report to the chief staff officer of an organization, it can just as logically answer to the chief operating officer—and with rather greater impact. Many T&D managers prefer this arrangement. Among its advantages:

- They are more clearly identified as solvers of operating performance problems.
- They are close to the operation and can give a quicker response to operational performance problems.
- Their proximity to operating managers permits quick access to key data needed for the analysis of performance problems.
- The entire T&D function is more clearly identified with "where the organization is"—a kind of organizational halo effect.
- The actual instruction is done by people affiliated with and responsible to operating authority, yet under the direct control of the T&D manager.
- Budgets for line operations are attractive: They are more flexible, therefore they can respond to sudden developments; they are inclined to be more realistic; and they are often more generous.

Of course, one disadvantage of this placement is that there is no natural mechanism by which the T&D manager can access performance problems on the staff side of the organization—and therefore no mechanism by which staff managers can access the T&D manager to ask for help. Obviously, such mechanisms can be devised, installed, and made to work just as they have in the reverse placement.

It is equally obvious that some organizations can afford—and do require—a T&D manager on both the line and staff sides at the executive level. About the only problem arising from this dual arrangement is the occasional skirmish over territorial imperatives. For example: Which one is responsible for management training and development? Who handles the training in a new technology that cuts across the line/staff barrier?

An answer to these questions is the final placement we might consider in answer to our question, "Where is the Training Department located?"

Placement with the Chief Executive Officer

How do you give proper authority to the T&D manager? How do you avoid wrangles about line and staff prerogatives? One answer is to have the T&D manager answer to the "big boss" to the chief executive officer; that person is often given the title of "Chief Learning Officer" (CLO). Although this arrangement is not the norm in all companies, it is happening more and more frequently, especially in large companies or those heavily dependent on human expertise for competitive advantage. There are some obvious advantages.

First, the position power is unquestioned. When it's necessary to arbitrate between departments battling for T&D assistance, there can be little doubt about the CLO's authority to make a decision. There can also be little doubt that from this position at the top of the pyramid, the CLO is more likely to be given the funds and support for resources, which would permit working on *all* the significant problems.

If it's hard to get at the facts, a person who answers to the top executive has rather a more forceful calling card than one whose boss is called Administrative Assistant or Staff Support Coordinator.

The view from the top provides a perspective permitting a proactive approach to T&D: Participation in strategic planning and crisis response permits far more effective decisionmaking for T&D policy, priorities, and programs.

Perhaps the most important aspect of the perspective is that the news about new directions and imminent crises comes *immediately*. The T&D department is far more able to prevent fires if it has direct access to the top manager of the organization. T&D managers who are peers to the key decisionmakers are key decisionmakers themselves. The same thing is proportionately true when the T&D manager answers to the top manager of either the line or staff organization.

Finally, the quality of the T&D decisions and programs tends to improve if the accountable person, the CLO, is in direct and constant scrutiny of the person who must make "the-buck-stops-here" decisions for the entire organization. Accountability rises in direct proportion to the position.

Summary

As T&D managers gain respect by solving performance problems, their analytical skills deepen and widen along with their knowledge of what the organization is about and how it works. They become acutely conscious of who is doing what work and in what direction they wish to grow. Thus it is no surprise that the T&D manager is asked to solve problems of increasing depth and breadth, problems ranging from simple knowledge deficiencies to organizational development needs involving the top managers.

Of the four inputs into an organization—people, technology, time, and material—the human resource is probably the only one capable of almost limitless appreciation in value. Directing the appreciation process is a big responsibility.

Robert R. Blake, of Managerial Grid fame, has been heard to say that the T&D manager and the chief executive officer should be the same person. That makes great sense. However, the facts of life are that chief executive officers do indeed delegate responsibility for a great many tasks—and human resource development is one they normally delegate. They can delegate the responsibility; but they cannot delegate active interest!

It is sheer delight to see chief executives enlist themselves in personal growth experiences, to hear them ask, "How are your new assertiveness skills working out on the job?" or to welcome them as active students rather than as quick visitors who say, "I wish I had time to stay longer, but I've important things to do!"

Chief executive officers make the most positive statement and the greatest contribution when they actively develop themselves, actively require the continuing development of their immediate subordinates, and visibly reinforce training at all levels of the organization. But they do have other things to do, too. So they characteristically delegate the T&D responsibility.

Where should they position the person to whom they make this delegation?

The training and development function should be positioned where it can give the best possible service to the largest possible number of organizational clients. The traditional dichotomy between "line" and "staff" is helpful only to the degree that it clarifies "who will do what" in solving performance problems. Since teamwork is imperative, and since the T&D specialists must have access to reliable data throughout their organizations, more and more T&D managers report directly to the chief executive officer.

It's a goal worth seeking—and an encouraging development.

Identifying Training Needs

Meeting Customer Needs

The "client" or "customer" will often have a preconceived notion of what the training needs are. However, it is important to note that their perceptions are not always accurately identified. Sometimes, the "fix" doesn't involve training at all. Therefore, we want to emphasize this point: In practice, the customer is seldom completely right. In the best of situations, customers are aware of the problems for which training interventions are needed. More typically, even their view of the problem is biased and often incorrect. Only in the rarest of situations do customers have the expertise to identify, design, and carry out effective HRD solutions. Following the customer's recommendation may satisfy the customer in the short run, but eventually the customers will determine that the T&D efforts they advocated added little value.

Yet many T&D and HRD specialists operate on the principle that customer service is a top priority. When T&D operates from a paradigm of customer service, the tendency is to anchor practice in the core principle of customer service: Ultimately the customer—the managers, trainees, etc.—is always "right" and gets what he or she wants. The end result is that ineffective and sometimes unethical practices are perpetuated and supported by HRD or T&D specialists.

What does that say about the value HRD places on its expertise? If the customer is ultimately always right, then HRD has nothing of value to add other than implementation. This notion is incorrect. HRD expertise is just as important and specialized as any expertise that engineers, accountants, lawyers, or architects have to offer. Furthermore, in an era where the intellectual capital is a competitive advantage, the impact of errors made in managing and developing human resources is at least as serious as the impact of errors in other professions. Ironically, it is the customer service model of practice that leads to lower professional esteem and reputation. In the short run, pleasing customers, even if they are wrong, is seductive. It appears to increase HRD's power and influence. Over the longer term, the end result is likely to be just the opposite. Customer satisfaction is important, but when defined as submitting to the customers' demands, it leads to diminished power and influence. Eventually, customers conclude that the providers of professional services have little value to add. Only when customer satisfaction is bounded by narrowly defined parameters of sound and ethical practice is it an effective performance measure for HRD.

Building Professional Integrity

Why do managers who can do a little training and deal with people decide they are experts in human resource development? The answer appears to be that HRD and T&D professionals themselves have allowed others to think this because of a customer service mentality. A customer service standard of practice leads to substandard practice and ineffective results; in turn, managers conclude that we really don't know what we are doing. Can you blame them? Customer service provides little in the way of a professional compass to guide practice. It allows the profession to be pushed and pulled by customers' whims. Ultimately, it provides little foundation for leadership and is atheoretical.

The challenge to the profession is to stop thinking like retail clerks and to start thinking like true professionals. At the core of most definitions of a profession is the notion that practice is anchored within a system of formal knowledge and expertise. We are not naïve to the pressures HRD professionals face in organizations, but it seems certain that giving into those pressures only makes them worse. The situation will not be changed overnight, but we must start the journey by abandoning the customer service model.

The proper vision of serving customers is one in which customers are satisfied because they got the right answer, even if they are unhappy because they could not get the particular program or service they wanted. A model of sound HRD practice means:

- Saying "No" to our customers and, when necessary, telling them that they are wrong
- Standing up for HRD/T&D practice that has ethical integrity by telling customers that we will not engage in practices that we know are misguided or simply wrong
- Opposing proposals for ineffective practices that we know are harmful to the human dimension of organizations from an ethical perspective rather than a political one

- Grounding practice in sound research and theory
- Spending more time defining "best practice" as what is most effective
- Spending less time talking about what is popular with customers
- Supporting field research to expand the body of HRD knowledge
- Maintaining the highest level of HRD expertise

If we do not value our profession enough to do this, how can we expect any-one else in an organization to view us as credible professional partners? Some might say that this is an arrogant view of HRD/T&D. If HRD/T&D is a core pro-cess for an organization whose success depends on the expertise of its employees, it can make substantial contributions to the organization's ability to accomplish its chosen mission, but only when practiced properly. To practice HRD/T&D properly, specialized expertise is needed. This is fact, not arrogance.

The appropriate vision of an HRD professional is something more akin to that of an architect, a lawyer, or an accountant. In areas of practice where there is room for professional artistry, customer input is sought and honored. But in areas in which specialized expertise is needed, there is no compromise. In those areas, the customer is almost never right. Thus, the T&D manager makes the ultimate decision about what training will be conducted within an organiza-tion. To make that decision, T&D managers must know a training need when they see one—and they must be able to discriminate between performance problems that are training needs and those that are not.

Distinguishing Training Needs from Other Performance Problems

The Swanson Diagnosis Matrix (Swanson, 1994) provides a convenient frame-work for diagnosing performance problems. Built on the Rummler and Brach model (1995), this diagnostic tool examines the mission/goal, system design, capacity, motivation, and expertise within the organizational, process, and indi-vidual contexts.

Key questions in helping to determine performance questions are listed below:

SAMPLE PROBLEM DEFINITION QUESTIONS

1. What opportunities do you see to improve the performance of this organization?
2. How do you know these opportunities exist?
3. When did you first notice the problem?
4. What data do you have that there are performance problems?
5. How are the problems affecting your unit now?

TABLE 5.1. Swanson's Performance Diagnosis Matrix

Performance Variables	Organizational Level	Process Level	Individual Level
Mission/goal	Does the organization's mission/goal fit the reality of the economic, political and cultural forces?	Do the process goals enable the organization to meet organization and individual mission/goals?	Are the professional and personal mission/goals of individuals congruent with the organization's?
System design	Does the organization's system provide structure and policies supporting the desired performance?	Are processes designed in such a way to work as a system?	Does the individual face obstacles that impede job performance?
Capacity	Does the organization have the leadership, capital, and infrastructure to achieve its mission/goals?	Does the process have the capacity to perform (quantity, quality, and timeliness)?	Does the individual have the mental, physical, and emotional capacity to perform?
Motivation	Do the policies, culture, and reward systems support the desired performance?	Does the process provide the information and human factors required to maintain it?	Does the individual want to perform, no matter what?
Expertise	Does the organization establish and maintain selection and training policies and resources?	Does the process of developing expertise meet the changing demands of changing processes?	Does the individual have the knowledge, skills, and experience to perform?

6. How are these opportunities related to the organization's goals?
7. Have you taken any action to address the problems?
8. What barriers do you see to making changes to improve performance?

Mission/Goals: Does the organization's mission/goals fit the reality of the economic, political, and cultural forces?

SAMPLE PERFORMANCE DIAGNOSIS
MATRIX QUESTIONS/ORGANIZATIONAL LEVEL

1. Does the organization have clear mission/goals?
2. Is the organization's mission/goals clearly articulated and communicated?
3. Is the organization's strategic plan compatible with the organization's mission/goals?
4. Does the organization's strategic direction support its mission/goals?
5. Has the organization's strategy/direction been articulated and communicated?
6. Does the organization's strategy make sense in terms of external threats and opportunities and internal strengths and weaknesses?
7. Given this strategy, have the required outputs of the organization and the level of performance expected from each output been determined and articulated?
8. Will the organization's strategic plan help, or at least not hinder, the organization's ability to meet external needs or demands?
9. Will the mission/goals help the organization either to obtain or to maintain a competitive advantage?
10. Have appropriate functional goals been set?
11. Have the economic, political, and cultural forces that potentially affect the organization's mission/goals been identified?
12. Are current economic conditions, both inside and outside the organization, conducive to efforts to meet the organization's mission/goals?
13. Is the political climate, both inside and outside the organization, a facilitator or barrier to efforts to meet the organization's mission/goals?
14. What role do cultural forces, both inside and outside the organization, play in efforts to meet the organization's mission/goals?

System Design: Does the organization's system provide structure and policies supporting desired performance?

1. Are the interfaces between the functions being managed?
2. Does the organization's current division into units or functions support the mission/goals and strategic plan of the organization?
3. Are workgroups or teams organized in a way that supports the mission/goals and strategic plan of the organization?
4. Are the current systems, such as information and rewards, centralized or decentralized in a way that supports the mission/goals and strategic plan of the organization?

5. Does the degree of consistency or variability of operations from one area to another support the mission/goals and strategic plan of the organization?
6. Do organizational systems currently have the degree of flexibility required to support the mission/goals and strategic plan of the organization?
7. Are all relevant functions in place?
8. Are all functions necessary?
9. Is the current flow of inputs and outputs between functions appropriate?
10. Does the formal organizational structure support the strategy and enhance the effectiveness of the system?
11. Have performance expectations been articulated and communicated for each function?

Capacity: Does the organization have the leadership, capital, and infrastructure to achieve its mission/goals?

1. Are resources appropriately allocated?
2. Will people have the budget or decisionmaking authority they need to implement the system design components?
3. Are there organizational measurements that will allow people to determine whether the organization's efforts have been successful?
4. Do the people who will implement the process possess the skills, knowledge, and experience necessary to make it work?
5. Are on-the-job resources available to support the organization's employees?
6. Are current time requirements or allowances for completing work compatible with the organization's mission/goals?
7. Is the predictability of workload compatible with the organization's requirements?
8. Will the overall workload be manageable?
9. Are management's expectations of people reasonable?
10. Does the current physical environment foster or inhibit the organization's efforts?
11. Do people have the equipment, tools, materials, and information they need to work effectively and efficiently?
12. Are support services or personnel needed and/or available?
13. Are the resources people need easily accessible to them?

14. Do current management and leadership practices support the mission/ goals and strategic plan of the organization?

Motivation: Do the policies, culture, and reward systems support the desired performance?

1. Is there typically a match between what the organization states as values and the kind of behavior that is actually recognized and rewarded?
2. Do current team norms about work behavior support the organization's mission/goals and strategic plan?
3. Are the organization's mission/goals and strategic plan compatible with people's beliefs about integrity and ethical behavior?
4. Is the way in which people receive feedback about their work compatible with the change in frequency, timing, and format?
5. Are people currently rewarded and recognized for behavior that is compatible with the organization's mission/goals and strategic plan?
6. Are current organizational expectations about work and work behavior compatible with what will be required to meet the organization's mission/goals and strategic plan?
7. Will the efforts required to meet the mission/goals and strategic plan of the organization contribute to increasing or maintaining employee satisfaction?

Expertise: Does the organization establish and maintain selection and training policies and resources?

1. Are current productivity levels sufficient to meet the requirements of the organization's mission/goals and strategic plan?
2. Are work standards or criteria currently compatible with those required by the organization's mission/goals and strategic plan?
3. Is relevant performance measured?
4. Are appropriate selection criteria in place?
5. Are effective training interventions developed and implemented?
6. Are adequate resources allocated to employee development efforts?
7. Are employee training policies focused on performance?
8. Are training interventions adequately evaluated?

Mission/Goals: Do the process goals enable the organization to meet organizational and individual mission/goals?

Process Level

1. Have appropriate process goals been set?
2. Are goals for key processes linked to customer and organization requirements?
3. Has the organization clearly identified the mission/goals for its processes?
4. Are the process mission/goals clearly articulated and communicated?
5. Are the process mission/goals compatible with both the organization's mission/goals and strategic plan and the mission/goals of individual employees?
6. Do the mission/goals identified for the processes support the organization's strategic plan and individual initiatives?
7. Do the process mission/goals make sense in terms of external threats and opportunities and internal strengths and weaknesses?
8. Have the required outputs of the processes and the level of performance expected from each output been determined and articulated?
9. Will the process mission/goals help, or at least not hinder, the organization's ability to meet external needs or demands?
10. Will the process mission/goals help the organization either obtain or maintain a competitive advantage?

System Design: Are processes designed in such a way to work as a system?

1. Is this the most efficient and effective process for accomplishing the process goals?
2. Does the workflow progress in a logical and systematic manner?
3. Have appropriate process subgoals been set?
4. Is process performance managed?
5. Have process performance expectations been articulated and communicated?
6. Have sufficient resources been allocated to each process?
7. Are the interfaces between process steps being managed?
8. Are the work procedures or processes supportive of the mission/goals and strategic plan of the organization?
9. Is the current workflow designed to give efficient and effective support to the mission/goals and strategic plan of the organization?
10. Is the design of work generally free of duplications of effort or gaps that could interfere with the mission/goals and strategic plan of the organization?
11. Do the processes work together as a system to enhance organizational effectiveness?

Capacity: Does the process have the capacity to perform (quantity, quality, and timeliness)?

1. Are the time constraints associated with the process design too restrictive?
2. Can the process produce a high-quality output given the related time constraints?
3. Are all resources required for the process adequately available?
4. Do employees have easy access to the resources needed for process implementation?
5. Are the resources required the most suitable for the process?

Motivation: Does the process provide the information and human factors required to maintain it?

1. Does the process produce intrinsic rewards that serve as motivators for individuals and employee groups?
2. Are feedback mechanisms built into the process that generate information to the employees required to work within the constraints of the process?
3. Does the process take the individual into consideration? In other words, does the process include components or steps that would serve as motivational factors to individuals involved in the process?
4. Is the technical design of the process user friendly for individuals working within them?
5. Is all the information needed for effective process performance readily available?

Expertise: Does the process of developing expertise meet the changing demands of the changing processes?

1. Is expertise defined for each step of the process?
2. When the processes change, are appropriate expertise development opportunities made available?
3. Is employee expertise sufficiently broad to allow processes to change?

Mission/Goals: Are the professional and personal mission/goals of individuals congruent with the organization's?

INDIVIDUAL LEVEL
1. Do the performers understand the job goals (the outputs they are expected to produce and the standards they are expected to meet)?

2. Do the performers know whether they are meeting the job goals?
3. Are the performers rewarded for meeting the job goals?
4. Are individual goals congruent with organization and process goals?

System Design: Does the individual face obstacles that impede job performance?

1. Are job outputs and standards linked to process requirements? Are process requirements in turn linked to customer and organization requirements?
2. Are process requirements reflected in the appropriate jobs?
3. Are job steps in a logical sequence?
4. Have supportive policies and procedures been developed?
5. Is the job environment ergonomically sound?
6. Can the performer easily recognize the input requiring action?
7. Is the current assignment of job functions or tasks appropriate to support the mission/goals and strategic plan of the organization?
8. Have barriers to performance been removed where possible?

Capacity: Does the individual have the mental, physical, and emotional capacity to perform?

1. Are adequate resources available to enhance individual performance (time, information, etc.)?
2. Is the individual "right" for the job?
3. Do people have the confidence they need to meet the organization's mission/goals?
4. Does the individual have the potential to improve or change performance when necessary?

Expertise: Does the individual have the knowledge, skills, and experience to perform?

1. Have the knowledge, skills, and abilities required to adequately perform the job been identified?
2. Has the individual been evaluated for the required knowledge, skills, and abilities (KSAs)?
3. Has the individual been adequately trained for the job?
4. Can the individual continue to develop to meet future job requirements?

We have already noted that the chief test for a training need is just this: Does the employee know how to meet the performance standards for an accountable task? Accordingly, you will note that there is only one cell in this entire matrix that pertains to training problems: the analysis of expertise at the individual level.

If the answer is "Yes, the employee knows how," there is no training need. There is a performance problem; but it isn't a training need because more training will not solve the problem. The employee already knows how. There must be other obstacles to satisfactory performance. Thus, the remaining cells in the matrix do not warrant training solutions.

We can look at those other obstacles later. For the moment, let's just make sure we know what a training need is. *A training need exists when an employee lacks the knowledge or skill to perform an assigned task satisfactorily.*

This statement implies standards of performance. That may or may not be true: Not every organization has established standards for every task—and lots of standards have been informally established, but never documented. If there are no standards against which employee performance can be measured, it's very hard to conclude that the employee is not performing properly. Nevertheless, the T&D specialist, in the role of consultant, often gets into precisely that situation. Managers are dissatisfied with employees performances, but haven't identified precisely what level of performance would satisfy them. That often happens when new jobs are established, when the technology is altered, or when procedures are modified. It can also happen when employees begin to neglect old tasks, or perform tasks indifferently, or perform in ways that are not up to their manager's tacit expectations.

What can the T&D manager do in the face of such vague specifications? Well, this is one time when questioning skills are very, very useful. The reputation of the T&D department doesn't gain much respect if T&D specialists just say, "Well, when you make up your mind what you want, get in touch!" This is the perfect chance to ask direct questions to uncover the facts and to ask open questions to discover feelings, and then to reflect upon the manager's frustration over the performance problems back on the job and the hard thinking you're asking for in this consultation.

Far better that the T&D specialist and the perplexed client-manager mutually explore the issue to determine what level of performance *would* satisfy the manager whose people present a problem. Thus T&D specialists, acting in the role of consultant, can be heard asking things such as, "When you envision workers doing this job properly, what do you see them doing?" "What specific things would you like to see them doing—but don't?" "When you walk up to workers to tell them they're doing well, what specific things do you praise?"

"When you correct them for doing things the wrong way, what specific things do you ask them to avoid?" "What do you ask them to be certain to do in the future?"

Even though the answers to such questions are not yet sanctioned (or is the proper word "sanctified"?) by being published in procedures manuals, the T&D specialist has begun the standards-setting process. The next decision is whether the new "specification" is a reasonable expectation of workers.

At this stage, astute T&D managers try (1) to involve *several* managers, (2) to reach agreement without pain or "lose/lose" relationships, (3) to clarify goals and start the evaluation process by discussing what "things will look like when we have succeeded," and (4) to plant the idea of positive reinforcers for those workers who meet standards after the change effort. The truly wise ones also (5) conduct a reality test by involving workers themselves.

Workers' comments will do many things:

- Explain whether prescribed/recommended standards are reasonable
- Uncover interesting and productive information about hidden task interferences and conflicting consequences
- Help identify useful feedback data that might let them know how they're doing while they're performing
- Tell the T&D specialist whether the job aids (present training, written procedures, and job descriptions) are accurate (all too often they are not)

In gaining helpful inputs from managers and workers while defining performance standards, T&D representatives will be implanting that important concept that organizations get their work done because people fill their positions properly. They "put out the proper outputs." Positions, in turn, are made up of responsibilities; these, in turn, are discharged by the proper completion of various tasks. To set standards, we define those tasks by specifying the actions to be taken and the criteria of successful completion.

In many standards-setting conversations, it's necessary to point out that "criteria" is just a big word to describe what makes the work "okay" and what makes it "not okay." This includes data about what's right and wrong; it also includes data about how many in what period of time.

Once the actions and criteria are identified, performance conditions need to be considered; these include what the worker is given to work with and what happens when there are variations in working conditions. For example: a customer service representative who deals with the public may be encouraged to ask a pleasant question of customers. That's a "standard of performance"—unless there are more than three people waiting in line! Under those conditions, the pleasant question may be sacrificed in favor of speedy service to all three customers.

When determining standards, it's useful to think in certain terms:

numbers—such as hours, units, requests, completions
dollars—sales, unit costs, resources consumed, hours-of-effort multiplied by salary-per-hour
percent—of overtime, turnover, rejects, or utilization
time lapse—such as flowtime, set-up, inventory turnover
completions—shipments, acceptance, milestones

Skill in writing performance standards, or at least in describing human be-havior, is a "must" for all T&D managers and specialists. Some organizations have begun to train managers from all departments in how to define perfor-mance standards. One such firm (Kemper Insurance Companies) has con-ducted workshops so that line managers become trainers for workshops at which still other line managers learn how to develop standards for their subor-dinates. Kemper stresses the importance of developing the actual standards as a joint effort between the manager and the subordinate—not as a product of staff trainers.

Once the standards are agreed upon by key people in the client department, the T&D specialist is ready to ask that all-important question: "Do the people who must meet these standards possess the knowledge and skill to do so right now?" If the answer is yes, no training is indicated.

For newcomers, that seldom happens. They rarely know how to do their new jobs perfectly. For them, we have discovered a training need. It does not follow, however, that newcomers need training in all facets of their positions. Even newcomers have some ability and some knowledge, and we call this their "inventory." If we match the inventory against the standard we have set, we have a possible training need.

What the employee must do to meet the standard can be represented by the letter M for minimum mastery, or "must do." From this M we subtract the in-ventory to discover what the newcomer needs to learn to perform properly.

The test is somewhat different for employees who are already incumbent in their positions. We can again let M represent what the worker must do; from that we still subtract the I, or inventory. But this time the inventory is what the worker is actually doing now. The difference between the M and the I is a po-tential training need. We now have a formula for potential training needs:

$$M - I = \text{A potential training need.}$$

The word "potential" is accurate. Why? Because with incumbents we are not yet certain that the reason for difference is lack of knowledge or skill. We don't yet know that *they do not know how.* Only if the reason for the difference is their not knowing how do we have a training need.

It's helpful to regard the distance between the "must do" and the "is doing" as a deficiency. We can put this into our formula by assigning it the letter *D*. Now our formula looks like this:

$$M - I = D.$$

At this stage we are now ready to consider several different types of deficiency. When employees don't know how, we call this DK for "deficiency of knowledge." All DKs are regarded as training needs. If the difference between the "must do" and the "is doing" stems from other causes, we consider it a "deficiency of execution" and call it a DE. What "other causes" might there be? To name a few: lack of feedback, badly engineered jobs, or punishing consequences. DEs are not solvable through training.

Sometimes people know how to do the job, but have so little practice that they cannot maintain a satisfactory level of performance. This might be called a DP, or "deficiency of practice." Training in the form of drill may solve DP problems. (But one just has to ask why the manager of these inventories let them go to waste!)

Individual Needs and Organizational Needs

Many T&D managers find it helpful to think of two classes of training needs: individual and organizational. The difference is very simple, but it has heavy impact on the response made by the T&D department. Of course, an individual training need exists for just one person, or for a very small population. Organizational training needs exist in a large group of employees such as the entire population with the same job classification. That happens, for example, when all clerks must be trained in a new procedure, or all managers in new policy. A manager in a specialized department, however, may develop an individual training need when some new technology is introduced into that field, or when performance as a manager reveals the noncomprehension of one facet of good managerial practice!

When new employees enter the organization, it is assumed that they know nothing of policies and procedures, nothing about organizational goals or structures. These deficiencies of knowledge are assumed to apply to all new people.

However, there may also be individual needs involving special tasks the newcomer will perform; it is a good idea to "take inventory" to see whether the individual meets the standards for some of the skills necessary to the satisfactory performance of a position.

Because there may be serious lapses in such areas, some organizations use "certification testing." These might be written exams, performance demonstrations, or both. They are tests requiring the employees to demonstrate their capabilities to *perform* a specific task or job duty.

One T&D manager describes the process for certification testing this way: "They are used as predictors of job performance to assure the company that employees are ready to perform job responsibilities safely and accurately following the completion of their training." In other words, there is individual testing or assessment before there is organizational assessment.

Potential Sources of Individual Training Needs

How does a conscientious T&D manager discover actual symptoms of these individual and organizational training needs?

Let's look first at the individual needs. What better place to start than by keeping an eye on the existing employee systems? The actions taken to maintain employee systems lead to the discovery of many training needs:

- *New hires.* Their individual need is the peculiar information required before they can feel comfortably and acceptably "at speed" in the new position. This information might include such organizational cultural factors as starting times, lunch and break schedules, the location of the necessary rooms, whom to turn to for help. If prehiring interviews or certification testing reveal deficiencies bad enough to correct (but not serious enough to deny employment), those are also individual training needs.

(Just a note about training needs for hires: Not all their needs should be met immediately. They should be trained only for tasks they will perform *soon;* they will be overwhelmed by—and forget—training in tasks they won't perform until later in their tours of duty.)

- *Promotions.* When one person moves into a position of greater responsibility, we may presume that there will be a gap between that person's inventory and the knowledge and skill required to perform properly in the new position.

- *Transfers.* Even if no promotion is involved, switching to new responsibilities is a signal that there may be a temporary mismatch between what the employee can already do and what must be done to perform satisfactorily in the new placement.

- *Performance Appraisals.* This system exists in many organizations for both management and nonmanagement positions. The "suggestions for improvement" are invariably triggers for individual education and development—and thus symptoms of training needs. Let's suppose a manager or supervisor tells a subordinate to acquire a new skill, or to master the conceptual framework for some phase of the present job that isn't being done as well as it might be; the T&D manager now has data that a perceived individual training need exists. Helping the appraised and the appraiser develop a plan for acquiring new or perfected skills is an important part of the human resource development activity. It matters not at all whether the growth recommended is meant to improve performance on the present position, education to prepare for the next assignment, or development to help the organization grow to fit new environments. Any suggestion calls for some response—an offer to help—from the T&D department.

- *Career planning programs.* Since these tell where employees want to go, they also can reveal lacks (deficiencies) in the current inventories of those people.

- *An accident.* An accident may signal that an employee is unaware of certain safety regulations. If the accident report indicates that the probable cause is ignorance, the T&D department has a trigger to see that the DK is quickly overcome.

- *Quality control records.* If the record shows the profile of individual workers (and it should if it's a dynamic management instrument!), then that profile reveals consistent errors. If the worker is making the same mistake again and again, it's time to find out why. Does the worker know better? If not, training is needed.

- *Grievances.* When a grievance is filed against a foreman, a supervisor, or a manager, alert T&D specialists ask whether these people know what they are entitled to do and what they are constrained against doing under policy or contract statements. When they act out of ignorance, a DK has been uncovered and some individual training is indicated.

- *New positions.* These are created occasionally as the way to handle incomplete or lagging workloads—and as a way to introduce new technology into the organization. When this occurs, the people who fill the new positions will almost assuredly have a need to acquire new knowledge and skill. If the position is filled with people from outside the organization, the newcomers will have a DK about the policies and procedures of their new employers.
- *Special assignments.* These are vehicles for educating and developing incumbent employees. People so assigned will inevitably have some DKs about the terms of their assignment as well as about the technology required in the special tasks.
- *Job descriptions.* Individual training needs are especially important if the job descriptions are under attack for being useless.
- *Research and development projects.*
- *Tuition refund programs.*
- *Job rotation programs.*
- *Cross-qualification decisions.* All these are possible sources of individual training needs. When people assume duties under any of these programs, they inherit some lack of knowledge about the terms of the activity. T&D managers who manage the *entire* T&D function establish communication mechanisms to keep themselves informed about routine activities in all such programs. They can therefore respond effectively with good counsel about how to overcome the DKs that are inevitably created in such programs. Usually they become actively involved in designing the learning experiences.

That represents a wide range of potential training needs for the individual employee. Isn't it nice that most of them result because a person or an organization has grown and will enjoy still more developmental training?

Potential Sources of Organizational Training Needs

Certain organization events trigger the proactive T&D manager to look for training needs involving large numbers of people. The first source of information is so obvious that many overlook it!

- *Regular management reports* tell about production, warehousing or inventory problems about trends in turnover, or grievances about an array of things that cause T&D managers to ask whether human performance could be a cause. A great deal of valuable news can be discovered by reading the reports the upper management requires to run the organization.

- *Special reports and requests* reveal future plans, shifting priorities, problem areas, successes, failures—many of which either result from human performance or will involve it. They reveal new strategies and programs that may require people to do things they have never done before. That means potential inadequate human inventories, and inadequate human inventories are symptoms of potential training needs.
- *New plants* usually mean new hiring, sometimes new positions.
- *New products,* which can result only if a new technology (or significant amendments to old technologies) are acquired by significant numbers of employees.
- *New equipment or machinery* can arrive when there are new plants or new products—or simply because somebody found a better way to handle old tasks. Examples: The Accounting Department gets a new computer, or the Print Shop buys new equipment. If many people become involved with these machines, there is an organizational training need.
- *Changes in standards,* as we have noted so many times, inevitably mean that large numbers of people must be informed—and sometimes trained. Frequently, incumbents need a chance to express their feelings about the change, to understand the reasons for the new standard so that they can accept it more easily—or at least respond effectively by "going along with it."
- *Trends* in any operating or management index are signals for training needs for populations of employees—especially if the trend is in the wrong direction. Thus sales reports, productivity indices, cost figures, waste reports, back orders, reject rates, turnover, grievance trends, and frequent recommendations in appraisals—all these are good data for the T&D manager who is deciding what training needs might exist in the organization.
- *New policies* frequently result from the changing position of the organization in the marketplace. If times are tough, the employment, layoff, benefits, and salary "package" may be changed. When that happens, the expectations of employees often change, too. How will they know the new policies, and where will they express the new expectations, unless in training-type sessions? The alert T&D manager sees that such sessions are considered.

It's quite apparent, then, that T&D managers receive signals about potential needs by constantly monitoring the ongoing operation!

Is that the only way to find training needs? No, but it is assuredly the most reliable and the most consistent way to remain relevant and responsive. Personnel moves and operating events and indices tell management where the organization is succeeding, where it is falling short, and where it is going. Paperwork that supports these activities can provide data that trigger the T&D manager to further investigation and analysis.

Furthermore, if T&D managers make intelligent use of these symptoms, they can avoid the "firefighter" trap. That is, instead of being purely reactive they can become proactive and take steps to solve potential performance problems before they become actual problems. By carefully scrutinizing personnel moves, operating activity, and planning documents, the best T&D managers generate good training programs before damaging deficiencies occur.

Surveys or Interviews?

In addition to the monitoring and anticipation, T&D managers often use surveys (for quantitative data) and interviews (for qualitative data) to poll managers for their perception of the training needs in the organization.

Unfortunate results sometimes grow out of such surveys and interviews if T&D managers fail to consider carefully what questions they ask and how they interpret the data.

A typical ploy is to concentrate on perceived training needs and ask managers, "What are your training needs going to be in the next year?" Line managers don't know their training needs! So they either ignore the survey or provide misleading and superficial data. Hotheads with deep personal agendas send very strong signals, only to give intense but distorted pictures of the situation. Conscientious managers who have nothing much to say but who think they ought to say something send back lots of data based on minimum thought or perceptivity.

Another problem grows out of asking managers to tell the T&D specialists their training needs: They come to believe that they do know how to determine training needs. Over time, they begin to demand training for performance problems that training won't solve. At that point, because the T&D manager is in a weak, defensive position, he or she tries to dissuade clients from doing training. It's an awkward position, even when training won't do any good.

Inherent in any survey is the problem that once line managers have responded, they feel they have totally discharged their responsibility for training.

They need only wait until a schedule is published, nominate a few subordinates to fill up their established "quota" of enrollments—and that's it.

The trouble with all this is that in relevant training systems, that isn't "it" at all.

In relevant T&D systems, line managers in all departments and at all levels of the organization see the direct relationship between their own operations and T&D programs. If they merely respond to surveys or interviews, line managers are in a purely passive position with no proactive responsibility and no proactive potential benefit. This passivity, which may result from a needs determination based on nothing but surveys and interviews, is unacceptable to dynamic T&D managers.

On the other hand, if the T&D department never takes its inquiry to the actual line-manager clients, it risks bad generalizations about the macrotraining needs of the organization. Thus, the most astute T&D managers use surveys and interviews to validate their own analysis of the data gathered in monitoring the ongoing operation.

Perhaps an effective summary of the relationship between surveys and interviews on the one hand, and monitoring the operation on the other, would go like this:

1. Basic signals about training needs come from monitoring the ongoing operation.
2. Signals about individual training needs are pursued, the T&D department using further inquiry and analysis with the manager of the potential trainees and, of course, with the trainees themselves.
3. Signals about the organizational training needs of the organization are validated by further inquiry in the form of surveys and interviews.
4. New signals that come from the surveys and interviews are validated by reference to the "hard data" from the operational monitoring.

By such a dual focus in determining training needs, the T&D manager can better validate the accuracy and completeness of the department's response to the training, education, and development needs of the organization.

There are also various actions the T&D manager can take to make certain that the surveys and interviews actually used are of maximum help.

First, one faces the question: Shall we use a survey or interviews? The answer depends on several criteria. The T&D manager must consider the size of the population, the sensitivity of the issues, and the time available.

Clearly, interviews are time-consuming and unfeasible when a vast population must be reached. An alternative is to interview a few and send surveys to larger numbers. If the population is extremely vast, the T&D manager may have to sample, even on the survey.

If the issue of training is especially sensitive, or if strong feelings exist about certain programs, then perhaps no survey can measure the depth of the feelings; only interviews can permit that two-way affective exchange. On the other hand, if people are taking training too much for granted, perhaps the "hot" interview medium will rekindle the interest the T&D manager would like to generate.

The issue of time involves at least two facets. There is the time available before the data must be collected and analyzed. There is also the time the data source is willing to invest in supplying the information. No matter which one uses, interviews or surveys, the decision should reflect a genuine concern for the responder. Short is best—so long as it can provide good data on which to base training decisions. Surveys should be as brief as possible, with the time for completion measured in minutes rather than hours. Interviews should be just as long as the interviewer told the interviewee they would last—no longer.

Perhaps the decision table shown in Figure 5.1 will provide some help in deciding whether to use surveys or interviews in the next data-gathering quest. Regardless of the medium (surveys or interviews), the same questions are useful. The two most useful questions are probably these:

1. What are your people doing that they shouldn't be doing?
2. What aren't your people doing that they should be doing?

These have the value of orienting the responder toward behaviors. They focus on visible behaviors—which are the only kind we can ultimately verify. Thus these two questions put the entire inquiry into the proper realm: human performance. In addition, they tend to be relatively open, yet relatively specific. However, most effective surveys and interviews contain a balance between open questions and directive questions.

We have already noted the futility of asking managers to tell us what their training needs are. They don't know. Besides, it's our job to determine training needs. It's their job to identify performance problems, ours to help them solve those problems. Training may be the solution—or it may not.

Another direct question, "What are your problems?" tends to be less than productive for the T&D specialist. The question itself may be too threatening: Managers probably can't afford to have problems—at least not publicly. Even if they share their problems, the question doesn't focus on human performance. It's likely to uncover such things as the inadequate plumbing, the

If the population is	And time is	And sensitivity is	Then
Big	Tight	Low	Use survey
Big	Tight	High	Interview a sample of the population
Big	Ample	High	Interview
Big	Ample	Low	Survey with limited interviews to validate
Small	Tight/Ample	High	Interview
Small	Tight	High	Interview (This is often the initial data-gathering activity in an organization development program.)

Fig. 5.1.

Deciding whether to use surveys or interviews.

deterioration of the community in which the office is located, or the tight labor market.

Client descriptions of performance problems are often a bit cloudy; it's easy for managers to contract a disease called "They Don't Make People the Way They Used To!"

However, when asked to do so, managers can usually describe what they would like their subordinates *not* to be doing. From that the T&D specialist can move to the next question: "What would you like to see them doing that they aren't doing now?" or "Just describe what you see your staff doing when you view the office the day after the new system has been installed." Then when that visioning step is complete, ask, "Now what do you see a week after the installation?"

For the client unskilled in visioning, a format or matrix such as the one shown in Figure 5.2 often helps.

Such formatting brings focus. Of course, there are other ways to help client managers specify what they want; for example, prioritizing exercises, such as the one in Figure 5.3.

Such lists of skills "prime the pump" and encourage client managers to envision specific behavior rather than make general complaints about the human condition.

A little of that "pump priming" can be a good thing; too much can be harmful. It limits the client manager's responses in several significant ways:

• A long list deters them from thinking of their own performance problems.
• A long list limits their creativity.
• A long list implies that the thinking has already been done by the T&D department.

ACTION (What you should see them doing)	OBJECT (What they do it to)	HOW WELL? HOW OFTEN? HOW MUCH?
Type	letters and reports	with *all* errors corrected.
Add 5%	sales tax	to *all* purchases, without error, by referring to chart on cash register.
Restock	all shelves	when no customers are in the department.
Serve	customers	whenever there are customers present.
Refrain	from chatting	with other salespersons if customers are anywhere in the department.

Fig. 5.2.

Matrix for identifying expectations.

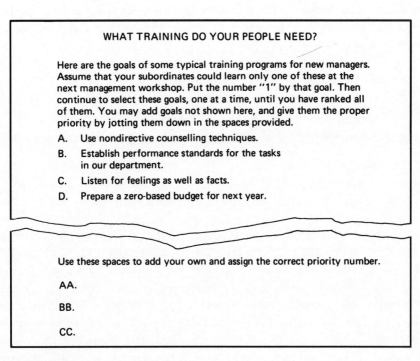

WHAT TRAINING DO YOUR PEOPLE NEED?

Here are the goals of some typical training programs for new managers.
Assume that your subordinates could learn only one of these at the
next management workshop. Put the number "1" by that goal. Then
continue to select these goals, one at a time, until you have ranked all
of them. You may add goals not shown here, and give them the proper
priority by jotting them down in the spaces provided.

A.   Use nondirective counselling techniques.

B.   Establish performance standards for the tasks
     in our department.

C.   Listen for feelings as well as facts.

D.   Prepare a zero-based budget for next year.

Use these spaces to add your own and assign the correct priority number.

AA.

BB.

CC.

Fig. 5.3.

Establishing learning goals.

Although Figure 5.4 brings focus by forcing the manager to rank items (as in Figure 5.3), it lists topics only; there is little implication of behavior and no mention whatsoever of standards or criteria. It would be more useful if, instead of topical lists, it listed skills such as "provides for two-way feedback when making assignments" or "voluntarily prepares zero-based budget forecasts for semiannual, annual, and five-year cycles." Nevertheless, as it stands, the format can help acquire data from client managers who are not accustomed to dealing with a training function that uses behavioral statements.

By completing such a question, line managers help the T&D director put proper priorities on training objectives and training needs—even as they give helpful data about performance problems.

It's important to include, in any structured question, a place for the responder to include fresh ideas—as the suggestions they may add to the bottom of the list in the "What Training Do You and Your People Need?" forms just examined. This is just as true of interviews as it is of surveys.

Respondents need a chance to inject their own ideas. On questionnaires, blank lines where they can add items reveal many interesting data. Open questions are excellent ways to involve respondents. For example, the T&D specialist might ask (on a questionnaire as well as face-to-face) the respondent's opinion about:

- The chief duties of the T&D department
- The respondent's own responsibilities for training and development
- The most significant changes this organization might make to improve its training and development activity
- The most significant skills the respondent could acquire with the help of the T&D department
- The most significant skills the respondent's subordinates could acquire with the help of the T&D department

One big advantage of the interview is its flexibility. When preplanned questions fail to hit pay dirt, or when the unexpected "agendas" of interviewees begin to appear, the interviewer can always move into an "open and reflective question" mode to accommodate and encourage the unanticipated data. When the responder gives extraneous answers, obviously not understanding the question, interviewers can always rephrase and redirect. In other words, a planned interview assumes that interviewer and interviewee alike can follow the structure—yet shift, add, adapt, or delete as the dynamics of the interview require. When the T&D specialists who conduct interviews cannot do so, there is a training need right in the T&D department, isn't there?

WHAT TRAINING DO YOU AND YOUR PEOPLE NEED?			
If you could divide 100 percent of the training effort among the following topics, how would you do so? Divide exactly 100 percent, but assign no effort at all to topics in which you don't want training.	For yourself	For your own direct reports	For those who report to your direct reports
Cashflow, budgeting, and economic planning			
Interpersonal relationships			
Time management			
Other (specify)			
Other (specify)			
TOTAL	100%	100%	100%

Fig. 5.4.

Getting training priorities from line managers.

This does not mean that interviews are loosely structured. There should certainly be some forced questions to test the depth of the conviction and to ensure some common basis for comparing data from all interviewees. Any forced choice would serve this need. A parallel to the list of desired learning objectives would be something like this: "Of the seven training programs listed here, assume you could have just one. Which would it be? Which one would you least likely use?" This process can then be repeated, with the same list of programs, by asking the manager to do the same selection—but as if the choices were for subordinates rather than for the manager.

Prioritizing Training Needs

It must be quite apparent that the T&D manager has many sources of data about potential training needs. Whether they seek micro- or macrotraining, alert T&D managers keep their eyes on the operation, on key communications, and on personnel moves even as they poll their client population.

If there are lots of signals from lots of sources, the training needs (or the need for some performance-problem solution) may exceed the resources available to meet those needs. On what basis does the T&D manager decide which needs to fill?

At such moments, a written policy statement comes in mighty handy. But on what basis does that policy rest? In most organizations, at least four criteria must be considered: cost-effectiveness, legal requirements, executive pressure, and the population to be served. Let's examine each criterion individually.

The cost of a performance problem can usually be determined. It's relatively easy if one immediately knows the cost of a defective unit. For example, if word processors are having to retype letters, you can take the number of letters they retype and multiply that by the cost per letter. To establish the cost per letter, one divides the total cost of the clerical pool by the number of letters produced for an equal time period. Therefore, if a letter costs $1.05 to type, and 40 percent of the 1,000 letters per week must be retyped, the deficiency costs $450 per week and $21,840 per year. If this research is too cumbersome, industry averages are available (as the $1.05 used here is) from many sources. Usually, they're available within the organization in some of the many management-control reports generated by the computer for the Controller.

Price tags for other behaviors, such as managerial skills, are more elusive—but not impossible. Consider a problem in which management complains that supervisors are "soft." Further probing reveals that this "softness" reveals itself in a refusal to give decisions in grievances. Supervisors just pass them to the next level of review. The T&D manager can use the salary costs for each level to establish the cost of a single grievance. Since there is no decision, that cost is waste. By multiplying this unit cost by the number of unanswered grievances, one can establish the cost of the deficiency.

For either the deficiency or the undecided grievances, it's then necessary to compute the cost of the solution: development costs, salary costs, special expenses. Do they add up to less than the cost of the problem? If not, these problems don't meet the cost-effectiveness criterion. If they do meet that criterion, they may need to go into a "waiting list" because they offer fewer cost benefits than other problems.

A second criterion is the legal requirement. Numerous government statutes dictate some of the decisions about what training to offer. Equal-employment legislation, occupational safety and health acts—all these make an impact upon the T&D director's priority system. It may be necessary to introduce programs for which no immediate tangible cost saving can be computed—it's the law.

Executive pressure is a third criterion. It usually comes from within the organization—and it's a criterion that smart T&D managers do not ignore. Executive desire for certain training is a reality of the marketplace for T&D managers—and it is also a pleasing symptom of management support. When T&D managers complain that they don't get support from the top, they should ask themselves how many suggestions from chief executive managers, vice presidents, or directors they turned down recently—or even in recent years.

Certainly this does not mean that T&D managers should roll over and be obedient puppies just because a major executive says, "I have a training problem," or "Why don't we have a program in assertiveness?" Executive T&D managers use the same performance analysis they would use with similar requests from any other place in the organization—they just do it more patiently and more gently! And indeed, there may be occasions when the decision is to go ahead with the program even if it doesn't pass all the tests. The long-range support such a concession may buy could be worth this once-only faulty decision.

Finally, there is the criterion of population. Sometimes this means simply that training goes to the most extensive problem. Macro needs may take priority over individual needs. Fortunately, it doesn't always need to work that way. The factor of influence and impact must also enter the decision table. Possibly the people who perform defectively occupy positions that affect the entire operations—for example, senior managers. Perhaps they have product hand-offs to workers in "downline" jobs. Perhaps the value of their product gives some priority to their need.

Performance problems that affect many workers, that are costly, that are related to the law, or that interest executives—all these deserve attention. Actual or potential knowledge deficiencies (DK) deserve training. Problems stemming from lack of practice (DP) should produce drill, or enforced on-the-job application. Problems stemming from other causes are probably deficiencies of execution (DE) and nontraining solutions are in order.

Summary

How about another figure (Figure 5.5) to give the "big picture" of the process by which you determine training needs?

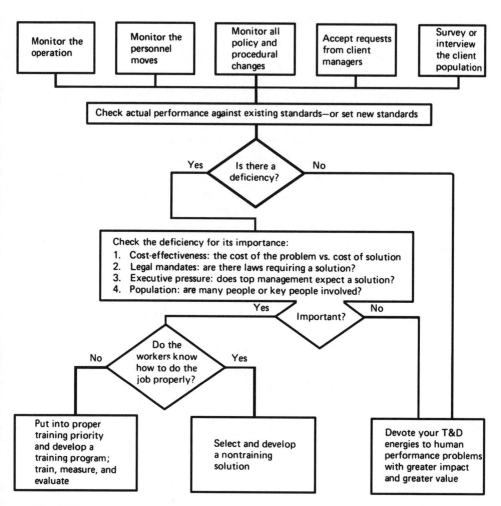

Fig. 5.5.

How to determine training needs.

Responding to Individual Training Needs

The Importance of Individual Training Needs

Once the T&D specialists have determined that a performance problem can be solved through training initiatives, the next step is to design or locate an appropriate program. The central issue? "How can we ensure that trainees acquire the necessary behaviors—and that they apply them on their jobs?" The two parts of that inquiry are equally important; acquisition without application is an inadequate response to individual training needs.

If we were dealing with organizational training needs, involving large numbers of people, we would want to make sure that the investment produced differences in the participants' on-the-job performance. Is it any less important when we solve an individual training need? Our response to an individual training need is important: It meets a genuine *human* resource need. When we meet individual training needs we "put teeth" into career planning, individual development, and assessment-center programs. We also take major steps in the total human resource development of our organizations.

Performance appraisals, assessment centers, selection certification, career planning, individual development plans (IDPs)—all provide data about individual training needs. And they are all hollow exercises unless there is a relevant and *implemented* development program as a result of the data gathering.

T&D specialists respond to individual training needs much as they would respond to any other request for help. They make certain that:

- There are some reasonably definite objectives
- The requesting manager is prepared to assign the "trainee" to work that will permit the use of new insights, skills, or attitudes

- The factors that facilitate transfer of training are attended to
- The requesting manager is prepared to reinforce the application of the new behavior
- The training, developmental, or educational activity can produce positive results in costs benefits
- The "trainee" understands the reason for the program

Because the cost of individual training cannot be spread across large populations, it is an expensive process no matter what source of help you use: (1) Developing a highly individualized program with existing resources may easily cost more than the new knowledge or skills could possibly contribute back to the organization. (2) Searching for a "precisely correct" outside program means reading many brochures and university catalogs, searching countless Web sites, making many phone calls, and taking risks on untested programs; indeed, it can seem like searching for a needle in a haystack. (All this presumes that no combination of existing in-house programs will meet the peculiar individual training needs.)

The range of individual training needs is very broad. Top executives frequently have individual training needs: They need cutting-edge information for their unique technology, they need leadership training, they need unusual help in solving unusual managerial problems, and very often they need perceptive skills so they will anticipate future problems. Where does the T&D staff locate that highly individualized program for them?

Executives are not alone in this position. Rapidly changing technology requires constant monitoring to lag just a bit behind their competition. Besides, as technology is upgraded throughout the organization, so many positions require knowledge and skill in a technology applied by very few employees. These are very serious, very expensive, and very *real* individual training needs.

A major decision in the search for programs to meet individual training needs is the answer to this question: "Do we have, within our organization, the resources for meeting this need?"

Before we examine those "inside resources," let's review the process: We have discovered a potential training need—a performance problem. What do we do first?

Well, first, of course, we validate the request to make certain that it is indeed for a *training* need. If the manager is distressed about skills that workers *once had* or *do have* but aren't using now, then we naturally work toward a nontraining solution.

But if we are dealing with a genuine training need, we estimate the size of the trainee population. If there are many employees involved (and it's a good idea to check that when the manager first becomes a "requester"), then that's an individual training need to be dealt with by establishing objectives for a class or workshop. If there are only a few trainees, or just one trainee, we start joint discussions.

Typically, three people should attend those discussions: ourselves as the T&D consultant, the potential trainee(s), and the immediate supervisor. At this discussion, the objectives are established and the search begins. At this point, we ask whether we use inside or outside resources. The logic of that joint analysis is essentially the process charted in Figure 6.1.

Inside Answers to Individual Training Needs

When the T&D department agrees that reasonable objectives have been clarified for a validated individual training need, it should first look within the organization to find solutions.

Take a typical case. A manager comes to you and says, "I have this training problem—and this seminar is just what we need." Now, that manager may be wrong on both points. Maybe there isn't a training need at all. Even if there were, the solution may be totally inappropriate. The manager may be totally mistaken! But that manager is supporting training—and should be reinforced for such support. Probing questions about the nature of the deficiency, the appropriateness of the proposed solution, and how the learning will be applied on the job are all in order.

Existing programs are the first place to check. Do the behavioral or learning goals for the need match or parallel those published for programs already in the curriculum of the organization? If there is a match, the obvious thing to do is to enroll the trainees in the next session of the existing program.

If that program has other, unrelated objectives, it may be possible to attend only certain modules of that program. An individual or small group "special session" might be arranged to solve the training need. If the established objectives vary only slightly, minor adaptations and tutoring by the regular instructors might be an inexpensive, quick, and effective way to respond.

Self-study programs are especially adaptable to individual needs. They are thus excellent answers to individual training needs. By omitting certain segments, or by combining several programs, T&D specialists can often "tailor-make" highly specialized programs with minimum effort. Many commercial self-study programs need trimming and adapting to fit the peculiar needs of an organization anyway. A "visit" or field trip may be an adequate solution for simple training needs. Such visits can be productive—but they require careful planning. Generic visits ("just to look things over") are seldom useful—and

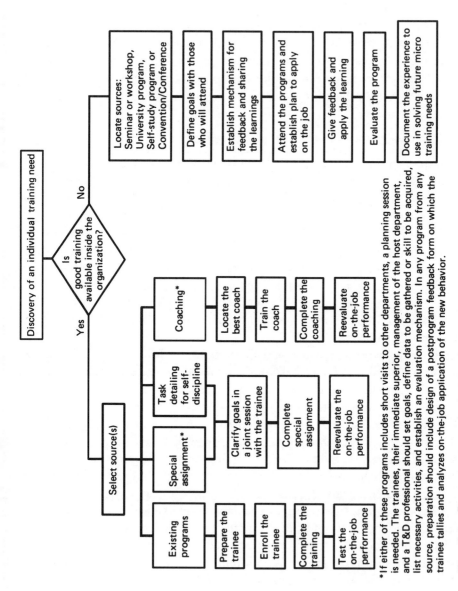

Discovery of an individual training need

Is good training available inside the organization?

Yes — No

No branch:
Locate sources: Seminar or workshop, University program, Self-study program or Convention/Conference

Define goals with those who will attend

Establish mechanism for feedback and sharing the learnings

Attend the programs and establish plan to apply on the job

Give feedback and apply the learning

Evaluate the program

Document the experience to use in solving future micro training needs

Yes branch:
Select source(s)

Existing programs | Special assignment* | Task detailing for self-discipline | Coaching*

Existing programs:
Prepare the trainee
Enroll the trainee
Complete the training
Test the on-the-job performance

Special assignment*:
Clarify goals in a joint session with the trainee
Complete special assignment
Reevaluate the on-the-job performance

Coaching*:
Locate the best coach
Train the coach
Complete the coaching
Reevaluate on-the-job performance

*If either of these programs includes short visits to other departments, a planning session is needed. The trainees, their immediate superior, management of the host department, and a T&D professional should set goals, define data to be gathered or skill to be acquired, list necessary activities, and establish an evaluation mechanism. In any program from any source, preparation should include design of a postprogram feedback form on which the trainee tallies and analyzes on-the-job application of the new behavior.

Fig. 6.1. Discovering an individual training need.

quite often annoying to the hosts. They easily result in superficial or misleading learnings. A planning session before the visit is a "must." The trainee, the trainee's requesting manager, a T&D specialist, plus a "host" manager should establish a general objective and compile a list of questions that must be answered at each position visited. It helps to regard the visit as an "Easter-egg hunt" that will answer questions, complete flowcharts, fill in organizational charts, and/or annotate manuals. After the visit, a follow-up mechanism should make an evaluation: "How much is the new information or skill being used?" "Did the visit pay off?" "Should others make the same visit?"

Special assignments within the organization may be the ideal way for individuals to acquire desired knowledge and skills. This is particularly true when specialists need knowledge of practices in other departments to manage "hand-offs" smoothly or when middle/staff managers need insight into how other departments operate. Examples:

- To develop empathy with departments they audit, auditors might work as regular employees for several months in other staff offices, local offices, or line plants.
- Procedures writers might work in operations to know how previous work fares in the reality of the workplace and to improve future procedures.
- Instructors might work for several months in departments they will relate to and for whom they may develop future programs.
- "Ready-to-promote" employees might rotate through various sections to gain experience, perspective, and new networks.

Task-analysis for self-discipline sounds a bit punitive and pedantic, but it really is an effective way to overcome individual performance problems in employees who are deficient in just one characteristic of their work. Typical of these deficiencies of execution (they are usually DEs) is carelessness, lack of attention to detail, missing parts of assignments, lack of follow-through, or unilateral decisionmaking. Such personal problems can best be overcome if the trainee is acutely conscious of the problem—and aware that the temporary assignment will give maximum experience plenty of chances to apply a good level of performance. *Coaching or mentoring* offers an important internal answer to many individual training needs. A coaching and mentoring program has many advantages:

1. It can be individualized.
2. It can ensure complete validity if the coach is the trainee's immediate superior. (That is the usual and ideal situation.) Since the "boss" is

coaching, there can be no doubt about management's valuing the behaviors that are to grow out of the coaching.

3. The close, one-on-one communication permits a dynamic feedback
   mechanism.
4. The close, one-on-one communication permits a dynamic reappraisal
   of the learning objectives.
5. Training responsibility is delegated to that point in the organization
   where it has the most immediate and direct payoff: the relationship
   between superior and subordinate.
6. Manager/coaches tend to learn a great deal about the inventories of
   the individuals whom they coach—as well as about the entire process
   of motivation, directing, and communicating with subordinates.

There is, in addition, a subtler benefit from widespread use of coaching in
an organization: Many managers become dynamically involved in the training
process. Furthermore, managers who have served as coaches represent an empathic population for all T&D activities. As decisionmakers or requesters of
T&D services, they know more "of the ropes" about learning—why it is important and how it works. They are certainly useful resources in meeting future individual training needs.

Mentoring is growing in popularity as an effective individual training strategy. Mentors provide opportunities for the growth of their protégés by identifying situations that will enhance their knowledge and experience. Mentoring
programs are also used to address equity issues by supporting the advance-
ment of women and minorities. Mentoring programs are also a successful
strategy for addressing external pressures on an organization (i.e., globaliza-
tion, workforce composition, mergers, acquisitions, etc.). Formal mentors can
provide job-specific training as well as techniques for coping with organizational culture and change issues. Because of the numerous and important benefits provided through the mentoring process, many Fortune 500 companies
have developed and implemented formal programs for the orientation and
socialization of new employees and to facilitate the rise of key employees.

None of these programs from within the organization is complete without
an ongoing planning and evaluating mechanism. That is another reason for
the active involvement of T&D specialists when any such solution is applied to
an individual training need. In every situation, the trainee, immediate superiors, "hosts" (if job rotation, special assignments, or visits are used), and a T&D
specialist should:

- Set goals
- Define the activity

- Describe the way in which the training content will be applied on the job
- Establish criteria and a mechanism for evaluating the experience

This strategy implies creating a postprogram feedback form on which trainees tally and analyze their on-the-job applications of the new skill. Such feedback not only gives data for evaluation but helps maintain the new behavior as well!

Outside Answers to Individual Training Needs

When searching for programs to satisfy individual training needs, T&D managers use such activities as seminars and workshops, university and college offerings, programs from local trade and night schools, self-study, or conventions, conferences, and so forth. Each of these options has some special value—and each requires some special consideration.

Membership in professional societies provide T&D managers and T&D staff members with a rich opportunity to find out what is new in the profession, to meet people who do similar things (often in innovative, useful ways) in other organizations, to get recognition for their own accomplishments—or just to find support groups, socialize, or hold an office if they need such fulfillment. The largest groups feature local chapters, regional and/or national conferences, publications, and seminars or institutes.

The American Society for Training and Development (ASTD), the Academy of Human Resource Development (AHRD), the National Society for Performance and Instruction (NSPI), and the Organizational Development (OD) Network are among the largest. The National Society of Sales Training Executives is one of the active groups that serve a particular discipline or specialty within the T&D population. The Office of Personnel Management sponsors programs to upgrade trainers in the public sector.

Seminars and workshops offer one of the more frequent answers to the T&D manager's quest. Their sponsors range from independent consultants to professional societies to colleges and universities. Their length ranges from one day (even a few hours) to several weeks. Unfortunately, their quality spans an even wider spectrum.

How do T&D managers locate such events? Usually, they need only open their mail. Membership in any professional society will get your name on mailing lists, which are then going to be sold to sponsoring agencies. Organizational listservers also announce upcoming events. Furthermore, attendance at any event by just one sponsor will guarantee future mailings—frequently multiple, because computer lists become cross-fertilized. If these methods haven't already produced more mail than there is time to read, phoning the associations or writing to nearby universities (or the American Management Association) will ensure lots of brochures in the future.

How do alert T&D managers separate the wheat from the chaff? How do they select the really "right" answer to the individual training need they face at the moment?

For openers, one might ask these "primary" questions about the workshop or seminar:

	Yes	No

1. Does the brochure publish learning objectives or "expected outcomes?" ____ ____
2. Are those outcomes stated in behavioral terms? ____ ____
3. Are the behaviors observable, measurable, reasonable? ____ ____
4. Is a topical outline included in the announcement? ____ ____
5. Does the brochure specify what types of employees should register? (Nature of position? Level of position? Experience assumed?) ____ ____
6. Does the outline provide time for participants to raise issues and ask questions? ____ ____
7. Does the time schedule look flexible? (Could it possibly be completed? Can it adapt to the unique needs of individual participants?) ____ ____
8. Is there provision for "process feedback" so participants can let leaders know to what degree their needs are/aren't being met? ____ ____
9. Does the brochure mention the learning methods that will be employed? ____ ____
10. Do those methods involve "action training" chances for your trainees to become involved in something other than just listening and watching? ____ ____
11. Is there workshop time so that your trainees can contemplate ways to apply the material they have learned back on the job? ____ ____
12. Is there an opportunity for your trainees to access the leaders in small group or one-on-one conversations? ____ ____
13. Are the leaders well known to you or to the managers in the department in which the individual need exists? ____ ____
14. Have the leaders published on this subject? ____ ____
15. Have the leaders worked for or consulted with corporate or bureaucratic organizations, or is their background entirely academic? ____ ____

A reliable seminar or workshop should score a "Yes" on at least ten of those questions. It certainly should score a "Yes" on five of the first six questions if it is to meet the unique learning needs of your trainees.

If the seminar looks marginal, there may be value in inquiring about the sponsor or the announced leaders. Has the sponsoring organization been in existence for at least two years? (New sponsors may be perfectly fine. But when sponsors are established you can uncover data about their past programs.) Has the seminar offered programs in these particular subjects for at least a year? Are the conference leaders offering similar programs throughout the area—or throughout the country? How long have the leaders worked for this sponsor? Remember, these questions become useful only if the more urgent questions in that "primary" list haven't given you the data you need.

If the program has been previously offered, T&D staff members can ask for rosters and check with other organizations who sent people—the T&D department as well as attendees. The point is to establish a mechanism for exchanging information on the usefulness and quality of public programs in providing data that's more user-oriented than the data you can hope to acquire from the sponsors or the leaders. They're marketing people while they're answering your questions. And be sure to ask the users how they're using the program—not how they liked it. Answers to the last question will be contaminated with data about the food, the meeting site, the trip to and from the program, and other participants. A useful list of questions to ask previous participants at seminars and workshops would include some of these:

- Did you or your participants institute new policies as a result of attending?
- Did you or your participants revise or eliminate old policies as a result?
- Did you or your participants revise procedures as a result of the participation?
- Did participants return to the organization with products they could immediately put to use?
- What specific problem was solved as a result of attending this seminar?
- Have you calculated a dollar payoff from participation?
- If the need still existed, would you send people to this program today?
- Did others who attended really reflect the audience appealed to in the advertising—or did the sponsors admit anyone who paid the money?
- Should our participants make special preparations?
- In what ways did your participants receive special individualized time and attention from the leaders?

Some of those questions are quite important, others far less valuable. What one probably does is select about two-thirds of the relevant ones, and then hope to receive concrete answers to about two-thirds of those. When previous participants are unable to identify unique assistance or specific applications, the program may be questionable. (Of course, there's a fallacy in that: Users can be incompetent, too—so check with more than one and with the T&D department.)

Even for one-person training needs, some organizations like to send teams of two to seminars and workshops. This is often a good idea. Dual participation can increase pressure on leaders to respond to the uniqueness of your organization. It can cause each trainee to stimulate the other toward active participation and active contemplation of on-the-job applications. Dual participation can make "honest people" out of your trainees; they tend to acquire the needed behaviors more consistently—especially if the "partner" is the boss. Not only do behaviors tend to be acquired at workshops—they tend to be *applied;* then on-the-job behaviors tend to be reinforced more readily if the boss has the same knowledge. This merely says that team attendance (especially superior-trainee teams) results in more dynamic change than attendance by just one person. For this, as well as for marketing reasons, some seminars offer discounted rates for the second person. Team members should be warned against isolation; they should be instructed to mix with the group.

University programs take a variety of forms. They may be short seminars. They may be "one-night-a-week" programs offered through regular channels or through extension services. They may also be a full-time investment of the trainees' time and energy during a period of release from normal work responsibilities. Such "release" programs sometimes lead to degrees—as a "year at Harvard" or an MBA from a state university.

Regardless of the money invested, regardless of the time and energy spent, regardless of the organizational level from which trainees come, university programs should be investigated and evaluated. As any training investment must, it should pay its way—if not in documented dollars and cents, then in ideas, which are brought into the organization.

How can T&D managers assure investments in university programs?

To begin with, they can check the programs for relevance and quality in the same way they check seminars and workshops. Colleges and universities will invariably have existed for more than a year; their reputations as sponsors have already been established. (Sometimes for good, sometimes for bad sponsorship.) But it's dangerous to be beguiled by good reputations. Colleges with good reputations in general may be poverty stricken in the department from which you need help. Institutions with shabby reputations in one department may excel in others. And besides, it isn't the institutional reputation that matters so much as it is the competence of the professors who will teach your trainees.

But beware. A glittering array of renowned authorities on the faculty does not guarantee that those luminaries will actually teach your people. Astute T&D managers check, and get a commitment about:

- The precise name of the instructor
- The amount of time the learners will be exposed to each faculty member
- The nature of that exposure (Will they listen to lectures? Get to ask questions? Get small-group or one-on-one time to discuss unique problems?)
- The size of the class
- The nature of the testing (Will your trainee be held accountable for the information learned?)

When no guarantees can be made about the faculty's willingness to deal with the special needs of your employees, a longer search may be a good investment of time and energy. Often, the truly motivated trainee or manager will do the searching—a healthy action that gives some "ownership" of the final decision.

To insure commitment to make learners accountable, a "contract" may be in order. T&D people, in concert with the manager and trainee, identify specific ways in which the knowledge will be applied on the job. For example:

- Delivering four oral reports within three months of completing a university course in public speaking
- An X percent drop in rejects after a welding course or
- An X percent increase in the number of decisions at meetings chaired by a manager who attends a conference/leading course

Although such "contracts" can and should be simple documents, they indicate that both student and manager accept accountability for the expenditure of money and energy and support by the organization. They also show both the businesslike and the supportive nature of the T&D function. What these contracts say is that the payment of the tuition (and sometimes compensation for time in class) is a business transaction in which evaluation criteria and accountabilities were established at the start.

Such commitment to learning and on-the-job application can erase some of the stigma of academia, some of the "ivory tower" reputation that tarnishes college programs. It is also a basic mechanism for meaningful evaluation, for encouraging immediate feedback when students find the program a doubtful route to the targeted application objectives. For general tuition aid programs, these contracts are recommended parts of the policy guidelines.

Self-study is another medium for meeting individual training needs. Sometimes, these self-study programs already exist within the organization; they've been bought for previous similar needs. Sometimes they are available through local educational institutions. More often they are available as books and computer-based training packages, sold through publishers or commercial vendors. Again, membership in professional societies puts the T&D director onto mailing lists describing such programs. Subscription to training magazines also uncovers many sources of such "software," as well as the names and addresses of suppliers. In addition, attending conferences (or local merchandising sessions by publishers) lets T&D specialists know what is on the market, which sources to respect, and whom to turn to when a really unique individual training need arises.

More important is the appropriateness of the presentation to the learning goals.

If the goals involve acquiring knowledge, then reading a book may be the best solution. Other training needs may involve a retention and application that is possible only through programmed instruction, or lessons mailed to and reviewed by an instructor on the vendor's staff. Other needs involve psychomotor skills, which can come only if the program provides visual displays—and perhaps equipment with which to perform the tasks.

In evaluating self-study programs, the usual questions arise:

- Are the behavioral (learning) outcomes clearly defined? (This may not apply to books, but it should be a minimum test for accepting any programmed text.)
- Is the scope of the content clearly specified?
- Are there indications of the "normal" time required for completion? (Beware of averages; look for upper and lower limits.)
- What do previous users say about their use of information from this program?
- What do other users say about the learning processes stimulated in this program?

Professional conferences and conventions provide another source of learning to meet individual training needs. They are seldom structured as behaviorally oriented learning systems; thus, they often become intellectual bazaars at which people discover new trends in their fields. As such, they can be an effective way to bring state-of-the-art and cutting edge knowledge into an organization. One hopes that people who attend conferences and conventions will bring back ideas and that they will try them out or, at the very least, share with them their peers.

A Control System for Solving Individual Training Needs

Individual training needs come from all parts and all levels of the organization. The solutions to individual training needs are elusive. Even the search for solutions can be expensive: Cost per trainee is likely to be high because the population to be trained is so small.

All these facts conspire to a requirement for steady but gentle control over the processes by which organizations meet individual training needs. In practice, many individual training needs come to the attention of the T&D manager because managers say they "have this problem" or "Can you help me with the funds to send some of my people, too?" Intelligent T&D managers reinforce such initiatives and also subject them to further analysis. That analysis tests the validity of both the request and the suggested program. It asks, "Will the people learn something *new*? Will the program supply what they need to learn? Will the content actually be put to use on the job? If not, will the experience permit intelligent rejection of the technology in the program?"

Even if the T&D manager is not informed or involved in all the decisions, the control system is needed—and it is the responsibility of the T&D manager to see that managers at all levels comprehend and apply the system whenever they solve an individual training need.

It's not a question of control for the sake of control. It's not a policy designed merely to keep the T&D manager informed about what's going on—although that is not an insignificant item. The reasons for a centralized, systematic decision process are many, and they go like this: A control system for meeting individual training needs:

- Eliminates duplicate searches
- Increases the probability of selecting an effective, appropriate solution to the individual training need
- Increases the probability of selecting an appropriately priced training program
- Increases the probability that the training content will actually be applied on the job (a feedback device can be designed for each program)

- Provides a data bank for meeting future individual training needs
- Establishes a databank about the quality of vendor's products and services
- Keeps the immediate superiors of all trainees actively involved in setting goals and following up each training investment
- Makes a statement to the entire organization that training is an investment that must be justified and evaluated
- Provides data to monitor the actual dollars being spent on training, education, and development
- Keeps the T&D manager informed about the genuine training needs (from this data, trends may emerge; and the organization learns when individual training needs have become organizational training needs)

In other words, astute T&D managers put special stress on steps 3, 8, and 9 of the control process in Figure 6.2. Step 3 deserves special attention. Especially important is the presence of three parties in the joint planning. The T&D department is obviously involved—but just as important is the active involvement of both the trainee and the immediate superior of the trainee. Without their inputs there is no real assurance that the learning content will be useful to the organization, that they will be properly reinforced after they have been acquired—or even that the trainee understands the purpose of the training.

However, the basic message of the process chart is the need for central control. When individual training needs are solved from any source (inside or outside the organization), the process should not be hit-or-miss. Such decentralization produces chaos in the form of poor decisions, wasted money, duplicated search, and lack of follow-up to ensure that the organization gets its money's worth and puts the learning content to work.

The theme of those advantages is application and accountability. A word of caution applies here. The reservation that needs to accompany the policy is an admonition: "Be gentle." In other words, the T&D staff must use tact during the performance or cost-benefit analysis of an individual training need—or when denying the funds for one. With diplomacy, the logic of the system (Figure 6.2) appeals to most managers.

If there has never been a control system to govern the way individual training needs are met, the T&D manager might very wisely institute the control system one step at a time. Perhaps it should start with only the most expensive investments; after that, it can gradually be applied to additional cases until it becomes the norm. It's probably just good psychology, good politics, and good management to reinforce with liberal decisions those managers whose requests

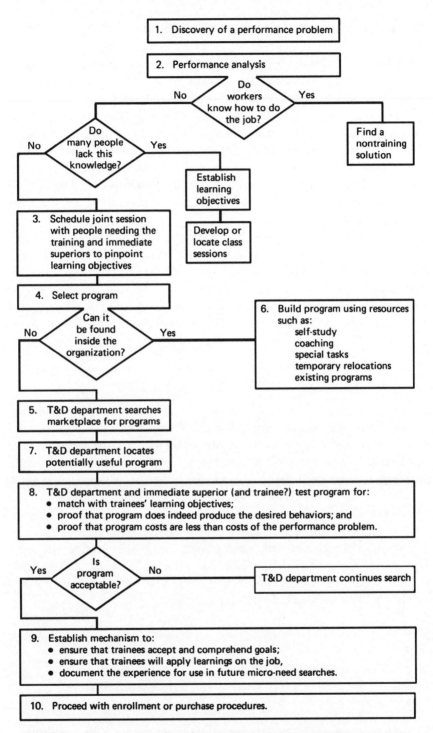

Fig. 6.2. Control process for solving individual training needs.

are most valid and most cost-effective. (If we were discussing reinforcement theory, we'd call it "successive approximations.") Furthermore, if the control system is valid, it will gradually earn its own good reputation.

The alternatives to such gentleness are frightening. T&D managers who are too rigorous, too hard-headed, will soon experience some unhappy consequences. First, they will receive fewer requests for their consultative services. Second, they will grow increasingly ignorant about the many employees who attend special training; that is to say, client-managers who want training will find a way to get it—whether they find the proper training through the proper channels or go the "bootleg route."

These are the days of assessment centers, appraisals, career development, and career planning through outreach programs and tuition assistance. At their best, all these are part of a long-range individual training and development system. The T&D manager wants to be a major factor in the design of those programs for individuals and in the follow-up and evaluation that refines the programs and gives their real impact to the individual and the organization.

Summary

A training need that exists for one person is just as real as a training need that exists for vast numbers of people. For this reason, individual training needs cannot be evaluated on the same priority system used for organizational training needs. In other words, the total impact on the organization may be smaller—but the need must be evaluated on its own merit. It cannot be thrown into the same general hopper as organizational training needs.

Whether it is a response to a performance appraisal, a career plan, or an assessment decision, the individual training need is part of the T&D manager's job.

Controls are necessary. Over time, a firm control system can be established by a gentle, intelligent analysis of each training need. When that system is fully operating, an organization is ready to process all its human resource growth needs—the little ones as well as the big ones.

Training Isn't Always the Solution

Why Training Isn't Always Useful

As we have often noted, there is no sense in training people to do what they can already do. Training is an appropriate solution to job-related problems for people who have what we call DK (deficiency of knowledge) or DP (deficiency of practice), both of which cause performance problems and deficiencies in knowledge, skills, or abilities.

But what about all those other occasions when workers *can* do their work properly—but just don't?

In this chapter we will look at a way to analyze these situations and examine the nontraining solutions used by T&D professionals to solve the performance problems in the organizations they serve. The chapter explores the expanding role of HRD or T&D managers: No longer do they merely see that "programs are implemented." They are expected to solve the human-performance problems for their organizations.

As we look at this expanded role, we will consider:

- The questions T&D managers ask when they consult with client departments
- The solutions they evaluate and select to overcome the problems that concern the client

Graphically, the process looks like Figure 7.1. Our focus is the left side (deficiencies of execution [DEs]), the problems that training will not solve. As solutions for the DEs, we will consider feedback systems, contingency management, job design/reengineering, and organizational development.

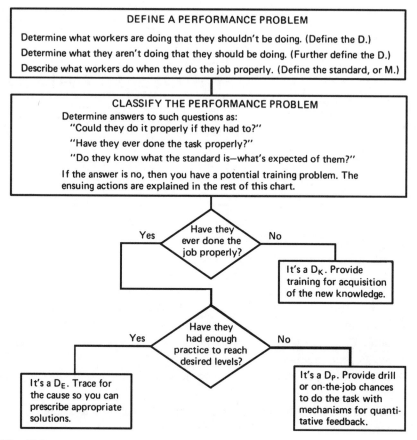

Fig. 7.1.

The expanded function of training and development.

Motivation and Feedback Systems

When T&D specialists discover cases where workers *can* do the job properly but are failing to do so, it's fitting to ask, "Do they know, while they do their work, how well they are doing?"

That question is really geared to discover whether the employees are receiving feedback. Why is feedback so important?

Feedback systems are attractive alternatives to training because they motivate workers, are inexpensive, and can be part of the regular management reporting system.

First, let's see why feedback is in itself something of a motivator. When employees are able to see their own accomplishments, they have more reason to be interested in their work, more reason to be satisfied with their assignments, a greater sense of being needed, and a keener awareness of their contributions.

Unless graduates of training programs receive on-the-job feedback about the skills they acquired in that training, they tend to lose the new behaviors. Feedback, on the other hand, can "control" their performances. In short, feedback gives workers more reason to care, more *motivation* to perform well. Motivation means "a motive for action." Put another way, motivation is the reason someone chooses to do some things and chooses not to do others.

Motivation is a fundamental component of performance. Supervisors and managers are responsible for achieving the goals of the organization through leading the performance or efforts of their employees. The HRD or T&D professional can be of tremendous assistance in the process. Individual job performance can be summarized as follows:

$$\text{Performance} = \text{Ability} \times \text{Motivation (effort)}$$

In this model, performance is the product of ability times motivation:

$$\text{Ability} = \text{Aptitude} \times \text{Training} \times \text{Resources}$$

- Aptitude refers to current skills and capabilities, education, and previous job experience.
- Resources are the tools that an employee needs to do the work (e.g., equipment, supplies, the work of other employees, time to complete the tasks, etc.).

$$\text{Motivation} = \text{Desire} \times \text{Commitment}$$

- Desire means wanting to perform the job, but desire by itself is not enough. An employee who wants to complete a task but who is easily distracted or discouraged cannot perform well (high desire/low commitment).
- Commitment means being persistent or trying hard to complete a task. However, without desire, an employee could be committed to his/her work but proceed slowly and produce only adequate results (low desire/high commitment).

The multiplication symbol (x) demonstrates that all elements are essential. Someone with 100 percent of the motivation and 75 percent of the ability needed for a job can perform at above average level. However, an individual with only 10 percent of the ability would not be able to perform acceptably regardless of how motivated he or she is.

What then are the elements of ability and motivation?

- Aptitude refers to current skills and capabilities, education, and previous job experiences.
- Training is a mechanism for improving employee job performance. Almost any ability can be improved through training.
- Resources are the tools that an employee needs to actually do the work (e.g., equipment, supplies, the work of other employees, time to complete tasks, etc.).

The fundamental elements of motivation include the following key concepts:

- Desire means wanting to perform the job, but desire by itself is not enough. An employee who wants to complete a task but who is easily distracted or discouraged cannot perform well (high desire/low commitment).
- Commitment means being persistent or trying hard to complete a task. However, without desire, an employee could persistently plod along but his or her work is barely adequate (low desire/high commitment).

The fundamental assumptions about motivation include:

- A supervisor's actions influence the day-to-day motivation of employees. People respond to the manner in which they are treated.
- A supervisor can simultaneously achieve department goals and be concerned about employee satisfaction at the same time.
- Positively reinforcing high performance employees is as important as dealing with motivation-based problems.

The first thing a manager or supervisor must do when faced with an employee performance problem is to determine whether the employee understands that there is a performance problem. Again, the HRD or T&D specialist can play a pivotal role in this process by providing a framework for the performance standards, investigating industry benchmarks, and so forth.

If the employee does not understand that there is a performance problem:

- The process of identifying the problem must be temporarily put on hold.
- The manager/supervisor should focus on resolving the differences in perception through two-way communication.
- The manager/supervisor may have to clarify current expectations.
- The employee does not have to like the fact that there is a performance problem, only acknowledge that there is one.

What happens if the employee understands that there is a performance problem?

When a supervisor has a performance problem to solve, he or she must identify whether poor performance is rooted in ability or motivation. Why? If a manager or supervisor incorrectly assesses the root case of the performance problem, that problem may get worse.

The story of Jack and Jill's work-based research shows that supervisors tend to apply more pressure on an employee if they believe that the employee is deliberately not performing to expectations. The following is an example of that approach:

1. Jill, the supervisor, decides that the performance problem of Jack, her employee, is rooted in motivation.
2. Jill increases the pressure on Jack.
3. Jack believes that Jill is insensitive to his real problem—lack of resources, lack of training, or unrealistic time schedules. Because the root of the performance problem has not been addressed, Jack continues to perform poorly. Eventually, Jack develops a motivational problem as his desire and/or commitment decreases under this misapplied pressure.
4. Jill notices this and is convinced that her original assessment of Jack was correct (it's become a self-fulfilling prophecy).
5. Things go downhill from there.

There are four general diagnostic questions to assist in determining whether the performance problem is an ability or a motivation problem. Supervisors, managers, and T&D specialists need four pieces of information to know the difference between an ability-related problem and a motivation-related one: the level of difficulty of the task; the employee's level of capability; how hard the employee is trying to complete the task successfully; and how much improvement the employee is making in his/her attempts to complete the task successfully.

Differences Between Performance Problem
Linked to Ability or to Motivation Low Ability

Performance problems linked to low ability stem from the inability of the employee to do the work. Possible factors include:

- Very difficult tasks
- Overall low level of skill and/or aptitude
- Evidence of strong effort yet a lack of improvement over time
- Inadequate resources
- Inadequate training

Low Motivation: Performance problems linked to low motivation stem from the employee's unwillingness to give the necessary effort. Possible factors include:

- Low commitment with high desire—the employee wanted to perform well, yet is distracted or discouraged easily.
- High commitment with low desire—the employee is very persistent at the job, but his or her performance is lackluster: of low or moderate quality.
- Both low commitment and low desire—over time this can result when the cause of the problem is not properly identified, or the problem is misdiagnosed or ignored.

If the employee does not agree that there is a performance problem, the following steps should be taken:

- The process of diagnosing the problem must be temporarily put on hold.
- The manager or supervisor should focus on resolving the differences in perception through two-way communication.
- The manager or supervisor may have to clarify current expectations.

(The employee does not have to like the fact that there is a performance problem, only acknowledge that there is one.)

When the employee agrees that there is a performance problem, use the following diagnostic points or questions to assess whether the problem is one of ability or motivation. You may recall from the earlier discussion that these questions involve: the level of difficulty of the task; the employee's level of capability; how hard the employee is trying to complete the task successfully; and how much improvement the employee is making in his/her attempts to complete the task successfully.

Other key considerations are whether the employee understands and accepts the performance expectations, and whether the employee believes that it is possible to achieve the expectations. This brings us to the subject of goals and objectives. The foundation of an effective motivation program is proper goal setting.

Employees are more likely to "buy into" goals if they are a part of the goal-setting process. Put another way, involvement in goals leads to commitment to goals. The HRD or T&D specialist can play an important role in this process by establishing parameters for performance goals and by designing and operating a performance appraisal system that focuses on performance expectations and standards for a specific timeframe.

A goal is a specific and measurable target for achievement within a specific timeframe and with a specific set of resources. For goal setting to be effective in improving or sustaining motivation, the goals must be:

- Specific—measurable, unambiguous, behavioral
- Consistent—logically possible to attain
- Appropriately challenging—high expectations encourage high performance; goals that are too easy to reach may not be rewarding or motivating

A well-written goal statement contains enough information to identify who is accountable, what is to be achieved, when the activity will be completed, and constraints and resources required for the process. Managers, supervisors, and the T&D specialist play an important role in this process.

In general, employees will accomplish objectives when consequences are attached to both the achievement and the nonachievement of those objectives.

- Rewarding is the consistency of linking desired behaviors with employee-valued outcomes. You should link positive consequences (rewards) to high-quality performance, not to nonperformance factors (e.g., seniority).
- Disciplining is responding negatively to an employee's behavior for the purpose of discouraging future occurrences of that behavior. You should use negative consequences (discipline) to reduce unacceptable performance.

Keep in mind that a supervisor is always reinforcing *something*. In other words, behavior that is repeatedly exhibited in front of a supervisor is being rewarded, regardless of the supervisor's intention. A supervisor should not ignore or minimize the seriousness of unacceptable employee behavior by personally fixing an employee's mistakes or by encouraging high performers to be tolerant.

Psychologists who specialize in adult behaviors stress that mature humans regard self-evaluation as having primary importance; evaluation by others is secondary. It just naturally follows that when workers have a simple method for continuing their accomplishments, they find the very process of counting both reinforcing and motivating.

Thus T&D "consultants" ask questions such as these:

- How do workers find out how many times they have completed the task successfully?
- How do they discover whether their units of work are satisfactory or unsatisfactory?
- Do they ever judge their own work to determine whether it is or is not satisfactory?
- What tally do they see showing the number of successful units, or the ratio of satisfactory to unsatisfactory units?
- Who keeps that tally? Themselves? Their immediate superiors? A quality-assurance specialist?
- At what intervals do they see the data about the quantity and quality of their work?
- What positive reinforcement is made as a result of high achievement?
- What follow-up (consequence) is made for low achievement?
- Do the workers themselves have control over the action that corrects their poor performance?

When such questioning reveals no feedback, the T&D specialist may have found not only the cause of the performance problem but also a possible solution.

The results of simple feedback systems generate many success stories. The trouble is, the stories are unbelievable because they produced such dramatic results in such short time. Yet they happened. In one firm, clerks retrieved millions of dollars in lost business each month simply by recording the dollar value of shipments resulting from matching backorders with unnoticed inventory in the warehouses. Performance went from the low teens to mid-eighties in one week. An air freight forwarder reported overnight strides as a big problem: the failure of agents to consolidate small shipments. Workers merely kept tallies of how often they might have consolidated—and how often they actually did. In both situations, the new high-performance levels were maintained for long periods just through feedback.

Several principles are important to successful feedback systems; for example:

1. The feedback mechanism must be simple. If it's cumbersome or time-consuming, requiring lots of work or lengthy reports, it will be an unpleasant task—and thus will erode motivation. Obviously, simplicity also contributes to the economy of maintaining performance.
2. The workers should check their own work and enter the data onto the feedback form. Why? Because adults perceive self-evaluation as more valid and more important than evaluation from anybody else.
3. The data in the feedback form should be quantitative. Many experts feel that if it can't be expressed in numbers, it shouldn't be entered. Thus workers can count units completed, opportunities captured, dollars of revenue. They can also make distinctions between "okay" and "not okay" units. By tallying the ratio between these two, they give themselves feedback on both the quantity and quality of their work. Other units of measurement can be time-taken-to-complete-a-task, or numbers of successive error-free performances.
4. If at all possible, the form on which workers give themselves feedback should be a part of the regular reporting system already installed to provide management what it needs to know about the operation.
5. The feedback should enable employees to modify their performance and the system itself. By checking themselves, they can modify their performance without feeling "snoopervised." If they repeat the same error for an external reason, their reporting the interference to management can lead to modifications in the system itself.

Skeptics ask whether employees won't "cheat" when given such control over the feedback. The answer seems to be, "Oh, now and then—but not as much as one might expect." And anyway, the form can be designed so that there is no payoff for cheating. For example, with the freight forwarder: There would be no sense in showing opportunities not taken, and the consolidations they actually did make are a matter of local record. In other words, there is no point in manufacturing data about units completed if the total system output won't support your data. But the main point is this: There is little evidence that people cheat very much on self-controlled feedback systems.

There is, however, strong evidence that when people have the mechanism for controlling their own output, they perform in the desired fashion—and do so more frequently. Such improvement in quality and quantity of performance is, after all, what both T&D managers and client managers want.

Contingency Management

"Contingency" is merely a technical word for "consequence" or "result" or "effect." Contingency management is based upon the belief that every human action causes some consequence. If employees find joy in the consequences (contingencies) of doing a good job, they will tend to repeat their good performance. It is often said that "that which gets rewarded gets repeated." Thus, a main thrust of contingency management is to provide positive consequences for performing at the desired standards.

Management sometimes (often?) argues that employees receive positive reinforcement for proper performance when they collect their paychecks. The trouble with that logic is that so many employees collect their paychecks whether they perform properly or not. One reason they ceased long ago to see a direct connection between proper performance and salary is that the checks come anyway.

Another reason is the considerable delay between the behavior and the consequences. Merit raises are granted months after the good work was completed. Anyway, the increments are usually very small; people who were truly outstanding get just a *little* bit more than those who were "above average." Finally, merit raises stir up lots of questions about why the other fellow "got more than I did!" Such jealousy is often based on pure rumor, since management works so diligently to keep confidential the amount of merit increase granted each employee.

For all these reasons, the merit raise is not seen as a positive consequence at all. Overtime, on the other hand, shows up directly and soon in the paycheck. (It also makes a statement that what the organization will pay for is "time at work," not the quality of performance.)

Most T&D managers have encountered situations in which management had mixed up its contingencies. Bosses think they are reinforcing positively, but they are perceived by the worker as punishing. Need an example? The new administrative assistant stays late to get some important work out on "voluntary overtime." Guess who is rewarded with the invitation to give some more voluntary overtime the next time the department is in a pinch? Another frequent example occurs when one level of management says, "Do it this way"—and a different level screams, "But that's all wrong!" Employees caught in the middle of these inconsistent responses can only wonder, "What do they expect around here?" From the employees' viewpoint, the standards are dim—all because of the conflicting verbal signals given in the reinforcements. Swing shift foremen may stress quality; dayshift foremen scream for more units of work. Whom is one to believe? And then there is always the supervisor who thinks that great praise has just been handed out with the words, "Not bad!" But the employee remembers only the word "bad" and wonders why praise or acknowledgement is never given. "Not bad" seems like faint praise indeed and just another glum bit of judgmental feedback from management.

HRD or T&D departments that go to work rearranging consequences may have a tough job on their hands. It isn't just that new schedules of rewards upset tradition: It's hard work to discover what the *real* rewards and punishments are. Consultation skills come into full play. Especially important is the ability to identify individual value systems—and to recognize honestly what the true contingencies are. Furthermore, in bringing them out into the open, it's necessary to see how workers perceive them.

Thus, to make contingency management effective, the real operative consequences must be identified, verified, and changed. That involves perceptual data from the organization and from the worker—they may not see the contingencies in the same light at all! Beyond that, the contingencies to the learner-worker need to be identified for both short-range and long-range time spans.

Thus successful contingency management requires an analysis which includes *all* the thinking illustrated in Figure 7.2. This means completing a matrix that honestly shows the positive consequences for "bad behavior" and the negative consequences for "good behavior."

The analysis in the Figure 7.2 matrix deals with a universal safety problem: exceeding posted speed limits.

Until all the areas have been filled in, the matrix is incomplete—and so is the analysis. When it is apparent that doing the job properly brings no positive consequences, the next step is to add some. In the example, rewards for accident-free periods of driving (such as one month) might be added as a positive consequence. When it is apparent that the system may actually be rewarding noncompliance, those positive reinforces should be eliminated. In the example, the organization might well afford to quit paying the fines for drivers who are caught speeding. When it is apparent that doing the job properly brings aversive consequences, the organization should try to remove them. In the example, supervisors would need to desist from reprimanding drivers who abided by the speed limits—even though that means late deliveries now and then.

	THE DESIRED BEHAVIOR IS: Driving within speed limits.		THE CURRENT UNDESIRABLE BEHAVIOR IS: Exceeding speed limits while driving.	
	Consequences		**Consequences**	
	Positive	*Negative*	*Positive*	*Negative*
To the worker Now	None	Customers often chew you out for late delivery; supervisors may chew you for "goofing off."	More deliveries mean more wages; might get time off with pay during accident investigation and hearing.	*Might* get hurt if an accident happens; *might* get reprimanded by supervisor; *might* get a speeding ticket *if* caught.
To the worker Later	None	Lower total deliveries mean smaller paycheck.	Get variety by going to court if you get a ticket; get paid for court time.	May waste time in court without incentive pay if you get a ticket.
To the organization Now	Less supervisory time spent in checking; fewer accidents; fewer speeding fines to pay.	May get behind schedule in deliveries.	More deliveries.	Downtime if drivers are arrested and have to go to court; cost of accidents; cost of fines if convicted of speeding.
To the organization Later	Lower costs for fines, accidents, and insurance; less downtime costs while drivers are in court	Fewer total deliveries; less total revenue.	More deliveries with greater total revenue.	Same as short-range, except cumulative totals impact on efficiency of the operation and adherence to budget.

Fig. 7.2.

Matrix for analyzing consequences.

This last example often happens in contingencies affecting safety practices. Management says it wants care and attention paid to details of the regulations, but actually it "chews out" all the people who slow things down by complying. It happens again when management says it wants careful workmanship but reinforces only volume of production.

The corrective process, once the real reinforcers have been determined, includes such steps as:

- Removing negative consequences for proper performance
- Removing positive consequences for improper performance
- Adding positive consequences for proper performance

Changing the contingencies imposed by long-established systems is arduous work—but there can be big payoffs. T&D departments have helped avoid more than one costly and fruitless sales training program by helping management see that they were actually punishing good performers by raising their quotas. Sizable reductions in safety training costs are available to organizations that find effective positive reinforcements for compliance. Management development becomes a reality under managers whose salary and promotions are directly related to their discovery and development of other managers. The T&D department attracts talented personnel when a T&D specialist's effective performance leads to responsible positions in other departments rather than to permanent "detachment in the T&D function."

Job Enrichment

Not all performance problems originate in people. Sometimes they are built into the position itself.

The problem can arise just because some workers are misplaced. People with poor writing skills probably shouldn't be asked to write manuals—or even many reports. But if the position demands writing, then those people are in the wrong job—and all the training in the world will help but little. Employees who like to tinker with machines may be ill-suited to managerial assignments. Creative systems analysts may make terrible supervisors.

Positions that require crisis management (aircraft pilots and hotline counselors) may require special mind-sets or value systems; people who must satisfy customers may need to demonstrate their extroversion—not to mention their patience; problem solvers probably need to demonstrate logical and creative capabilities, and so on.

However, placement/employment specialists in Human Resource (HR) departments are usually responsible for fitting the person to the position. They sometimes use "Selection Certification," a test for personal adjustment, or an inventory of an applicant's values as ways to put the right people into the right job.

But when T&D managers think of job enrichment as an alternative to training, they have a different technology in mind. Job enrichment is generally concerned with positions that are either too demanding or too simple. Sometimes job enrichment is little more than an attractive fad for an organization that likes to keep up with the times. On other occasions, job enrichment has begun with the T&D manager's own position—and to good effect for the T&D function and the entire organization. At its best, job enrichment is an attractive and important new tool for the T&D manager's kit.

Whether T&D staff members actually manage job-enrichment projects or merely recommend them (handing them off to specialists to carry out) is a moot point. The central question is the ability of the T&D specialist to know when job enrichment is appropriate and how to launch a job-enrichment project.

To do so, today's T&D specialists need to know what constitutes an enriched job. Several factors are involved.

A complete piece of work emerges from an enriched job. An automobile might be a complete piece of work. Indeed, one manufacturer once boasted that its workers made automobiles—not transmissions. A right front wheel placed on the car does *not* qualify. A letter written for another's signature, a complaint recorded but not processed, a sketch for a visual aid that someone else will develop—none of these seems to represent a complete piece of work.

Enriched jobs *do not damage, humiliate, consistently bore, or degrade* the worker. That says a lot! It pleads for variety, for safety, for dignity, and for challenge.

Frequent feedback about performance is another dimension of enriched jobs, but this chapter has already said enough about that subject.

Utilization of the worker's valued existing skills is a mark of an enriched job. In his study of andragogy (adult learning theory), Malcolm Knowles (1977) points out that during their time as learners, adults want to apply their past skills and experience in acquiring new learned information. Job-enrichment technologists apply this same human need to the way workers relate to their jobs. People skillful in communication enjoy investing that skill in activities in which they've never before been responsible for communicating; people who have solved other problems like to be part of the problem-solving team in issues that affect their work.

An opportunity to acquire other skills characterizes enriched jobs. Instructorships should qualify very well on this. Instructors need to develop—and then develop some *more*—skills in communicating both as senders and as receivers! They can grow in their comprehension of learning theory, methodology, feedback, and evaluation techniques. But teaching the same old course again and again and again and using the same old materials is not an enriching trend in what is basically an enriched position.

Enriched jobs *enhance (or at least do not impair) the employee's ability to perform other life roles.* Strangely enough, many managerial positions rate rather low on this. How many times have you heard managers complain, "My time isn't my own any more! The job takes twenty-four hours a day!" Or the exasperated question, "Just what does this outfit expect out of me?" Enriched jobs leave something over; they permit incumbents to be parents and citizens to coach the little leaguers or to lead the scout troop.

Now that we know the elements of an enriched job, let's look at steps in job-enrichment projects. Professional "job-enrichers" know that there is much more to it than the seven steps we'll examine here. They also know that in a given project, not all these steps will apply. But generally job enrichment takes place when one or several of these things can be done:

1. Remove controls—but raise the accountability.
2. Add accountabilities. This often means providing training; there will be knowledge deficiencies about how to discharge the new accountabilities.
3. Add new authorities for decisions.
4. Find natural units that can result from the way tasks are assigned to individual workers.
5. Add feedback decisions for the employee to make about accomplishments. For example: "Does the product meet all standards?" or "Shall I speed up or slow down to avoid bottlenecks in the total system?"
6. Assign specialized tasks to the total job requirements. This is often an effective way of letting the worker use existing skills and to become an "expert" in one part of the operation. Note that this is an *added* specialization. It doesn't substitute the specialized skill for the total task; rather, it gives a new dimension to the job.
7. Introduce more difficult tasks. The degree of difficulty is important. Just adding more of the same type doesn't enrich a job; it merely adds what some experts call "horizontal loading." For example, a gardener who pulls up ragweed scarcely occupies an enriched job when the scope of the job is extended to pulling up dandelions, too.

It must be apparent by now that employee performance is not the sole cause of performance problems. When turnover is high, or when absenteeism and tardiness afflict a work unit or an organization, the job design should be considered. Astute T&D managers who find these symptoms consider the possibility that job enrichment is an appropriate solution for the DE they face.

Organizational Development (OD)

When is organizational development a useful solution to performance problems? Why would the T&D manager, or a staff member serving as consultant to a performance problem, suggest OD?

Organizations have an overall mission. As they grow, they add to the structure subsections with which they carry out that mission. These subsections develop missions of their own. On occasion, the missions of the subsections may be in conflict. They may even become counterproductive to the mission of the parent organization. Sometimes, individuals within an organization are more motivated toward their personal goals than toward organizational goals. They then begin to invest their energy and influence in activities that are destructive to the goals of the larger organization.

When such conditions exist, it's quite possible that changing the behavior of individuals will not overcome the problems. And "problems" is the right word! There are apt to be so many of them that one can truly say that it is the organization that needs fixing—not the individual behaviors or the jobs themselves.

Organizational development may be required when trust levels are low or nonexistent. It can be needed where gossip is prevalent—or worse, where gossip is used as the basis for decisions. Other symptoms may be decisions that are slow to come or missing altogether; personal frictions that are high and pervasive; and persistent progress reports that are misleading, ambiguous, or downright falsified. All these are symptoms of organizational illness. In short, when the environment of the organization prohibits or seriously deters the proper performance of individual tasks, then OD may be the solution.

Let's examine one of the standard definitions: Organizational development is a change effort within an organization, managed from the top, and uses planned interventions to reallocate resources to improve processes and attain organization goals with maximum effectiveness, satisfaction, and efficiency.

That last part ("attaining organization goals with maximum effectiveness, satisfaction, and efficiency") may sound a little like a testimonial to motherhood and Pollyanna—but it is, after all, a description of what most organizations would like to be. The other elements of the definition merit individual analysis.

"*A change effort.*" This is essential. There is no point to developmental efforts that merely maintain the status quo. By definition, "development" implies change in mission, structures, policies, and/or relationships. Unless the management of a distressed organization is open to change, there is no reason for the T&D staff to invest energy. Consultants in OD efforts are often heard to say, "We're testing to see whether there is energy here." They say that during all phases, but especially for early activities.

The phrase is often completed with words such as "if there is energy to change communications channels, or reporting relationships"—and even "the way we relate to one another"; or, more often, "to change our mission statement."

"Within an organization." The organization need not be the entire organization. It might be the accounting department, one plant within the manufacturing department, or even one office within that plant. But it must be a unit, and the person at the top of that unit must be involved. Thus the next item.

"Managed from the top." If the person at the "top" of whatever unit is being developed is absent from the activity, there will be no sanction for change from the power structure. Active involvement and assent for the effort to change is vital. It is equally vital as each change is analyzed and adopted. Consensus with the consultant about what will and what will not be permitted during the developmental activity is essential, too.

A written "contract" usually specifies constraints. For example, if no participant can lose a job due to disclosures made during the OD process, that fact is specified. If there may be no changes in reporting relationships or salary reductions, that, too, is specified—though if such constraints are applied, one must wonder whether the change manager at the top has any real energy for changing anything.

The contract may also detail whether changes may be made in the span of control, in the distribution of responsibilities, or in the communications channels. These things must be specified at the very beginning, since the active involvement of all managers (perhaps of all employees) is required if the organization is truly to r*edevelop* itself. If peoples' positions and powers and accountabilities are going to be altered, they are entitled to know the rules of the game.

"Using planned interventions." Based on a set of behavioral science theories, the strategies and techniques used in OD efforts must be carefully planned and systematically carried out. The planning and systematic implementations are vitally important.

"To reallocate resources." This is an apt way of explaining what goes on during typical OD interventions. The human resources in particular may be fulfilled in many ways; and OD process considers reallocation in ways that individuals find fulfilling and that are more effective, pleasant, and efficient in reaching the organization's mission.

One objective of an OD effort is for the organization to identify and solve existing problems. An equally important objective is to develop a mechanism for identifying future problems and for solving them before they once more paralyze the organization. Thus the third-party consultant seeks to eliminate the need for similar services just as soon as that mechanism is designed and ready to function. The sooner the consultant can depart the OD intervention, the more effective the consultancy.

Definitions don't always say much about the process. The definition we have just analyzed *does* reveal quite a bit about what happens during an organizational development effort. For an activity so shaking to the organization, no one formula can be developed. Even if OD practitioners (a term they like to use when referring to themselves) have a standard approach, they will need to vary it so that it fits the initial contract with the "change manager."

"Change manager." Change manager is an excellent name for the person at the top of the organization. This person manages the developmental change process and takes responsibility for it. The initial plan, made with the active involvement of the consultant and the change manager, may need amending when data emerges from early activities. The original plan may even be dropped in favor of a new plan and a new contract. Thus flexibility if a key attribute for the consultant and for the program.

Nevertheless, some similar and inevitable phases tend to occur in all organizational development interventions. First comes the problem identification phase. The principal members of the organization get together to try to identify the problem and its causes—or their perceptions of the problems and what is causing them. Because this identification may be more difficult than one would think, most consultants use structured devices to stimulate and maintain honest communication.

Small teams may postulate their ideas about problems and causes and then compare these in reports to the total group. There may be "More and Less" exercises when subunits or individuals make lists of "I wish you'd do more" and "I wish you'd do less" for every other unit or every other person. These exercises relate closely to "Role Identification" exercises in which members define their own roles and then hear what other people think their roles should be.

There are also "polling" activities in which members fill out a blank form with information about work partners with whom they most—and least—enjoy working. Such data are later shared as part of the problem definition and in action plans for personal change.

Polling can take the form of "Physical Representations" in which group members position themselves along a wall to express personal concepts of how they behave or make an impact. For example, on an "Influence Axis," those who see themselves as the most powerful, stand at one end; those who feel ineffectual stand at the other end. Not until everyone is placed so that each person accepts his or her position is the exercise complete. To attain the final representation, each person must do a bit of influencing, even if that means doing a bit of influencing to prove one's lack of influence.

Another type of physical representation tells members to stand very near those with whom they enjoy comfortable working relations—but far away from those whom they find difficult. The participants keep moving until everyone is happy with his or her position in relation to everybody else. This maneuver may require some deep conversations. And those deep conversations have been known to result in changed relationships—at least in changed perceptions. It's easy to envision the potential emotion generated by such "hot" data-gathering techniques. Quite clearly, OD assumes that feelings are facts in organizational behavior; these facts must be identified, examined, and managed if human resources are to work together toward effective organizational processes.

Second-step activities involve generating optional solutions to the identified problems. This is feasible when participants have agreed upon the nature and the cause of the problems. Note, however, that when the entire group is dynamically doing this analysis, the analytic and communicative process itself solves some of the problems.

The OD specialist will probably urge the group to a literal translation of the word "options." If they have choices about solutions, they will find greater satisfaction in their involvement in planning and carrying out the action. These action plans are, of course, another facet of this second phase. In addition, this is the point at which many consultants start to work with the group in developing a mechanism to identify and solve future problems before they become serious. Perhaps "mechanism" is an unfortunate word; avoiding future crises may merely depend on patterns of responsibility, communication, and accountability that permit individuals to spend their energies constructively. The open communication of the facts of feeling is inherent in nearly all the activities—and assuredly implied as a part of the "mechanisms" of the future.

When an action plan and a mechanism for evaluating the organizational health are adopted, the consultant is ready to exit. Note that the second phase is not regarded as complete until all the participating parties have agreed to the evaluation criteria and mechanisms.

Evaluation constitutes the final phase—but of course this was started near the beginning when the group agreed upon a vision of "how it will look and how it will feel around here when we are working together to achieve our departmental and personal goals." Such group visions offer a rich exercise in participative goal setting; revisiting it from time to time is a potent way to measure progress toward becoming a nice organization in which to work and live.

In addition to data gathering to measure results and satisfaction levels, to agreement that old problems have been eliminated or alleviated, and to the processing of new problems as they arise, the final evaluation also requires agreement that the developmental process has given the group a skill (or an enduring mechanism) that it can use in dealing with future problems before they again paralyze the organization so badly that it needs OD. When that agreement happens, the organization may be presumed sound and, indeed, "developed."

The organization now offers an environment in which behaviors acquired in training can persevere on the job. Above all, the energy of "human resources" is being expended in ways that contribute to organizational goals and pleasantly reinforce the contributors.

Quite clearly, organizational development is a comprehensive program. It is appropriate to profound and widespread distress within an organization. Astute T&D managers will know through the accurate analysis of performance problems within the organization when OD is necessary. Proficiency in OD interventions involves a vast technology—a great many skills not in the inventory of all T&D managers. Yet large numbers of T&D specialists know that many performance problems cannot be solved with anything less than OD. They are therefore busy acquiring the necessary skills—or actively recruiting staff members or consultants who can help solve the problem of a sick organization.

Summary

Today's T&D manager is expected to solve performance problems—not just to run training programs. The logic used in locating the appropriate solution is graphically expressed in the "Decision Tree" of Figure 7.3.

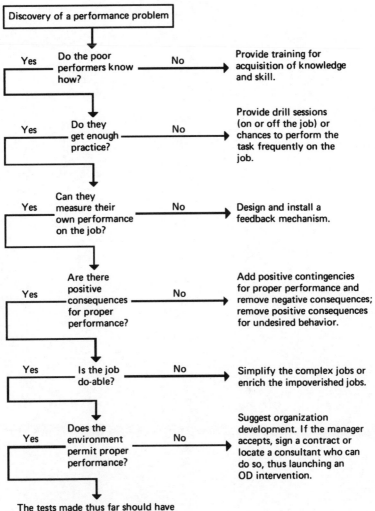

Fig. 7.3.

Decision tree for locating appropriate solution.

Learning Objectives

Robert F. Mager (1962) made a major contribution to the T&D profession by publishing *Preparing Objectives for Programmed Instruction.* Its thesis was simple: Effective training requires clear objectives in order to achieve outcomes.

The book was a big hit. Later re-titled *Preparing Instructional Objectives,* it sold more than 1 million copies. Few other books about training and development can make that statement. In some parts of the world, pirated copies were sold under the counter to escape copyright constraints. The second edition, which appeared in 1975, retained the fundamental principles of the first, but suggested that performance objectives might be a better word for the goals of training. A third edition was published in 1977.

Despite the success and impact of the book, a few resisted its thesis and technology. For such readers, Mager ended his preface with the words, "If you are not interested in demonstrating achievement of your objective, you have just finished reading this book" (Mager 1984, vi).

Some T&D managers took Mager at his word; they still ignore objectives. But if there is a current contention about learning objectives, the issue is not "Do they have value?" Rather, people ask, "Must every objective be totally observable and precisely measurable?" Or, "How can we avoid the limiting effect of such total precision?"

Today, most T&D managers expect themselves and their staff to write objectives. Why? Their consultation includes establishing learning goals; their course designs are guided by these expected outcomes; their learning experiences include an early examination of the objectives; their evaluations ask, "Did the learners achieve these learning goals?"

The Case for Writing Learning Objectives

As we've noted, a great many T&D specialists took Mager at his word—but read beyond his preface. As they put the technology of specifying performance objectives to work, they discovered significant reasons for attempting to define what the learner would do as a result of the training. Among these reasons:

1. Trainees who know precisely what is expected of them are much more inclined to invest energy in pursuit of the goal—and thus to get there more quickly.
2. Instructors can better control the stimuli they use on students and can better re-respond to the learners' reactions when they have a clear statement of the desired behavior to be produced by all this stimulus-response/re-stimulate/re-respond activity.
3. Management knows what it is getting for its investment when it sees statements of the outcome.
4. The bosses of the trainees have a tool for motivating the learning, for communicating expectations. They can establish accountabilities for the learning and for applying it on the job after the training.
5. The T&D department can more honestly evaluate its own achievements when the T&D manager and instructors have a clear statement about what they are supposed to produce.
6. Clear statements of learning accomplishments can validate performance standards, or set them if there are none. If standards are set for the first time, the learning objective should be approximately equal to the expected performance standards.
7. The distribution of printed objectives makes a documented statement to the organization that training means business and that learning is work.

The "work" to be done in training is achieving the objectives—just as work on the job is typing letters, assembling or repairing machines, providing a product or a service.

But writing performance (or "behavioral" or "learning") objectives is hard work. Thus there is predictable resistance. It's probably helpful to look at the arguments against learning objectives—and at the same time to examine questions to raise for each objection. We can learn something from this process. In Table 8.1, the left-hand column you'll find typical objections; the center column poses counterquestions; the right-hand column draws some conclusions about the legitimate role of learning objectives in an effective T&D system.

TABLE 8.1. Pro/Con Analysis of Learning Objectives

Arguments against	Counterarguments	Conclusions for the T&D Staff
You just can't define some jobs!	Then how does this job survive during a crisis? Who would miss it if it were eliminated?	One way to determine the learning (behavioral) objective for an ambiguous task is to identify the product (or "accomplishment") resulting from successful completion of that task. Example: Managers are decisionmakers; therefore the product of that process is a decision. What are the qualities of effective decisions in their organization? The objective of the training program would be to produce decisions that meet those criteria.
They take too much time!	Did you cancel your vacation just because it took a long time to decide where you wanted to go?	To get at behavioral objectives, ask such questions as: Describe them (or yourself) doing the job perfectly. What do you see? When you see others doing the job the wrong way, what do you see that you don't like?
There are no standards to work from!	Then how do you now know when the work is okay? When it should be rejected? When to insist that the work pace be accelerated? Whom to promote? Are you certain? Better check again for manuals or documents which specify standards	When standards do exist, that's where learning objectives start! Thus learning objectives may be a way to validate existing standards—and to generate them when they're missing. Sometimes standards "vanish" because nobody ever enforces them, because there is no steady feedback about their achieve-ment—or because they are not realistic and people conveniently "rise above them"!
We've been getting along just fine without them!	Are any of your people getting by with less than good on-the-job performance? Well, maybe that's what we've been doing by not trying to define the output of our training.	Resistance to change is one of the perpetual realities with which T&D specialists learn to cope in themselves as well as in others.
	Do you agree that we might find a better way to do training?	The technology with which training is accomplished is the peculiar domain of the T&D staff. If that staff says it wants learning objectives specified, then it has final authority to try to do so.

How to Write Learning Objectives

To be useful, learning goals should contain:

- Performance (Mager says it describes what a learner will be able to do)
- At least one criterion (*measurable*, says Mager)
- Conditions of performance (*usually*, per Mager). (Mager 1984, 21)

The recipe sounds simple, but it requires rigorous thinking. Observable actions are hard to find; we tend to think of covert actions that we assume to be "hidden inside people somewhere." These are *affective* goals, and we need to find an outer observable action. We're also reluctant to pin down precise criteria—even more reluctant to insist that they be measurable.

Observability and measurability are important if we wish to evaluate; without actions that we, as well as learners, can see, or criteria that we can measure, how will we know we have succeeded? For people who *want* them, observable actions and measurable criteria can be established. It's always helpful to start with the clause, "After training, the worker will be able to . . ." Note the magic phrase: *"will be able to."*

Next, let's think of verbs and objects. For example, "compute the tax" or "relieve tension." With these verbs and objects we have our observable action.

Now for "measurable criteria," which answer such questions as "How often?" "How well?" "How many?" "How much?" "How fast?" and "How high?"

"Conditions" can best be expressed with prepositional phrases such as "without reference to the manual" and "unless course attendance is mandated."

Through such grammatical/mental exercises, we can translate ambiguous objectives such as "counsel effectively" or "understand adequately" into concrete performance standards, which are also learning goals. These are behaviors that learners can see and give themselves feedback for achieving as they progress in class; these are behaviors managers can see and reinforce when graduates apply them on the job.

Let's look at a range of tasks from the very concrete to the somewhat abstract. Table 8.2 shows four examples: salesclerks are learning beginners' skills in the example across the top; the middle example deals with drivers; the third is from customer relations training; managerial skills appear in the example at the bottom. The vertical columns identify the action, criteria, and conditions of performance for each of these four cases.

Success in establishing useful learning goals depends largely upon the willingness to do the necessary thinking and to make the effort to envision successful performers.

TABLE 8.2. Standards for Learning Behavioral Objectives

	The Observable Action May Be Expressed As: Verb (or action)	Object	Measurable Criteria — Answer Questions As: How often? How well? How many? How much? How will we know it is okay?	Conditions of Performance — What's given?	What are the variables?
After training, the clerk will be able to	Add	6% sales tax	Exactly 6% on all sales	By checking a chart on the cash register	
	Identify	corporate officers	18 of the top 20	By looking at a photo or by hearing the title	
After training, driver will	Activate the turn signals		For all turns	By using the automatic signal in the car	
	1. raise	left arm	Upward at elbow for	Right turn	If no automatic signal
	2. extend	right arm	straight left for 0.8 mile before turning or	Left turn	When driving in country. When driving in the city.
	3. give	proper signal	0.25 block before turning		
After training, the worker will be able to	Smile	At all customers	Even when customer is exhausted or ill		unless irate
	Express concern at the fact that the customer is unhappy		With all irate people Be brief (fewer than ten words) apology only after customer has stopped talking	No matter how upset, or abusive, or profane the customer becomes!	
After training, the manager will be able to	Ask open questions		Which cannot be answered yes or no or with facts	Whenever probing for feelings	
	Relieve tension in subordinates		By asking open questions	When employee seems angry, frustrated, confused, or tense	

TABLE 8.3. Useful Words for Learning Objectives

Observable Action Words		Measurable Criteria
Choose	Collect	At least ___(#)___ correct
Categorize	Trace	At least ___(%)___ correct
Copy	Count	With no more than ___(#)___ errors
Chart	Classify	With at least ___(#)___
Define	Describe	Accurate to ___(?)___ decimal points
Diagram	Designate	In _____ (amount of time)
Detect	Distinguish	At ___(#)___ per hour
Differentiate	Discriminate (between)	
Document	Repeat	
Locate	Identify	
Find	Label	
Isolate	Match	
Mark	Note	
Name	Place	
Rank	Order	
Provide	Select	
Quote	Underline	

There is no magic formula for writing good learning objectives, no list of "right and wrong" words. However, for novice writers, the words listed in Table 8.3 are often "doorways." If accompanied with some honest analysis, these words can lead to the actions and criteria desired in some of those ambiguous tasks.

Three Domains: Cognitive, Affective, and Psychomotor. Another tool for specifying learning behaviors is the Bloom (1956, 1964) *Taxonomy of Educational Objectives.* Compiled by a committee of college and university examiners and published by David McKay of New York City, this list arranges objectives into three general domains. The three domains parallel what industrial T&D departments have always said *they* did: produce new knowledge, different attitudes, and new skills. The three domains are *cognitive,* for mental skills; *affective,* for growth in feelings or emotional areas; *psychomotor,* for manual, physical skills. The Bloom group produced an intricate analysis for each of the first two domains, but none for the psychomotor domain. Their explanation: They have little, if any, experience in teaching manual skills at college levels.

In the cognitive domain, the taxonomy cites six distinct types of behavior:

TABLE 8.4A. Types of Cognitive Behavior

Behavior	Definition	Examples
Knowledge	Recall of data	Names of the officers of an organization. Recite the pledge of allegiance. Quote a policy.
Comprehension	Translation; Interpolation or Interpretation	Explain the principles of performance objectives. State a problem in one's own words.

(continued on next page)

TABLE 8.4A. *(continued)*

Behavior	Definition	Examples
Application	Unprompted use of an abstraction; Using a concept in a new context.	Use an organization manual to calculate your own sick leave. Apply laws of trigonometry in practical situations. Solve a discipline problem by relating it to the union contract.
Analysis	Breaking down systems or communications into components	Troubleshoot a machine that isn't working properly. Distinguish facts from hypotheses. Outline an essay.
Synthesis	Building a structure or pattern from elements found in diverse sources	Write an essay. Design a simple machine tool to perform a specific operation.
Evaluation	Making judgments about the value of ideas, works, solutions, materials	Select the most efficient solution from an array of options. Select the most qualified candidate for a specified position.

The affective domain covers learning objectives that change interests, values, or attitudes. This would include the development of appreciations and adjusting to new systems or policies. The affective domain specifically identifies:

TABLE 8.4B. Types of Affective Behavior

Behavior	Definition	Examples
Receiving	Attending; Awareness; Willingness to hear; Controlled or selected attention	Develops tolerance for a variety of types of music. Listens to others with respect. Listens for and remembers the names of people to whom one is introduced.
Responding	Willingness to react; Acquiescence or satisfaction in responding	Keeps still when the situation calls for silence. Forces oneself to participate with others. Willingly serves the group of which one is a member.
Valuing	Sensing worth; Commitment; Conceptualizing a value	Feels self to be a member of a group. Speaks up at a discussion in class or at meetings. Writes management on matters about which one feels deeply.
Organization	Organizing values into a system; Determining the interrelationship of values; Establishing dominant or pervasive values	Forms judgments about an organization's responsibility to practice ethically. Develops techniques for controlling aggression in socially acceptable fashion.

(continued on next page)

TABLE 8.4B. *(continued)*

Behavior	Definition	Examples
Characterization	Reliable performance of value systems; An individual's unique characteristics	Revises judgments and changes behavior in the light of evidence. Develops a plan for regulated rest in accordance with job demands.

The two volumes of the "Bloom Taxonomy" further subdivide each objective into even more specific levels of behavior. They do regard these as "levels," each successive behavior being more difficult than the previous. It's easier to teach Knowledge than Comprehension. Either of those is definitely easier than Valuing, they contend. This is partly because each behavior involves earlier learnings. For example, people cannot make evaluations without having analyzed, and they cannot analyze without possessing knowledge. Yet one wonders about all those people who constantly make judgments based on no facts at all. The point is that educated minds do insist upon facts first.

From the Bloom list, T&D specialists are particularly influenced by the conclusion that affective behavior is more difficult to develop than cognitive—and that psychomotor is the most difficult of all! One rationale for this conclusion is that useful manipulative, physical behavior does indeed rest upon highly trained minds and emotions. Then, as the books themselves say, "We find so little done about it [psychomotor skill] in secondary schools and colleges" (Bloom 1964, 1:6–7).

Other educators have developed a set of subobjectives within the psychomotor domain, but this domain has never been the problem in organizational training. The manipulative skills very easily reveal observable actions and measurable criteria. It's easy to define learning objectives in the psychomotor domain.

There is a lesson here—particularly for T&D specialists who find their organizations reluctant to define learning objectives, or for T&D managers who find that some of their very own T&D specialists resist all the hard work that goes with "pinning down" the learning objectives or performance standards. Why not begin in the psychomotor domain? Why not obtain good observable and measurable statements for programs that demand manipulative skills? The "smell of success" there can often encourage reluctant T&D specialists to apply the technology to more ambiguous tasks. It can gradually create the norm that states, "We like crisp learning objectives in this organization." It's a place to start in creating good objectives for future programs. Later on, managers come to expect and demand that there will be good objectives for all learning programs.

Who Writes Learning Objectives?

By now, it must be apparent that useful and valid learning objectives result from a collaborative effort between the client management and the T&D department. But writing these objectives is hard work, and only the T&D specialists are masters of the technology. Does it follow, then, that they should be held accountable for the initiative and for the final product?

Precisely! But it also follows that T&D specialists should never do the work alone. The statement may be for a totally observable action with a thoroughly measurable criterion and well-defined performance conditions. It is worthless if it isn't also a realistic statement of what the client organization needs and of what it will reinforce on the job. Thus a team approach seems critically important in the process of creating professional but practical learning objectives.

Who should be on that team? Ideally, several elements need to be represented. First, the top management in the client department must approve the final objectives. These top managers may not be actively involved in selecting the words—but their final "sign-off" is critical, and they must be involved in a two-way conversation while reviewing those statements. Only such scrutiny by top client management can ensure the legitimacy of the program.

Actually, three elements are usually necessary representatives of the client (line) organization: (1) top management, at least for review and approval; (2) typical, or representative, superiors of the workers who will attend the training; and (3) representative workers. Without those superiors and actual performers, total realism and reasonableness in the final version of the learning objectives are less likely.

And, of course, the T&D department should be represented. Typically, two types of T&D expertise are needed: the consultant who helps analyze the performance problem and defines behavior, and the designer who must create learning systems to develop those behaviors. These functions may very well be combined in or performed by just one person, but the process requires both skills: pinning down the behavior and making certain that some learning method can be devised to achieve it. Without the consultant's active involvement, it is possible that the real problem will go unsolved; without the designer's participation, it is possible that unrealistic learning outcomes or inappropriate methods will be attempted.

The team that produces the learning objectives should probably be organized, as shown in Figure 8.1.

Summary

Should every training program have a behavioral objective?

Should every developmental effort have a predetermined behavioral outcome?

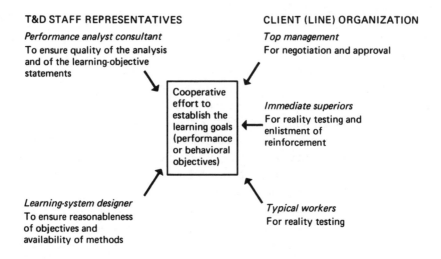

Fig. 8.1.

Team for establishing learning objectives.

Should learning objectives be precisely defined?

What about tasks that aren't so easy to define?

To be certain that the T&D department is giving the organization what it wants, learning objectives are highly desirable. They document the behaviors and imply a pledge that client managers will reinforce those behaviors when the T&D department produces them. They give managers from all departments a clear picture of "what things will look like around here after we've solved this performance problem."

There is great value in the joint effort by T&D people and client personnel such as the subject matter experts (SME), or top performers. The SME help define the task, criteria, and conditions. Client managers *may* help define, but they *certainly* approve the final version of the behavioral objectives. Their involvement obviously has great long-range value for the T&D function.

It seems apparent that even if T&D specialists cannot establish precise goals for all learning, there is value in doing it for those tasks for which they are able to establish observable, measurable behaviors.

Perhaps the most sensible conclusion is this: To the degree that the learning can be specified, instructors have a better basis for making good decisions, learners have a better sense of why and how well they are learning, and the organization has a better idea of what it is getting back from its training investment.

How Do People Learn?

Learning Theories

How do people learn? Although experts can't agree on a single learning theory, T&D designers need to know certain core theories. Since experts can't agree, you might ask, "Why worry"? Well, T&D designers need some learning theory upon which to base the activities they specify in the learning systems they create. Professional instructors need some theoretical basis from which to operate. Consultants and administrators, who serve as change agents for the client organization, need a theory about learning if they are to produce change. After all, change begins with learning that there may be a better way.

But which learning theory should you use? Chances are you will use many theories and do what must be done to help people change. By observing your successes and failures, you will develop an eclectic but consistent learning theory of your own.

This chapter can help you launch your growth toward that objective. Newcomers can think of opportunities to try out these ideas; old-timers can guard against the temptation to dismiss them because they're unfamiliar, or because they tried them once and they didn't work the first time.

In this chapter, we take a closer look at representative theories and research on learning in Human Resource Development (HRD); these are based in large part on the work of Richard Swanson and Elwood Holton (2001). First, five meta-theories of learning are discussed. Then, representative midrange learning theories at the individual and organizational level are reviewed.

So our learning objective reads: "After reading this chapter, the reader will comprehend the similarities and differences among four learning theories: Sensory Stimulation, Reinforcement Theory, Facilitation, and Andragogy." An application objective would be: "Will develop a personally satisfying and realistic theory about helping others learn."

Meta-Theories of Learning

Table 9.1 below provides a summary of five meta-theories of learning for T&D and HRD. These five are meta-theories because they apply to learning in all settings, for all age groups, and to all types of learning events. In this section, each meta-theory is described along with its primary contribution to HRD. Each has been the subject of extensive thinking, writing, and research.

Table 9.1 clearly shows that each approach represents a fundamentally different view of learning. Each would define learning differently, prescribe different roles for the teacher, and seek different outcomes from learning. Each has made a substantial contribution to learning in HRD, and will continue to inform practice. This section provides only a brief summary of each.

It is important to realize that very few HRD professionals or HRD interventions use only one of these meta-theories. Most are quite eclectic, using a combination of approaches that fit the particular situation. Thus, these five approaches should not be read as either/or choices, but rather as five approaches to be drawn upon as appropriate to your particular needs. In practice, they are usually adapted and blended to accomplish specific objectives.

Behaviorism

Behaviorists are primarily concerned with changes in behavior as a result of learning. Behaviorism has a long and rich history, having been originally developed by John B. Watson, who introduced the term in 1913 and developed it in the early decades of the twentieth century. Six prominent learning theorists are commonly included in this school: Ivan Pavlov, Edward L. Thorndike, John B. Watson, Edwin R. Guthrie, Clark L. Hull, and B. F. Skinner. Pavlov and Skinner are the best-known contributors, Pavlov having developed the classical conditioning model and Skinner the operant conditioning model. Although each of these six men had different views of behaviorism, Ormond (1999) identifies seven core assumptions that they share (10–11):

1. Principles of learning apply equally to different behaviors and to different species of animals.
2. Learning processes can be studied most objectively when the focus of study is on stimulus and response.
3. Internal cognitive processes are largely excluded from scientific study.
4. Learning involves a behavior change.
5. Organisms are born as blank slates.

TABLE 9.1. Five Orientations to Learning

Aspect	Behaviorist	Cognitivist	Humanist	Social Learning	Constructivist
Learning theorists	Thorndike, Pavlov, Watson, Guthrie, Hull, Tolman, Skinner	Koffka, Kohler, Lewin, Piaget, Ausubel, Bruner, Gagné	Maslow, Rogers	Bandura, Rotter	Candy, Dewey, Lave, Piaget, Rogoff, von Glaserfeld, Vygotsky
View of the learning process	Change in behavior	Internal mental process (including insight, information processing, memory, perception)	A personal act to fulfill potential	Interaction with and observation of others in a social context	Construction of meaning from experience
Locus of learning	Stimuli in the environment	Internal cognitive structuring	Affective and cognitive needs	Interaction of person, behavior and environment	Internal construction of reality by individual
Purpose of education	Produce behavioral change in desired direction	Develop capacity and skills to learn better	Become self-actualized, autonomous	Model new roles and behavior	Construct knowledge
Teacher's role	Arranges environment to elicit desired response	Structures content of learning activity	Facilitates development of whole person	Models and guides new roles and behavior	Facilitates and negotiates meaning with learner
Manifestation in adult learning	• Behavioral objectives • Competency-based education • Skill development • Skill development and training	• Cognitive development • Intelligence, learning, and memory as function of age • Learning how to learn	• Andragogy • Self-directed learning	• Socialization • Social roles • Mentoring • Locus of control	• Experiential learning • Self-directed learning • Perspective transformation • Reflective practice

SOURCE: Merriam and Cattarella 1999.

6. Learning is largely the result of environmental events.
7. The most useful theories tend to be parsimonious ones.

Behaviorism teaches that a behavior is controlled by its consequences. Humans will repeat a behavior that seems to produce pleasant consequences, and will avoid behaviors which seem to lead to unpleasant consequences. If one applies this to learning theory, the conclusion is simply that people learn because of what happens to them. To translate that to the instructor-learner relationship is a simple (but dangerous) step: Teachers can cause students to behave in desired ways by "rewarding" or giving positive, pleasant consequences to students who "got it right." In classic behaviorism, the role of the learning facilitator is to structure the environment to elicit the desired response from the learner.

This *is* a dangerous conclusion because it is terribly incomplete and partly incorrect. Why incomplete? Because it ignores that reinforcement is a two-way transaction between humans. Learners are constantly shaping the behavior of instructors, just as instructors are attempting to shape the behavior of the learners. How incorrect? Because behavior isn't that simple.

Behaviorism has played a central role in HRD. Its key contributions include:

- *Focus on behavior.* The focus on behavior is important because performance change does not occur without changing behavior. Thus, behaviorism has led to popular practices such as behavioral objectives and competency-based education.
- *Focus on the environment.* Behaviorism reminds us of the central role the external environment plays in shaping human learning and performance. An individual in an organization is subjected to various factors (e.g., rewards and incentives, supports, etc.) that will influence performance.
- *Foundation for transfer of learning.* Behaviorism also provides part of the foundation for the transfer of learning research. Transfer research, for example, Rouillier and Goldstein (1993), shows that the environment is at least as important, if not more important, than learning in predicting the use of learning on the job.
- *Foundation for skill development training.* As indicated in Figure 9.1, behaviorism has provided much of the foundation for skill or competency-oriented training and development. Behavioral objectives are another contribution from behaviorists.

When using behaviorism, reinforcers should be *positive*. Why? Because happy consequences teach behaviors and unhappy consequences teach the avoidance of behaviors. Slot machines never tell their "one arm" to attack the player in the chest or stomach! They carry no taped recording to chide, "You jerk! I just paid off two spins ago!" When slot machines reinforce, they reinforce with happy consequences, with good news, and with *positive* contingencies. Gamblers continue to insert coins because they never know when or how much that positive payoff will be.

Psychologists urge positive rather than aversive (negative) reinforcement because positive reinforcement can instill the desired behaviors, but negative reinforcement can only get rid of undesirable behaviors. Thus spankings follow naughtiness; jail follows lawbreaking; suspensions follow infractions. Wade Burck, tiger master for Ringling Brothers, and Barnum and Bailey's Circus, trains his pupils by way of the reward method: a piece of meat for a job well done. "But if an animal is good for two months, then all of a sudden doesn't do a trick, I don't beat the animal." Most organizational trainers have no desire to experiment to prove Burck wrong!

The *principle of individuality* is expressed in the old cliche, "One man's meat is another man's poison." Thus it is that time off without pay is a negative reinforcer for those who value doing their own thing. This individuality of reinforcers sometimes makes contingency management systems very hard to administer. Varying the reinforcers can conceivably clash with organizational policy, union contracts, laws, or standard management practices. Many managers can tell you that they've driven themselves desperate trying to treat each person as an individual and yet treat everybody alike. Perhaps this very problem offers insight into its solution. If people are individuals, and if managers are hoping to reinforce them with their peculiarly individual "stroke," then the manager must know a great deal about every worker on the staff.

The *principle of immediacy* is also important. A consequence will control a behavior if it follows the behavior at once—or at least soon enough that the performer subtly perceives the consequences. Behaviors really have two consequences: one immediate and one delayed. The immediate consequence will control future behavior more than the secondary contingency.

In *About Behaviorism,* B. F. Skinner (1974) explains it this way (178): Drinking alcohol has an immediate, positive, and pleasant consequence—feeling "high." Unfortunately, there is also a delayed negative consequence. It's called a hangover! During this delayed, aversive consequence, drinkers may resolve never to touch the stuff again. But they do. Why? Because the immediate consequence is so pleasant. That's what controls their consequences. In the same vein, suspending an employee next month for yesterday's infraction will not produce desired behaviors. A good performance appraisal next year for last winter's extra effort will not be very reinforcing.

The *principle of strength* means merely that the consequence needs to be noticeable. Weak reinforcers don't control behavior; witness the gentle taps that some parents call a spanking, or the small variations in salary increases spread across an employee population. Unless the reinforcement is perceived to be significant, it doesn't encourage a repetition of the desired behavior. Slot machines know that; if they give you back anything at all, they usually give you back at least twice the amount you inserted—which takes us to the next principle.

The *principle of variability* ties in closely with strength. The strength must not only be noticeable; it must vary. Slot machines are programmed perfectly for this principle. Sometimes, they return twice as many coins as the player inserts; sometimes they pay off at a rate of five-to-one, ten-to-one, or even with jackpots! The players just never know when they're going to get paid—or how much. Some sociologists feel that our criminal justice systems are actually encouraging criminal behavior by the erratic penalties applied to identical crimes. The logic of the criminal goes: "Even if you get caught, you might get off easily. You can always get a soft judge, you know." Slot machines are also programmed to apply another important principle of contingency management.

Mutuality is another principle that governs the transaction of reinforcers in interpersonal relationships. We don't always stop to think about it, but we are constantly cross-reinforcing one another for our behaviors. Consciously or subconsciously, we give either positive or negative reinforcement to the people with whom we interact—*and they are continuously doing the same thing to us!* People who don't believe this need only observe how quickly little tots teach their parents to shout. Instructors who introspect can agree that cooperative students control the instructor's behavior at least as much as the teacher controls the student.

It takes real discipline to pay less attention to those who are constantly smiling than to those who seem not to be responding at all. Also, it is often easy to over-respond to troublemakers at the expense of learners who are investing constructive energies in acquiring the new behaviors.

Successive approximations represent another significant principle of reinforcement theory. Those big words simply describe the small steps people take toward the ultimate objective; those small steps are "successively approximate" to the desired behavior.

Students rarely "get it all right" the first time. They certainly don't get the complex objectives of most adult learning programs totally correct when they first try out the new skill, the new idea, the new value. They do, however, do *some* of it properly during their early efforts.

Learners approach mastery one step at a time. Rarely do they sit down at a sophisticated computer and write a successful program the first time; hardly ever do they embrace a quantitative feedback element in a new appraisal system the moment it is first explained to them.

Successive approximations work for all of us from infancy to senility. Instructors of adults need to understand this phenomenon.

Why? Because adults so often need to reacquire the skill of open inquiry. Too many adults have closed their minds to new ideas, methods, or options. A learner's experience is a double-edged sword. It can be "a rich resource or an impenetrable defense" against new learnings.

Just recall classroom situations in which you've participated. You will surely remember plenty of times when instructors missed the opportunity to reinforce learners who, though a long way from mastery, were moving in desired directions. You can probably also recall times when trainers actually punished learners for successive approximations. Teachers who exclaimed, "But you forgot to cross the 't' in the second word!" are ignoring all the other words the student completed properly. Phrases such as, "Not bad!" may seem to be praise to the instructor, but rejection to the learners who aren't at all sure of their progress. They may, indeed, not be at all sure they want to acquire the new learnings, and such ambiguous reinforcement may help them make up their minds—in the wrong way!

Instructors easily "put down" adult learners who challenge the instructor's ideas. What does that put-down really say to the class? It says, "Hey, fella! We don't want inquiry in this session." Instructors need to nourish questions that challenge the system or policy rather than argue with the questioner. After all, such questions show interest, some slight willingness to receive, and are thus successive approximations of the valuing that will ultimately bring compliance.

Behaviorism has also been heavily criticized, primarily by adult educators who prefer a more humanistic and constructivist perspective. The chief criticism is that behaviorism views the learner as being passive and dependent. In addition, behaviorism does not account for the role of personal insight and meaning in learning. These are legitimate criticisms and explain why behaviorism is rarely the only learning theory employed. On the other hand, certain training interventions are appropriately taught in a behavioral approach. For example, teaching police officers how to respond when attacked is an appropriate use of behavioral methods because officers have to respond instinctively.

Cognitivism

Cognitivism arose as a direct response to the limits of behaviorism, particularly the "thoughtless" approach to human learning. The early roots can be traced back to the 1920s and 1930s through the work of Edward Tolman, Jean

Piaget, Lev Vygotsky, and the Gestalt psychologists of Germany. However, contemporary cognitivism did not begin to appear until the 1950s and 1960s.

Ormond (1999, 168) identified seven core assumptions of contemporary cognitivism:

1. Some learning processes may be unique to human beings.
2. Cognitive processes are the focus of study.
3. Objective, systematic observations of people's behavior should be the focus of scientific inquiry; however, inferences about unobservable mental processes can often be drawn from such behavior.
4. Individuals are actively involved in the learning process.
5. Learning involves the formation of mental associations that are not necessarily reflected in overt behavior changes.
6. Knowledge is organized.
7. Learning is a process of relating new information to previously learned information.

Cognitivists are primarily concerned with insight and understanding. They see people not as passive and shaped by their environment, but as active shapers of the environment. Furthermore, they focus on the internal process of acquiring, understanding, and retaining learning. Because of that, they suggest that the focus of the learning facilitator should be on structuring the content and the learning activity so that learners can acquire information optimally. Some very well-known names within HRD fit under this umbrella, including Kurt Lewin (organizational development), Jean Piaget (cognitive development), Jerome Bruner (discovery learning) and Robert Gagné (instructional design). Contemporary cognitivism can be thought of as having three perspectives: information processing theory, constructivism, and contextual views (situated cognition).

Cognitivism has made significant contributions to HRD and adult learning:

- *Information processing.* Central to cognitivism is the concept of the human mind as an information processor. Figure 9.1 shows a basic schematic view of the human information processing system. Notice that there are three key components: sensory memory, short-term memory, and long-term memory. Cognitivists are particularly interested in the processes shown by arrows in this schematic. These arrows represent the mental processes of moving information from sensory memory to short-term memory, from short-term memory to long-term memory, and retrieving information from long-term memory.
- *Metacognition.* Along with these basic information-processing components, cognitivism also focuses on how individuals control their cogni-

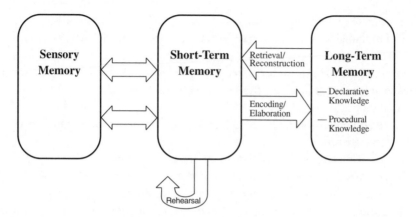

Fig. 9.1. Information processing model.

SOURCE: Bruning, Schraw, and Ronning 1999, p.16.

tive processes; this is called metacognition. This concept is more commonly known in HRD and adult learning as "learning how to learn."

- *Cognitive development.* Another important contribution has been the focus on how cognition develops over the life span. It is now generally accepted that cognitive development continues throughout adulthood.

Cognitivism has not received the same degree of criticism as behaviorism. For the most part, cognitivism has made important contributions and is widely used in HRD, especially in instructional design. At the same time, it is viewed in some circles as incomplete because it views the human mind as too mechanical.

Humanism

Humanism did not emerge as a learning meta-theory, but rather as a general approach to psychology. The work of Abraham Maslow and Carl Rogers provides the core of humanistic psychology. Buhler (1971), a leading humanistic psychologist, suggests that the core assumptions of humanism are these:

1. The person as a *whole* is the main subject of humanistic psychology.
2. Humanistic psychology is concerned with the knowledge of a person's entire life history.
3. Human existence and intention are also of great importance.
4. Life goals are of equal importance.

5. Man's creativity has a primary place.
6. Humanistic psychology is frequently applied to psychotherapy. (382)

Carl Rogers (1969) put forth his principles of significant learning by saying that such learning must have the following characteristics:

1. Personal involvement: The affective and cognitive aspects must come from within.
2. Self-initiated: A sense of discovery must come from within.
3. Pervasive: The learning makes a difference in the behavior, the attitudes, perhaps even the personality of the learner.
4. Evaluated by the learner: The learner can best determine whether the learning experience is meeting a need.
5. Essence is meaning: When experiential learning takes place, its meaning to the learner becomes incorporated into the total experience.(5)

Rogers places far greater emphasis on the learner's involvement in the process. He examines far more deeply the relationship between the learner and the instructor, identifying this relationship as the primary ingredient in the process.

The Rogerian approach is called "Facilitation." Why? Because Rogers sees the role of the instructor as a facilitator rather than a stimulator or controller of the learning process.

Rogers believes above all that humans have a natural capacity to learn—even an eagerness to do so. Yet he describes this eagerness as "ambivalent" because significant learning involves two kinds of pain: one caused by the learning itself and the other caused by giving up previous learnings. That is why he believes that external threats must be kept to a minimum. The instructor is there to facilitate the resolution of this ambivalence and to assist (never to force) the student in accomplishing the goal.

When learning involves changing one's concept of oneself, says Rogers, it is all the more difficult. Indeed, it is threatening—one of those "significant learnings" that truly interests Rogers.

But Rogers goes even farther. He points out that facilitative instructors are:

• Less protective of their own constructs and beliefs than other teachers
• More able to listen to students—especially to their feelings
• Able to accept the "troublesome, innovative, creative ideas which emerge in students"
• Inclined to pay as much attention to their relationship with students as to the content of the course

- Able to accept feedback, both positive and negative, and to use it as constructive insight into themselves and their behavior (164)

Thus Rogers's concept of facilitation involves permitting students to make responsible choices about the direction of their learning, and to live responsibly with those choices.

How does this relate to the course content in a typical T&D department training program? There may be a sharp conflict. Facilitative objective setting and the established performance standards may not turn out to be the same thing. The learning objectives have presumably been established and validated by management, and revalidated through reality testing with typical workers. One hopes these objectives will be reinforced by the managers of all successful graduates.

The potential conflict is quite obvious: Organizations are unwilling to alter standards just to permit craftspeople to fulfill themselves. However, in programs for supervisors, managers, executives, and staff professionals, many apply Rogers's advice. They stress individual development programs growing out of appraisal and goal-setting sessions with the immediate managers. In a few workshops, participants may select individualized learning goals relevant to their current positions or to those they may reasonably be expected to occupy soon—but the most frequent example of "Learner Controlled Instruction" in most organizations is employee participation in selecting which programs or conferences they will attend.

Learners increasingly select the sequence with which they will acquire new skills, or the materials they will use. Sometimes, the learner and the trainer work together to describe adequate tests of their learning accomplishments. This last activity reflects the principle of self-evaluation—a critical facet of Carl Rogers's philosophy. He insists that self-evaluation is basic and that evaluation by others is secondary.

One principle of facilitative learning is compatible with organizational T&D efforts: the belief that learning should be oriented toward the solution of significant problems—not to the history of the task or the profession. As a result, both seek students who become self-disciplined professionals attempting to cope with significant issues. What organization wouldn't like to have that sort of employee working at every level?

Some proponents of facilitative learning designs and relationships feel that there is an impenetrable barrier between the beliefs of behaviorists such as B. F. Skinner and the tenets of Carl Rogers. Others contend that good positive reinforcement is merely facilitation between two humans with mutual respect for one another's values. They argue that one must care enough about other people to discover what they find reinforcing. It's facilitative, they say, to see that others are positively reinforced for behaving in a mutually desirable fashion. That, they say, is facilitation at its most practical level.

Humanism adds yet another dimension to learning and has dominated much of adult learning. It is most concerned with development by the whole person and places great emphasis on the affective component of learning largely overlooked by other learning theories. The learning facilitator has to take into account the whole person and that person's life situation in planning the learning experience. Humanists view individuals as seeking self-actualization through learning and of being capable of controlling their own learning processes. Adult learning theories, particularly andragogy, best represents humanism in HRD. In addition, self-directed learning and much of career development is grounded in humanism. Andragogy will be discussed in much more detail in the next section of this chapter.

Social Learning

Social learning focuses on how people learn by interacting with and observing other people. This type of learning focuses on the social context in which learning occurs. Some people view social learning as a special type of behaviorism because it reflects how individuals learn from people in their environment. Others view it as a separate meta-theory because the learner is also actively finding meaning in the interactions.

A foundational contribution of social learning is the view that people can learn vicariously by imitating others. Thus, central to social learning processes is that people learn from role models. This view is in direct contradiction to what behaviorists believe; they say that learners have to perform for themselves and be reinforced for learning to occur. Thus, the facilitator must model new behaviors and guide learners in learning from others. Albert Bandura is probably the best-known name is this area. His works fully developed social learning theory in the 1960s through the 1980s.

Ormond (1999, 116–117) lists four core assumptions of social learning theory:

1. People can learn by observing the behaviors of others and the outcomes of those behaviors.
2. Learning can occur without a change in behavior.
3. The consequences of behavior play a role in learning.
4. Cognition plays a role in learning.

Social learning also occupies a central place in HRD. One contribution is in classroom learning where social learning focuses on the role of the facilitator as a model for behaviors to be learned. Facilitators often underestimate their influence as role models, and they forget to use role modeling as part of their instructional plans.

Social learning may make its biggest contribution through learning that takes place outside the classroom. One area is in the development of new employees, where socialization processes play the largest role. Socialization is the process by which organizations pass on the culture of the organization to new employees and teach them how to be effective in the organization. It is an informal process that occurs through social interactions between new employees and organizational members. Another key area is mentoring, a primary means of on-the-job development in many organizations. It is often used to develop new managers. This is clearly a social learning process because mentors teach and coach protégés. Yet another key area is on-the-job training whereby newcomers learn their jobs from job incumbents, in part by direct instruction but also by observing the incumbent and using the incumbent as a role model.

There are few critics of social learning because it mostly contributes to learning theory in HRD without inciting sharp arguments. Social learning is widely accepted as an effective and important learning process. When properly applied, it enhances learning and contributes learning that often can't occur in the classroom.

Constructivism

While controversial, especially in its more radical versions, constructivism is emerging as a useful perspective for some adult learning situations. Constructivism stresses that all knowledge is context-bound, and that individuals gain personal meaning from their learning experiences. Thus, learning cannot be separated from the context in which it is used. They also stress the cumulative nature of learning; that is, new information must be related to other existing information if learners are to retain and use it. For adults, experience might be conceptualized as creating a giant funnel of previous knowledge. When new information enters the top of the funnel and cascades downwards, it eventually falls out unless it "sticks" to some element of prior knowledge. The role of the facilitator is to help learners find meaning in new information.

Many learning theorists, including Ormond (1999), do not view this as a separate meta-theory but rather as a special type of cognitivism. Adult learning theorists, such as S. B. Merriam and R. S. Cafferella (1999), are more inclined to differentiate it from cognitivism because of its importance for adult learning.

The contributions of constructivism to HRD are still emerging. The emphasis on how adults make meaning of new information by relating it to previous experience largely supports the andragogical view of learning. In fact, the parallels between moderate views of constructivism and andragogy are striking. Both stress ownership of the learning process by learners, experiential learning, and problem-solving approaches to learning. However, andragogy and the more extreme views of constructivism are not compatible. Constructivism plays an important role in understanding informal and incidental learning, self-directed learning, and perspective transformation.

Middle-Range Learning Models at the Individual Level

In this section, three middle-range models of learning are reviewed. First, andragogy is discussed as a core adult learning model that has played a central role in adult learning within HRD. Next, David Kolb's (1984) experiential learning model is discussed, followed by transformational learning.

Andragogy—the Adult Learning Perspective

To become an elementary teacher, a person may study "pedagogy." T&D specialists in the past few years have become interested in "andragogy." The difference is quite simple. *Ped* is a Latin root meaning "child"; "andra" derives from the Greek *aner*, meaning man, not boy. Thus andragogy studies how adults learn. It asks whether they learn in ways that are significantly different from the ways in which children acquire new behaviors.

In the late 1960s, when Malcolm Knowles introduced andragogy in the United States, the idea was groundbreaking and sparked much subsequent research and controversy. Stephen Brookfield (1986), positing a similar view, asserts that andragogy is the "single most popular idea in the education and training of adults" (91). Adult educators and human resource development professionals, particularly those beginning their careers, find them invaluable in shaping the learning process to be more effective with adults.

Leading this inquiry was Malcolm Knowles (1973). He points to several differences in the inventory adults bring to the learning. Children are dependent, but adults see themselves as self-directing. Children expect to have questions that must be answered by outside sources; adults expect to answer parts of their questions from their own experience. What may be more important, children expect to be told what they need to do; adults have a very different viewpoint on that issue.

In part, these expectations stem from their view of their own experience. Children are well aware that they haven't been around for long. Thus they put a rather low value on their experience. But adults weren't "born yesterday," and they do value their experience. They value it so much that they want to invest it in the learning experience; they want to test new concepts and behavior against what they have previously learned; and they want to test what they now think against new research.

You can recall from your own schooldays the times when the teacher said, "Now, someday this will come in handy." Children may buy that; adults ask, "How soon?" Children accept a delayed application, but adults tend to demand an immediate application of the learnings. This harmonizes with Rogers's (1969) viewpoint that learners want to be problem solvers.

The Core Andragogical Model

Popularized by Knowles, the original andragogical model presents core principles of adult learning and important assumptions about adult learners. These core principles of adult learning are believed to enable those designing and conducting adult learning to design more effective learning processes for adults. The model is a transactional model (Brookfield 1986) in that it speaks to the characteristics of the learning transaction. As such, it is applicable to any adult learning transaction, from community education to human resource development in organizations.

Depending on which citation is consulted, various authors present andragogy in different ways. This difficulty has arisen because the number of andragogical principles has grown from four to six over the years as Knowles refined his thinking.

Today there are six core assumptions, or principles of andragogy (Knowles, Holton, and Swanson 1998, 64–68):

1. Adults need to know why they need to learn something before learning it.
2. The self-concept of adults is heavily dependent upon a move toward self-direction.
3. Prior experiences of the learner provide a rich resource for learning.
4. Adults typically become ready to learn when they experience a need to cope with a life situation or perform a task.
5. Adults' orientation to learning is life-centered and they see education as a process of developing increased competency levels to achieve their full potential.
6. The motivation for adult learners is internal rather than external.

These core principles provide a sound foundation for planning adult learning experiences. Absent any other information, they offer an effective approach to adult learning.

The second part of the andragogical model is what Knowles (1973) called the andragogical process design steps for creating adult learning experiences. Originally, Knowles presented as seven steps, but later (1995) added a new first step (preparing learners for the program), which brought the total to eight steps:

1. Preparing learners for the program
2. Establishing a climate conducive to learning
3. Involving learners in mutual planning
4. Involving participants in diagnosing their learning needs
5. Involving learners in forming their learning objectives
6. Involving learners in designing learning plans
7. Helping learners carry out their learning plans
8. Involving learners in evaluating their learning outcomes

Figure 9.2 shows the andragogical process elements and andragogical approaches as presented by Knowles.

These andragogic concepts have tremendous implications for the T&D specialist. Early activities need to allow maximum participation by learners so that they can invest their experience and values in the learning process—and so that instructors can note this inventory. Andragogic instructors use more questions because they realize that learners do know a great deal; that tapping that inventory permits the learners to invest more energy in new learnings.

For example: If learners know how digits are positioned in a decimal system, they can be expected to interpret displays in binary or octal numerical systems. This is sometimes called "letting the learners go from the known to the unknown." But note the use of those andragogic words "letting learners go" rather than the pedagogic "taking learners from the known to the unknown."

A major aspect of andragogic systems is the learner's active involvement in establishing the learning objectives. And so we have the same potential conflict between the needs of the organization and the needs of the individual. As we noted earlier, in management development learners may be able to select their own learning objectives; in skills training, that doesn't happen very often.

Not all organizational T&D programs can permit the full delegation of the learning goals to the learners themselves—but none of them prevents an activity that allows learners to analyze learning goals and understand why they are important to the organization—and to the individual learner.

Process Elements	
Element	**Andragogical Approach**
Preparing learners	Provide information Prepare for participation Help develop realistic expectations Begin thinking about content
Climate	Relaxed, trusting Mutually respectful Informal, warm Collaborative, supportive
Planning	Mutually by learners and facilitator
Diagnosis of needs	By mutual assessment
Setting of objectives	By mutual negotiation
Designing learning plans	Learning contracts Learning projects Sequenced by readiness
Learning activities	Inquiry projects Independent study Experiential techniques
Evaluation	By learner collected evidence validated by peers, facilitators, and experts. Criterion referenced.

Fig. 9.2. Process elements of andragogy.

SOURCE: **Knowles 1992, 1995.**

Understanding the reasons for (or "owning") the objectives is sometimes called motivation. One popular theory insists that until the learner has this ownership, little useful learning will take place.

But even when learning objectives are predetermined, the processes of andragogic sessions vary sharply from those in pedagogic classes. In fact, andragogy raises interesting questions about the proper role of the instructor. Are the best instructors those who can speak well? Those who can maintain a benevolent but consistent control? The andragogic learner-instructor relationship escapes the dominant-teacher and dependent-learner image altogether. It features reciprocity in the teaching-learning transaction.

The primary function of the instructor is to manage, or guide, andragogic processes—not to "manage the content," as in traditional pedagogy. To achieve this, learning designs involve establishing the norm for a great deal of two-way communication. This may very well include learner inputs, querying, or establishing the objectives and the methods.

It follows that the andragogic climate stresses physical comfort, variety, and mobility. (Learners need to get to their chosen resources for the learning; class or conference rooms may not be the ideal environment for this.)

Instructors need to focus on goals and inventories to use frequent skillful questions and empathic reflection to help learners invest their energies so that growth occurs for both the learner and the organization.

Thus in andragogic designs, trainers serve as facilitative counselors to each learner. This requires a wide range of the competencies listed in the American Society for Training and Development (ASTD) model: Understanding of adult learning, of organizational behavior, and of the organization itself, of the Training and Development Field and of Training Techniques; plus skill in Writing, Counseling, Questioning, Feedback, Group Process, Intellectual Versatility, Performance Observation, Objectives Preparation, Negotiation, Research, and Writing!

When T&D departments adopt andragogy as the philosophical basis of their learning designs, they are saying that they intend to make maximum use of student inventories. Remember that standard formula, $M - I = D$, or "Mastery minus Inventory equals Deficiency". Learners are encouraged to invest their considerable pretraining experience in new learnings. Skilled instruction is required to make certain the investment is a wise one—particularly in organizations that are unaccustomed to andragogic designs.

Andragogy in Practice: A Set of Flexible Assumptions?

In early works, Knowles presented andragogy as an integrated set of assumptions. However, through the years of experimentation, it now seems that the power of andragogy lies in its potential for more flexible application. As others have noted, over the years the assumptions became viewed by some practitioners as somewhat of a recipe implying that all adult educators should facilitate the same way in all situations. There is clear evidence that Knowles intended that they be viewed as flexible assumptions to be altered depending upon the situation.

It seems clear that Knowles always knew, and then confirmed through use, that andragogy could be used in many different ways and would have to be adapted to fit individual situations. Unfortunately, Knowles never offered a systematic framework of factors that should be considered when determining which assumptions are realistic when adapting andragogy to the situation.

The Andragogy-in-Practice Model

Andragogy in Practice, the framework depicted in Figure 9.3, is an enhanced conceptual framework to enable more systematically applied andragogy across multiple domains of adult learning practice. The three dimensions of Andragogy in Practice, shown as rings in the figure, are: (1) Goals and Purposes for Learning, (2) Individual and Situation Differences, and (3) Andragogy: Core Adult Learning Principles.

In contrast to the traditional model of andragogy, this approach conceptually integrates the additional influences with the core adult learning principles. The three rings of the model interact, allowing the model to offer a three-dimensional process for adult learning. The result is a model that recognizes the lack of homogeneity among learners and learning situations, and illustrates that the learning transaction is a multifaceted activity. This approach is entirely consistent with most of the program development literature in adult education that in some manner incorporates contextual analysis as a step in developing programs (Houle 1972; Knox 1986; Boone 1985).

Goals and Purposes for Learning

Goals and Purposes for Learning, the outer ring of the model, are portrayed as developmental outcomes. The goals and purposes of adult learning serve to shape and mold the learning experience. In this model, goals for adult learning events may fit into three general categories: *individual, institutional, or societal.*

- *Individual growth.* The traditional view among most scholars and practitioners of adult learning is to think exclusively of individual growth. At first glance, andragogy would appear to best fit with individual development goals because of its focus on the individual learner.
- *Institutional growth.* Adult learning is equally powerful in developing better institutions, as well as individuals. The adult learning transaction in an HRD setting still fits nicely within the andragogical framework, although the different goals require adjustments to be made in how the andragogical assumptions are applied.
- *Societal growth.* Societal goals and purposes that can be associated with the learning experience can be illustrated through Friere's (1970) work. This Brazilian educator sees the goals and purposes of adult education as societal transformation and contends that education is a consciousness-raising process.

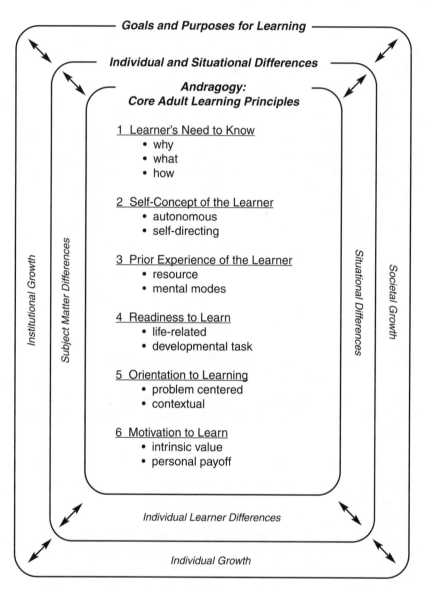

Fig. 9.3.

Andragogy in practice.

SOURCE: Knowles, Holton, and Swanson 1998.

Individual and Situational Differences

Individual and Situational Differences, the middle ring of the Andragogy in Practice Model, are portrayed as variables. We continue to learn more about the differences that affect adult learning and act as filters to shape the practice of andragogy. These variables are grouped into the categories of *individual learner differences, subject matter differences,* and *situational differences.*

- *Subject matter differences.* Different subject matter may require different learning strategies. For example, individuals may be less likely to learn complex technical subject matter in a self-directed manner.
- *Situational differences.* The situational effects category captures any unique factors that could arise in a particular learning situation and incorporates several sets of influences. At the individual level, different local situations may dictate different teaching/learning strategies. For example, learners in remote locations may be forced to become more self-directed, or perhaps less so. At a broader level, this group of factors connects andragogy with the social context that may include social influences prior to the learning event that affect the learning experience, as well as the social milieu within which the actual learning occurs.
- *Individual differences.* This may be the area in which our understanding of adult learning has advanced the most since Knowles first introduced andragogy. Several researchers have expounded upon a host of individual differences affecting the learning process (Dirkx and Prenger 1997; Kidd 1978; Merriam and Cafferella 1999). From this perspective, there is no reason to expect all adults to behave the same way, but rather our understanding of individual difference should help to shape and tailor the andragogical approach to fit the uniqueness of the learners.

Experiential Learning

Kolb (1984) has been a leader in advancing the practice of experiential learning. His definition of learning: *The process whereby knowledge is created through transformation of experience* (38).

For Kolb, learning is not so much the acquisition or transmission of content as the interaction between content and experience, whereby each transforms the other. The educator's job, he says, is not only to transmit or implant new ideas, but also to modify old ones that may get in the way of new ones.

Kolb suggests that there are four steps in the experiential learning cycle (see Figure 9.4):

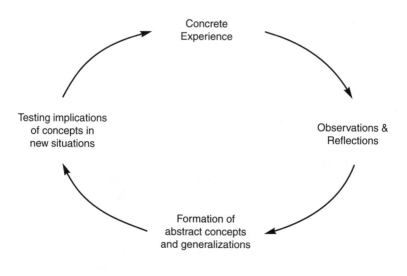

Fig. 9.4. Kolb's experiential learning model.

1. *Concrete experience*—full involvement, new here-and-now experiences
2. *Observations and reflections*—reflecting on and observing their experiences from many perspectives
3. *Formation of abstract concepts and generalizations*—creating concepts that integrate their observations into logically sound theories
4. *Testing implications of concepts in new situations*—using these theories to make decisions and solve problems

Kolb goes on to suggest that these four modes combine to create four distinct learning styles.

Kolb's model has made a major contribution to the experiential learning literature by (a) providing a theoretical basis for experiential learning research and (b) providing a practical model for experiential learning practice. The four steps in his model are an invaluable framework for designing learning experiences for adults. Programs and classes can be structured to include all four components, as well as units or lessons. Shown below are examples of learning strategies that may be useful in each step.

Human resource development practitioners, while always valuing experience, are increasingly emphasizing experiential learning as a means to improve performance. Action reflection learning is one technique developed to focus on learner's experiences and integrate experience into the learning process.

TABLE 9.2   Learning Strategies

Kolb's Stage	Example Learning/Teaching Strategy
Concrete experience	Simulation, case study, field trips, real experience, demonstrations
Observe and reflect	Discussion, small groups, buzz groups, designated observers
Abstract conceptualization	Sharing content
Active experimentation	Laboratory experiences, on-the-job experience, internships, practice sessions

Learning transfer researchers are also focusing on experiential learning as a means to enhance the transfer of learning into performance and to increase the motivation to learn. Structured on-the-job training has emerged as a core method to capitalize more systematically on the value of experiential learning in organizations and as a tool to develop new employees more effectively through the use of experienced coworkers. Experiential learning approaches have the dual benefit of appealing to the adult learner's experience base, as well as increasing the likelihood of performance change after training.

Transformational Learning

Transformational learning has gained increasing attention in HRD. The fundamental premise is that people, just like organizations, may engage in incremental learning or in deeper learning that requires them to challenge fundamental assumptions and meaning schema they have about the world. This concept has appeared in a variety of forms in the literature. Rummerlhart and Norman (1978) proposed three modes of learning in relation to mental schema: *accretion, tuning, and restructuring.* Accretion and tuning involves no change, or only incremental changes, to a person's schemata. Restructuring involves the creation of new schema and is the hardest learning for most adults.

Argyris (1982) labels learning as either "single loop" or "double loop." Single-loop learning is learning that fits prior experiences and existing values and enables the learner to respond in an automatic way. Double-loop learning is learning that does not fit the learner's prior experiences or schema. Generally, it requires the learner to change his or her mental schema in a fundamental way.

Mezirow (1991) and Brookfield (1986, 1987) are leading advocates for transformational learning in the adult learning literature. Mezirow calls this perspective transformation, which he defines as (1) the process of becoming critically aware of how and why our assumptions have come to constrain the way we perceive, understand, and feel about our world; (2) changing structures of habitual expectation to make possible a more inclusive, discriminating, and integrative perspective; and finally, (3) making choices or otherwise acting upon these new understandings (167).

The concept of deep transformational change is found throughout the HRD literature. It is easy to see that transformational change at the organizational level is not likely to happen unless transformational change occurs at the individual level through some process of critically challenging and changing internal cognitive structures. Furthermore, without engaging in deep learning through a double-loop or perspective transformation process, individuals will remain trapped in their existing mental models or schemata. It is only through critical reflection that emancipatory learning occurs and enables people to change their lives at a deep level. Thus, transformational change processes are vitally important to HRD.

Summary

Most learning theories in HRD can be embedded in one or a blend of these five meta-theories of learning. Each meta-theory makes unique contributions and adds power to learning practice in HRD. Readers should understand and master each one so that they can be employed in appropriate situations. We reiterate that no one approach is best, but in any given situation one or a combination of approaches is likely to be most powerful.

Instructional Methods

What Are Methods?

Interstate I-70 is a fine highway if you want to get to Topeka—but don't take it if Birmingham is your destination. The Ohio Turnpike is great for travelers from Ohio to New Jersey, but it's not the road to take if you're going from Fresno to San Francisco. Reverse role playing is great for learning to see the other person's point of view, but not much help for people trying to learn to read light meters.

And that's the point about instructional methods—more happily called "learning methods." They are only as good as they are contributive toward the achievement of a learning objective. In fact, it's often helpful to think of methods as highways that lead to cities (objectives) and of training materials (visual aids, case study write-ups, role-playing descriptions) as the ingredients of those highways.

Students may need to travel several highways before they reach a given destination. Certain students may progress most rapidly if they engage in discussion; others may learn more rapidly and more significantly through programmed instruction. For other goals, there may be several equally appealing and productive routes. When these issues arise, and at all phases of the design activity, the T&D specialist faces the question, "What methods shall we use?"

The decision is multidimensional. It involves the learning objectives, the inventory of the learners, and the norms of the organization—to say nothing of the available budget. But a fundamental criterion in selecting a learning method should be the appropriateness of that method to the learning objective.

There is a strong trend toward "experienced-based" or "experiential" training in programs that seek to alter the behavior of adults. Figure 10.1

merely indicates three approaches to the use of "experience" in learning systems. Approach "A" is the rather traditional system and places little emphasis on learning through experience; Approach "B" increases learners' activity, or experience; Approach "C" allows many variations, but includes learners' actual experience as part of the process.

When learning goals involve on-the-job use of new skills, the drill involved in Approach "B" is essential. When the expected future behavior involves application of new values, or when it implies that people will respond in unfamiliar ways to familiar stimuli, the kind of experience in Approach "C" is useful. These kinds of training programs are often referred to as "attitude development"; they invariably involve behaviors in the affective domain of the Bloom taxonomy (1964).

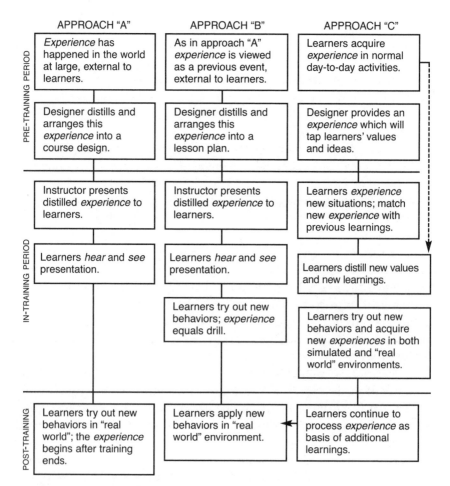

Fig. 10.1. Three approaches to the use of experience.

A Look at Specific Methods

All modern learning theories stress that adults must have a degree of owner-ship in the learning processes and that they want to invest their previous expe-rience in those processes.

Such ownership and investment are achieved by designs in which the learn-ers actively talk about what they've done in the past, or what they are thinking and feeling right now as they experiment with new behaviors during the learn-ing process.

The document of these designs is called a "lesson plan." It describes learners' activities under headings such as:

Time and A/V
Instructor Says and Does
Student Activity

Figure 10.2 shows a duo-dimensional array of methods that notes both in-structor control of content and learners' activity levels.

One logical sequence for examining learning methods is in order of increas-ing learners' involvement; another is by the delegation of content. The duo-dimensional matrix does both.

Does student involvement automatically bring a delegation of content? That can happen—but needn't if the participative activity is designed properly. Do participative methods take more time than pure lecture? No question! But the issue is this: Should instructors cover content or cause learning?

Those who opt for delegated content call it "the discovery approach" and they design activities; these enable learners to discover the content the instruc-tor would otherwise have to "tell" the class.

However, delegating content control does not automatically increase learn-ers' participation; in open forums the learners control all the content except the topic, yet they aren't necessarily more involved than when manipulating hands or arms in trying out a psychomotor task.

Delegating content does not mean withdrawing control of the processes. In a critical incident, for example, learners supply all the cases and examples, but an instructor leads discussions. The real control, however, comes in the *design* of the activity, not from an instructor's forceful leadership during the session.

For example, the in-basket materials provide their own control. During the class session, the instructor merely gives a few preliminary instructions, then watches the process while staying available for students' questions. If the in-strument has been well designed, there should be few, if any, questions.

The sequence of the methods on the chart makes a helpful sequence for us to use in analyzing all those methods. Let's look at each method and proceed

CONTENT

Set by the instructor ←——————————————————→ *Determined by learners*

Low

Learners listen and watch.

    Lectures
    Readings (assignments, handouts)
    Demonstrations (live, filmed)

Learners listen, watch, read, and/or move.

    Skits
      Field trips
        Free form note-taking

    Structured note-taking
    Programmed instruction

Learners listen, watch, read, move, write, or respond.

    Panel discussions (guests)
      Structured discussions
        Panel discussions (students)
      Topical discussions

      Question-answer panels

      Cognet
        Open-forum discussions

      Behavior modeling

Learners manipulate.

    Interactive demonstrations
      Performance try-outs

Learners make decisions or products; invest values and experience in decreasingly explicit designs.

      Brainstorming
     Traditional case studies
    Action mazes
      Incident process
    Jigsaws (right answers)
      Jigsaws (optional patterns)
     In-baskets
        Team tasks (traditional)
          Agenda-setting buzzgroups
     Roleplays
     Reverse roleplays
       Doubling roleplays
      Rotation roleplays
        Finding metaphors
      Simulations
      Games
        Critical incident
        Clinics
       Fishbowls
        T-groups
        Hot roleplays
        OD data gathering

High

LEVEL OF LEARNER PARTICIPATION

Fig. 10.2.   Duo-dimensional list of methods.

from those in which learners are least participative to those in which their activity levels are highest.

Level 1: Low Participation

Methods requiring a low level of trainee participation include the following.

Lectures.   The lecture is, by definition, words spoken by the instructor. It is thus a verbal-symbol medium and a relatively passive and unstimulating experience for learners unless the speaker has unusual vocal and rhetorical talent. The lecturer needs plenty of interesting examples to illustrate theory, colorful and persuasive language to enhance a well-organized pattern of ideas, and a pleasant and stimulating voice.

Lectures were popular in the Middle Ages when the *tabula rasa* theory of education prevailed. The mind of the learner was perceived as a blank tablet upon which ideas were inscribed by a great teacher, lecturer, or professor. It still prevails in many universities. Though under constant attack, the lecture method has apparently proved overwhelmingly appealing to professors who enjoy the security blanket of dog-eared lecture notes and the absence of feedback.

At the very minimum, lecturers should:

- Speak loudly and clearly enough to be heard. Amplification is recommended for classes of more than twenty-five learners; of course, microphone technique is a requisite skill for the lecturer.
- Organize each lecture around a theme, or "thesis."
- Develop inherent, mutually exclusive "areas of discussion" that thoroughly and relevantly develop the thesis.
- Develop each area of discussion through a variety of evidence; this includes analysis, concrete incidents, illustrations, quotations, statistics, and (if possible) physical objects to display.

Speakers should supplement their words with visual aids, such as PowerPoint slides or flip charts. This adds a new dimension to the sensory stimulation. Nor is there any good reason why speakers cannot be interruptible. They can offer "Swiss cheese" lecture presentations with "holes in them." In this way, learners can make inquiries and comments that accelerate their comprehension. Nor need all the questions come from the learners, though that's probably the most productive arrangement. No law prohibits the lecturer from asking questions or pausing for discussion.

Added accountability for receiving the content can result from supplying learners with a syllabus that can be used as a carefully structured notepad on which they can take notes. The careful structure ensures their copying down key words; it establishes key relationships through charts and tables as well as incomplete sentences, or the "bare bones" of the topical outline.

In itself, the lecture is a nonparticipative medium. It does offer an efficient way to *deliver* material. To qualify as an effective teaching method, lectures must also contain provisions to test *receipt.*

Readings. Reading assignments don't do much to stimulate the senses; they merely require some concentrated seeing of words on pages. They can, of course, efficiently expose learners to large quantities of content. Reading assignments, like the lecture, should be accompanied with feedback activities that measure and assist the retention of the content.

Presumably, even slow readers will read more material than they could hear in the same length of time. If the reading relates to illustrations or diagrams, some added interest (sensory stimulation) may result.

To make a reading assignment more meaningful, astute instructors build in accountability. They announce discussions or tests on the content—activities in which learners apply new concepts to real-world problems, projects, and products. If the tests and discussions are oriented to application (rather than memory recall), they need not be academic and sterile.

Another approach to this accountability is to supply a syllabus, or a structured notepad. Students complete this while reading, thus being guided to focus on the most important points. The reading experience thus becomes a kind of "Easter-egg hunt": Readers search out the critical data hidden in the reading assignment.

When instructors use reading as a postclass exercise, such accountability may appear less necessary. That assumption needs to be sharply challenged. Any reading that does not permit further growth is a questionable investment. Any growth deserves follow-up. Such follow-up might include discussion, participation on a panel of students, testing, or application to a simulated problem. Without such follow-up, the post-training reading assignment risks a very low return on investment.

Demonstrations. Demonstrations are merely illustrated lectures or presentations. We usually think of manipulative activities in a demonstration, though mere pictures of the process sometimes replace the "model" that the demonstrator manipulates. Such pictures are appropriate for processes, which can be comprehended through schematics or drawings. Demonstrations are especially suitable for psychomotor objectives, but can, of course, be used (as in "modeling") to illustrate interpersonal skills, interviewing, communication, discipline, and counseling.

The key to a successful demonstration is the close integration of the spoken and the visual stimulus. One hopes they will be simultaneous. If there must be a lapse, let the verbal stimulus precede the visual—but only by a split second. This means that good demonstrations probably proceed one step at a time, all visual materials being concealed until they come into play. Careful planning and ample rehearsal help. Good demonstrators:

- Analyze the process, breaking it into small sequential steps.
- Have all their materials in place.
- Check the operation of all equipment just before they start the demonstration.
- Position, or scale, their models so that all learners can see all the parts all the time.
- Explain the goals of the demonstration at the beginning, preferably in a two-way discussion with learners.
- Present the operation one step at a time according to the task analysis completed earlier.
- Allow the earliest possible tryout of the demonstrated skill. This probably should be at the end of the first step. Performance tryout can then be repeated at the end of each successive step in the operation. If andragogy is correct, adults want immediate application of all acquired skill and knowledge. Why make them wait until the end of a complete operation to "demonstrate" that they are learning and growing?
- Reinforce everything learners do correctly in their tryouts. Instructors need to reinforce these successive approximations of mastery of the total task. This also becomes part of an ongoing goal-setting process; learners themselves identify the differences between their tryouts and their ultimately desired performances.

Level 2: Some Participation

Moving up the scale of level of participation required by trainees brings us to the following training methods.

Skits. A skit is a prepared enactment. Precise dialogue is provided for the "actors," who are usually students reading their roles from scripts. They may sit at their regular positions, or if movement is required, stand and move about to simulate the actions of the situation they enact. Rehearsals are usually unnecessary.

Skits effectively transfer to learners the task of "modeling" verbal behaviors: what to say when counseling, asserting, giving directions and reprimands. Skits may also reflect differing points of view: Several "characters" face a common crisis and approach it with dramatic differences that reflect to their contrasting value systems. The skit personifies and vivifies what might otherwise be a dull theoretical lecture.

Field Trips. Field trips, excursions, observations, or tours may or may not be participative learning experiences. That depends pretty much on how well instructors set up expectations and objectives *before* the trip takes place—and upon the mechanism developed to make sure that learning happens.

Again, the image of the "Easter-egg hunt" seems helpful. Here's how that works: Instructors give each trainee a set of questions for which answers must be supplied. These answers can be discovered on the field trip. They can be reviewed at a feedback session in the classroom following the tour. If different learners are asked to locate different "eggs" on the tour, there can be a mutual sharing and comparison in the discussion that "debriefs" the participants after the tour.

If such accountabilities for learning seem inappropriate, then at the very minimum the instructor should preview the tour with the class. This means setting up expectations about what to look for. It means letting class members determine, in a mutual exchange, how the field trip will contribute to the announced objectives.

A major argument in favor of field trips is that they permit learners to experience sensory impressions that could never occur in classrooms or conference rooms—but that are characteristic of the environment in which the new behavior must persevere. The trip thus assists the "generalization" process by permitting behaviors acquired in an isolated or unnatural environment to persist in a less-focused "real world."

Further, field trips effectively let people who work in one part of the system comprehend the impact and dependencies they have upon other departments. This desire for organizational empathy is highly commendable, and field trips are probably infinitely more successful than "guest lecturers" from alien departments. These guests often manage to be not much more than mediocre lecturers. Too many orientation programs are just "parades" of people who assume far too much about the learners' inventories and curiosities. They thus do a great deal to confuse and to dampen enthusiasm for the new employment.

But when field trips are used to develop insights and empathy into other parts of the operation, accountability for gathering answers is critically important. The best method is probably to let the learner actually work with an employee of the visited department rather than stand apart and watch the operation. Specially planned "Easter-egg hunts" are in order. The questions need to ask such things such as, "How many times did the clerk have to . . . ?" How did the agent handle . . . ?"—or even some specific technical information such as "What is DFT?" or "What does ARUNK mean?" Such questions more nearly guarantee that the learners will come home with a clear, definite comprehension of how they depend upon other departments—and of how other departments depend upon them. The learners can also better comprehend how these "downline" and "upline" dependencies in the total system require close adherence to established performance standards. In any event, managers of both the visited and the visiting departments need to be involved in setting precise goals, action plans, and evaluation mechanisms for the field trip program.

Taking Notes. Note taking by learners is somewhat controversial. Theorists like to argue about its value and about the proper way to control taking notes. Does note taking enhance or impede learning? Chances are the answer is yes to both alternatives. For some people, taking notes may be necessary to "imprint" the data. These people need to hear it, to see it in the visual aids, and then to see it again as they begin to "own" the idea by writing it down. They may need to "hear it again in their mind's ear" several more times as they reread the notes they have taken. For others, all note taking may be a distraction.

At any rate, when notes are taken in a free form (as in most college lecture halls), the students are in almost total control of what they transcribe to the paper. That conceivably can be a bad thing. They may write down what they *think* they hear, or they may abbreviate in ambiguous ways that later produce misinformation. Knowledge is the probable objective of a lecture, and misinformation is detrimental to the acquisition of knowledge. Some lecturers are shocked and appalled when they see the "pure fiction" that shows up on students' notepads.

To prevent such distortion, many lecturers provide learners with a syllabus. The syllabus may take the form of a sheer topical outline with room enough for learners to complete the headings and statements as instructors say things such as, "The third category is minerals" while students write the words in alongside the "3" in the syllabus. Even more structured is the syllabus that includes most of the key statements and leaves blank spaces left for essential words. For example, the syllabus for a lecture on andragogy might have an entry like this:

"A child's self-image tends to be _____. Adults see themselves as _____."

(Note that this is a pedagogical approach to teaching, rather than an andragogical one.)

From the lecturer's comments, the learners are able to fill in the proper words: "dependent" and "self-directed or increasingly self-dependent."

A variation is a matrix onto which students make notations as the lecture or demonstration continues. As the lecture or discussion reveals the answers, students can put words such as "dependent" and "self-directed" and "limited and of little value" and "extensive and worth investing in the learning process" in the proper boxes.

As that example reveals, the answers to be inscribed in a syllabus need not be supplied by the lecturer; they can just as easily come from reading or discussion among the participants. This is especially true in review sessions where the learners bring a big inventory to the learning situation. Used this way, the syllabus is more a training aid than a learning method—but if it contributes to the achievement of the objective, who wants to quibble about categories?

Programmed Instruction. Programmed instruction, although not widely known today by that name, enjoys heavy support from its advocates for two major reasons:

1. It requires the active involvement of the learners. They make overt responses to a question-stimulus, which follows the presentation of small bits of information.
2. It provides immediate feedback about the quality of the learner's response. Learners are told the "correct" answers right away, and can compare their responses with the preferred answer.

Although effective programming requires mastery of an extensive expertise, these two virtues reveal a great deal about the nature of the method. Small-step learning is perceived to be important: Learners are given just a bit of data, then asked a question about that data. The "program" (whether it be printed in a book, presented in some audio-visual "teaching machine," or stored in a computer) supplies an appropriate answer. Learners access this answer as soon as they have made their own responses to the question. The program then does one of two things: If the answer is correct, the program directs learners to another bit of data so that they can continue their study; if the answer is incorrect, the program *may* redirect them to a previous or an altered stimulus so they can either change their insights or supply a more appropriate answer.

The bits of data are called "frames," and the two methods are called "linear" or "branching." In linear programs, the learners are usually given the next bit of information regardless of their answers; they control the decision about revisiting previous frames to clear up misunderstandings. (Advocates of this linear approach contend that if the program has been properly validated, it will control the stimulus so carefully that there is precious little chance of mistaken answers.) In "branching" or "intrinsic" programs, learners are routed to different frames depending upon their choices at any given frame. They thus proceed through the program on branches that may be entirely different from those followed by other students studying the same program.

As noted, the total technology is complex. Sizing and sequencing and wording the frames requires patient validation. What does this validation imply? First, that there will be trial drafts of each frame. Second, that these trial drafts will be tested on typical learners. Third, that each frame will be redrafted as a result of the experience gained from analyzing student responses. Most T&D departments will publish and carry out only programs that are validated at 85 percent or higher. This means that every frame of the final program has been answered correctly by at least 85 percent of the test audience before the program "goes to press." Some organizations insist upon more than 90 percent validity before they publish.

Programmed instruction obviously represents total control of the content by the designer or instructor. Andragogic T&D departments therefore like to use PI (the short title of Programmed Instruction) in conjunction with live instructors. Another problem with some PI is that the frames have been excessively simple. There is little thrill in the learner's soul when asked to copy a word from one frame as the answer to that frame. For example:

"The president of your company is R. J. Frieder."
Who is the president of your company?

_____

(Write your answer here.)

However, problems such as the absence of a human facilitator or stupid frames can easily be overcome. Therefore, PI is an important method in modern training systems, *even though it is not often called PI anymore.* It is especially helpful in organizations that:

- Hire only a few people at a time in any given classification
- Are widely separated geographically and must train individuals on a one-at-a-time schedule

- Employ minimum numbers of instructors and need to delegate the teaching function to some mediated instruments
- Have a heavy commitment to mediated programs, but need a mechanism to provide feedback to learners about their progress
- Need to teach intricate procedures that aren't easily communicated in classroom visual aids or group-instructional modes
- Have a heavy commitment to individual education and development and thus need a wide range of programs to serve a small population

Many computer-based training programs (CBTs) borrow from PI principles.

Level 3: Medium Participation

These training methods require a little more participation:

Panel Discussions.　Panel discussions represent a variation on the structured discussion format. Sometimes they are called colloquies; sometimes they are called symposiums (symposia). Panel symposiums tend to be a series of short lectures given by a variety of people rather than one long lecture by a single lecturer. In effective panels, each speaker concentrates on one subtopic and delivers a unique thesis (clearly different from that of any other panelist) and relates that thesis to the unifying objective.

The problem with many panels is that they tend to be so structured that learners' participation is very low. Thus the control of the content (to say nothing of the control of the processes!) rests too heavily with the panelists. An antidote for this problem is a question-answer session after the final presentation. (If the question-answer session comes too soon, later panelists may be seriously impeded in what they say, or influenced to amend a viewpoint necessary to the total achievement of the objective.) Another antidote for the low vitality and one-way communication of the panel format is a postpanel structured discussion in which one leader channels comments as well as questions from the listeners—or between the panelists themselves.

To increase learners' involvement in panel discussions, many instructors assign advance readings to class members; then they let learners serve as members of the panel. The reading is thus given greater meaning, and the learners take greater responsibility for developing the subject. As this happens, accountability for comprehending the subject and achieving the objective is transferred to the learners' shoulders.

Structured Discussions. Structured discussions are conversations between trainees aimed toward specific learning objectives. Such objectives distinguish them from mere social conversation as well as the discussion at staff meetings.

For structured discussions, this learning objective should be clearly announced in advance or during the first moments of the discussion itself. It is usually helpful to post a written statement of the objective where all can see it throughout the discussion. Structure can be further imposed (and meandering correspondingly controlled) by using a syllabus or a publicly posted agenda. These agendas may even include an estimate of the appropriate amount of time to devote to each subtopic.

Facilitative instructors like to let the class develop these agendas and their timetables. This permits the learners to own the entire proceeding. A heavy instructor-supplied agenda may be totally inconsistent with the climate needed for adult learning. Yet even structured activities planned by the leader permit learners to share their experiences and feelings. While this is going on, the instructor receives data about the learners' initial inventories and their progress toward their desired learning goals.

In these situations, the instructor may opt to use no control devices. They feel they can always inject control when irrelevant excursions or counterproductive dynamics might prevent the posted objective from being met. How? Simply by reminding the group of the objective, or by challenging the relevance of the current activity.

Thus, a typical "preparation" for leading a discussion is to predefine the objective and then build a list of questions for the group. These preplanned questions are used as the initial stimulus; when each subtopic has been thoroughly developed; when discussion wanders; or when the group needs re-stimulating. The "lesson plan" merely lists the objectives and questions; the teaching materials sometimes include printed versions of these for display or distribution to individual participants.

The structured discussion is appropriate when there are predefined objectives and when the learners do not bring a negative viewpoint to those objectives. Open forums are indicated when the learners need a chance to ventilate their apathy or hostility toward the learning goals.

Panel Discussions by Participants. The panel, though deadly if poor speakers are invited from outside the class, may prove a lively affair when a topic is broken down into subtopics and assigned to the best participants in the class. Some tips and precautions apply:

1. Give the panelists adequate time to prepare to read some specified material, analyze it, and synthesize it into an effective presentation.
2. Allow time for other participants to ask questions.
3. Delegate the role of moderator, too. Then brief the student moderator on (1) the relationship of the subtopics, (2) how to communicate that overall design to the class, (3) how to keep the discussion moving, and (4) how to provide a lively atmosphere without uncomfortable confrontation.
4. Select as panelists those participants who have shown unusual speed in acquiring and synthesizing information; make this an "enrichment" and a positive reinforcement for good work in earlier parts of the program.
5. The criterion for selection is always the ability to present and interact in the discussion, not social roles inside or outside the class.

Topical Discussions. Many people call these "general discussions." If that implies a general topic and minimal prescribed substructure, great! If it implies that instructors just name a topic and immediately launch a discussion, well, not so great! Impromptu chitchats, too, often meander, miss the mark, and bore the learner.

For useful topical discussions, instructors should:

- Announce the discussion far enough in advance to permit a bit of required reading, plus time to analyze and synthesize that *new* information.
- Announce precise time limits.
- Announce one or more specific objectives; and then lie low! From there on in, it's up to the group to meet the objectives of their analysis of this topic.
- Tell the group that it's up to them to keep the discussion on track and to meet the objective(s).

Question-Answer Panels. In more controlled Q-A sessions, instructors announce a topic and a reading assignment, then the key requirement: a list of questions to be brought to the session itself. The session may be the next meeting of the class; it may also be "after an hour of research and analysis." When the time for the Q-A session arrives, the instructor calls on the learners for their questions. The answers may come from a panel of the students in a sort of "stump the sudden experts" activity. The answers may come from the instructor—but that will prove only that the instructor is smart; it won't develop much learning in the participants. The answers may come from invited guests, though that also allows minimum growth in the learners. Whenever the answers come from someone other than the instructor, the instructor need participate only when the data given as answers are inaccurate or incomplete. Of course, instructors may be chairpersons, but that arrangement robs a learner of a participative opportunity.

In Q-A sessions there may be no panel at all. Since participants generate the questions (individually or in small buzz groups), they may also be the "experts." They can acquire their expertise by special reading, research, or experimentation achieved during the training program! In fact, "stump the experts" or "information please" panels of students have been known to enliven many classes that once covered less content through instructor-driven lectures.

When making the assignment to develop questions, instructors need merely point out a general objective for the session while reminding the question developers that each item should contribute toward that overall goal. Sample goals might be

• to make a personal decision about using zero-based budgets;
• to decide which operations in my office might effectively be computerized; or
• to complete a Pro/Con analysis on the use of robots.

Cognet. Cognet is short for cognitive networks, and is—you've guessed it!—appropriate for cognitive objectives. All participants do some reading and answer the same questions before they gather—but only several people read the same material. When they gather, these "homogeneous" groups meet to prepare group answers that they share in reports to the other teams.

For example, biographies of Harry Truman, Howard Hughes, Colin Powell, J. Edgar Hoover, Joan Crawford, Geraldine Ferraro, and Henry Ford might be assigned as pre-reading accompanied by questions about their planning strategy, leadership style, interpersonal relations, management of meetings, and behavior in crises.

After the initial report, there is usually another phase of Cognet when people who want to probe further into those subpoints form new teams. Thus there will be new and different reports on planning strategies, people handling, and leadership style—or new issues may emerge as positions on womens' liberation, unionism, technology, armaments, and/or politics.

The virtues of the method are that (1) a lot of information can be processed at whatever depth the group (or instructor) chooses; (2) the information is analyzed from at least two dimensions; (3) each participant is able to "network" with different people; and (4) each learner can integrate the reality of his or her own situation and perceptions into the theory contained in the literature.

Open-Forum Discussions.   Open-forum discussions are useful when learners can accept full responsibility for the content of the discussion, or when they need to "ventilate" their feelings and opinions. Generally, only the topic is announced—although more dynamic discussions result when that announcement involves pre-session readings or analysis. Learners tend to filter their experiences and biases through the reading, thus arriving better prepared to learn.

In the forum format, any member of the group may speak to any other member. A moderator is usually there to prevent everybody from speaking at the same time, or to "patrol" debates when more than one person is speaking simultaneously. Of course, simultaneous speaking isn't always a bad thing, and forums tend to encourage such interchanges. Free-for-all catharsis can be a useful way to ease threatening learnings—especially if those learnings involve affective behaviors where feelings run high. Objectives involving responding or valuing often profit from open-forum discussions.

Behavior Modeling.   The words of this method tell what it is. A "model" or ideal enactment of a desired behavior lets learners discover what actions and standards are expected of them. Typical behaviors to model would be managerial skills such as making assignments, delegating, counseling, asserting, or disciplining. The model is usually presented through a medium such as videotape, but may be performed by instructors in what amounts to a skit.

Behavior modeling differs only slightly from a demonstration, but it fits intellectual-cognitive rather than psychomotor objectives, and it usually presents the total skill before learners try out a behavior themselves. This technique has the virtue of offering a gestalt, or "big picture" overview of what may be rather complex interpersonal behaviors.

Level 4: Moderate Participation

A moderate level of participant involvement is required for the following methods.

Interactive Demonstrations.   All good demonstrations are interactive—but unfortunately there are a lot of bad demonstrations!

The difference is that interactive demonstrations allow learner-watchers to do something instead of merely observe. They have things in their hands and they move those things in purposeful ways; they start doing so at the earliest possible moment. They move around, they ask questions, they *interact.*

Job Instruction Training (JIT).   Job Instruction Training (JIT) is a perfect format for interaction. Once the climate is set, the instructor tells and shows the first step of the task, and learners *perform* that first step right along with the instructor. This technique permits cumulative repetition and the practice that makes perfect. After seeing and hearing how the second step is done, learners perform the first two steps, and then the first three, and then four, and so on.

Performance Tryouts.   Performance tryout is probably a necessary element in any "tough-minded" learning experience. Performance tryouts serve as ongoing feedback activity during the learning and as "criterion" tests at the conclusion of the program. Lest this imply that the performance tryout is used only for measurement and evaluation, let's remind ourselves that it is a significant learning experience, too.

Trying out the new skill offers the "immediate application" andragogical facilitators urge for adult learning. Facilitative learners such as Carl Rogers point out that much significant learning is acquired through doing. Trying out the new behavior starts the practice required to form habits. If tied into the rest of the learners' jobs, this practice can make the relevance of the new skill apparent to all learners.

"Performance tryout" is an integral, inevitable step in the four-part JIT used so successfully during World War II to train quick replacements for drafted workers. At its best, JIT lets learners try out the first step of a new task as soon as the trainer has completed the "tell and show" for that step—and before the "tell and show" of the second step, and is therefore an interactive demonstration.

Psychologically, a performance tryout is a perfect chance for learners to give themselves positive feedback for what they have already achieved, and also to do some goal setting for what they can still improve. By making this analysis, they reexamine the ultimate criteria and buy into the necessary self-improvement to get there. They have concrete evidence about the criteria they didn't achieve on their first attempt; they can better individualize their further efforts. But above all, they have evidence about what they *did* achieve. This is a practical application of the "Look, Ma! I'm dancin'!" effect that makes learning and instruction so exciting.

A performance tryout implies:

- Completing the entire task, not just successive steps
- Remembering and adhering to the proper sequence
- Coordinating all the necessary skills and knowledge
- Meeting criteria for each step in the task
- Demonstrating mastery, proving that the skill is available for use on the job

We naturally think of tryouts of psychomotor skills, yet demonstrated mastery is just as vital for cognitive and affective learnings. When managerial and interpersonal behaviors involve a step-by-step process, an intellectual formula, or an emotional discipline, then performance tryouts are necessary. It would be unthinkable, for instance, to use behavior modeling that wasn't followed with performance tryouts by all learners.

Role-plays or simulations, or any exercise in which students do the calculations or the paperwork of a process, are effective vehicles for performance tryouts. Sometimes the environment in which the behavior will be performed on the job is critical; if so, some simulation (noise, interruptions, temperature, outages) should be provided.

Level 5: High Participation

Methods requiring a higher level of trainee participation include the following.

Brainstorming. Brainstorming is a specialized form of discussion. It is commonly used in real problem-solving situations. As a training method, its most frequent use is to teach learners to suspend judgment until a maximum number of ideas have been generated. A second use is to train people to listen positively to the ideas of others and refrain from negative comments that might cause the creative process to run dry.

Brainstorming applies the synergistic theory that groups can generate more ideas, and better ideas than the individual members could produce if they worked independently. It is therefore a useful method only when there are several trainees; five or six is probably the minimum for a workable brainstorm.

The learning occurs because participants must discipline their inputs to the discussion. The controls occur through the instructions and through the behavior of the leader. Those instructions usually include these points:

1. Generate, don't evaluate. There will be time for evaluation later. In brainstorming, quantity is the goal: the more ideas, the better. This doesn't mean that quality is unimportant—only that when people stop to challenge quality during the creative processes they inhibit their creativity by moving into a judgmental mode too soon.
2. Create new ideas by amending those already suggested. This amendment can take such forms as increasing, decreasing, adding, deleting, consolidating, substituting elements, or reversing. The "reversing" specifically prohibits negative statements. For example, one participant might say, "Promote her." It's okay for another to say, "Demote her," but it's not okay to say, "Don't promote her." To offer an alternative (demotion) is to generate another option; to state the suggestion negatively is simply to start the analytical debate.
3. Post all suggestions on a visible list in front of the group. This strategy reinforces those who contribute and encourages further participation. When participants begin to analyze or question or debate, the leader uses "neutral reinforcement." That is, the leader at first ignores such behavior. Because there is no visible posting to the list, and no verbal response, the tendency to debate or analyze generally "goes away." If this neutral reinforcement doesn't work, the leader may remind the group that the analysis will come later.

The total brainstorm includes three phases: generation, analysis, and action planning. In the second step—analysis—participants ask the contributors to explain strange terms or an unfamiliar idea. Analysis also includes evaluation. At this step, the participants establish criteria for selecting the best ideas, then test each idea against those criteria. As ideas "fall out" because they don't meet the criteria, the group is left with a workable list of options. From these, they can select the "best" solution. They are then ready to move to the third phase, action planning. This consists of outlining the steps needed to put the adopted solution into operation.

Case Studies. Case studies have been a popular way to encourage involvement and to bring the discussion down to a realistic level. Case studies are thus antidotes for the tendency to avoid real issues by talking about theory rather than about its application.

In traditional case studies, participants receive a printed description of a problem situation. The description contains enough detail for learners to recommend appropriate action. The printed description must therefore include enough detail to enable some recommendation, but not so much that learners are distracted from central issues—unless, of course, sharp analytical skills and ignoring trivia is part of the learning objective.

Control of the discussion comes through:

- The amount of detail provided
- Time limits, frequently rather stringent
- The way the task is postulated, often a description of the desired output, such as a recommendation, a decision, or the outline of an action plan; and sometimes
- A list of questions for the group to answer on their way to the final total product

There are numerous commercial sources of case studies. Training reference books contain a rich supply of tested cases. Creative T&D designers can develop cases typical of the organization for which the learning is designed. Andragogic instructors permit participants to write their own cases from real-life problems. They then exchange or share these homegrown cases as the material of the learning experience.

When participants generate the cases, the control of the content is assuredly more in their hands than in the hands of the instructor—and there can be little question about the perceived relevance. To make certain that pre-prepared cases are equally relevant, good T&D specialists ensure that each case contributes toward identified insights or a specified learning objective.

To increase the total participation, instructors often divide the class into small teams, or buzz groups. Because there are fewer people in each group, individual learners are more inclined to participate at higher levels than they would or could if only one large discussion were going on.

Action Mazes. An action maze is really just a case study that has been programmed. Participants usually receive a printed description of the case that has enough detail to take them to the first decision point. The description gives them options from which to select. After the group discusses these alternatives, they request the leader to supply them with the next "frame." That frame will explain the consequences of their individual decisions; not by a theoretical background, but in terms of the case itself. Let's look at an extremely simple sample:

> Donald Lipson has been on your shift for nearly seven years. You regard him as a marginal worker at best. At times he comes close to insubordination, and once he was sent home without pay for three days for fisticuffs at the office luncheon.

He has been tardy seven times in the last two weeks. Today he arrives for work forty-five minutes late. You feel you should:

A. Give him one more chance, so you do nothing
B. Discuss this with him, so you ask him to see you at the next break
C. Discuss his tardiness with him, so you stop at his work post just as soon as he reports for duty
D. Suspend him for one day without pay

The group would discuss this phase. When they reach a decision, they inform the instructor, who then gives them a prepared response to their choice. Let's say they opted for "S." The prepared "consequence" might very well say this:

> When you tell Lipson of his suspension, he merely shrugs and gives you a sneer as he packs up his tools and walks out. You wonder how anyone can be that cool and clearly feel superior to the situation.
>
> Three days later, the shop steward hands you a written notice of Lipson's formal grievance. The basis of the grievance is that as a member of management you have interfered with Lipson's personal affairs and prevented him from discharging his duties as the parent of a minor child, a handicapped daughter.
>
> On the basis of this, you decide to . . .

Of course the case continues with additional options appropriate to the current state of the situation. When participants have made wise choices, they should face a new set of increasingly desirable options. When they choose badly, they may be offered another chance at a previously rejected option, but in general bad choices lead to limited numbers of unattractive options. It's just good reinforcement theory, however, to leave them one chance to retrace their actions and work their way successfully out of the maze. It is sometimes an effective way to let people discover the value of dissent, debate, confrontation, and compromise.

Even greater involvement is possible by allowing groups to generate original options when they are restless with the printed alternatives. The instructor may reinforce these by "inventing" desirable consequences—or route the group directly back into the maze if their solution would bring consequences similar to the published options.

Incident Process.   The incident process is a specialized form of case study. It is usually used to teach analytical skills, or techniques for special problem-solving tasks such as handling employee grievances.

The incident process differs from normal case studies by giving participants far too little data to reach a decision—even preliminary decisions, as in an action maze. The data are available to the instructor, usually in easy-access printed form. However, the instructor reveals the data only when asked a specific question to which the datum is a correct and relevant answer.

Learners thus acquire skill in knowing what questions to ask, how to phrase them, and how to draw inferences from the data thus uncovered.

Because it teaches skills of interrogation, analysis, and synthesis, the incident process is a popular tool for courses in labor relations, grievance handling, accident investigation, investigative techniques, and problem solving.

Jigsaws. Jigsaws are about what their name implies. We all know what a jigsaw is: Participants put pieces together to complete an integrated "picture." When the jigsaw is applied to the learning situation, participants may be given parts of a design or an organization; they assemble these into a "System" or an "Organization Chart." They may be given the elements of a letter or a report; they put it together into a logical outline. They may be given the key variables of a decisionmaking problem; their task is to select from the pieces of the jigsaw the proper action to take for every conceivable combination of variables.

When instructors are teaching a prescription, there is only one way to assemble the pieces properly, and the review makes that clear. When the objectives are more individualized or creative, the design provides for ambiguities: Different people (or teams) may assemble the pieces in different ways, then discuss the reasons and relative merits of each pattern.

Jigsaws are thus useful in teaching synthesizing skills, problem-solving skills, or organizational skills.

In-Baskets. In-baskets are a form of simulation that gets at the realities of a job through the paper symptoms of that job. Learners get all the materials one might expect to find in an "IN" basket on a typical work day. They must then process that paperwork until all the items are in the "OUT" basket. Usually, the situation is described so that participants must use only their own resources. For example, the directions may read: "You are alone at the office, and will be out of town the next week. You have just sixty minutes to dispose of the items in your IN basket. Complete as much work as you possibly can. Do not delegate decisions or actions unless it is proper for you to do so when you are actually at your desk."

Quite typically, the exercise contains more work than can reasonably be completed in the allotted time, thus training learners in managing stress as well as in the content of the basket: Learners deal not only with the rational decisions of the management problems but also with the added realism of working against the clock. To enhance this exercise, some instructors simulate emergency interruptions that add to the pressure by requiring new decisions about priorities.

Needless to say, there is a review of how learners handled each issue raised by the paperwork. To provide feedback in time to be useful, instructors may have to do homework on their "evening off." They can ease this burden by using numbered check sheets on which often-used comments are printed. For example:

#11. Glad you handled this first.

#17. Right! This section should be eliminated from the report.

#23. How about putting this idea up into the first paragraph?

#24. Would phrasing it as a question make it less "demanding"?

Instructors can also add some individualized comments, but a copious amount of basic feedback can be communicated by merely writing numbers on participant papers.

After the comments are returned, group discussion is productive. It can (1) clear up misconceptions, (2) reexamine common problem areas, (3) reinforce class-wide achievements, and (4) allow self-evaluation and goal setting. Because of this high potential as a measurement tool, in-baskets are attractive before-and-after instruments. Assessment centers also make extensive use of in-baskets in their task of determining management potential.

Team Tasks, Buzz Groups, and Syndicates. Team tasks for buzz groups (small teams of participants) result in some product, decision, or recommendation to be shared with similar groups in the class. For example, case studies may be assigned to small teams rather than to the entire class. Whatever the task, the small groups report their findings or present their "product" in a report to other buzz groups.

Typical products for these buzz groups, also called "syndicates" in many parts of the world, are reports, decisions, or a set of recommendations or Pro/Con analysis of some issue. The assigned task can run the entire gamut of the designer's or instructor's creative imagination. It is limited only by its relevance to the announced objective and by the learners' perception that it is a useful endeavor.

Here are some samples:

1. On the enclosed chart of a typical organization, indicate where the training and development responsibilities should rest. Specify the title, responsibilities, and reporting relationship of each T&D position.

2. By referring to your instructor-outline for a training program now filled with lectures, identify: (a) content which the learners could probably supply from the inventory they bring to the class, and (b) the specific questions or tasks you would use to get them actively sharing what they already know about the subject.
3. List the key criteria to be considered when selecting locations for branch sales offices in a metropolitan area. Include everything you can reasonably consider for such a decision.
4. Do a Pro/Con analysis of short-interval scheduling applied to the revenue-accounting function. Be certain to consider variations within the sub-departments of Revenue Accounting.

Buzz-group tasks can range from the one-level activities of those samples to more sophisticated tasks. Buzz groups can also be used to permit the members to generate an agenda for extremely andragogic programs. In any event, buzz-group activity early in the learning process permits an andragogic investment of the learners' inventories. It also permits the instructor to become acquainted with the goals and personal styles of the participants.

Team tasks may be time-limited—such as "Spend ten minutes developing your findings"—or open-ended. For open-ended tasks, the instructor says something like, "Let's keep at this as long as it seems a profitable investment of our time. I'll be around and amongst you, so give me a signal when the task is completed or when you begin to feel restless with the value of the task." In this approach, instructors need to be "sound sensitive." The noise levels of the buzz groups tell instructors how teams are progressing through a task.

A four-person group is reasonably effective, but for best results, five or six should be in the group. In groups of eight or nine, subgroups or splinter discussions occur.

Agenda-Setting Buzz Groups. Teams of buzz groups for agenda setting constitute a special use of the "small-group concept." We have already noted that they present an andragogic method of gathering inventory and goals-data from participants. This implies that the members determine all or part of the course content. This can mean that they decide on the objectives and areas of discussion; it can also mean that within an assigned list of objectives or within an assigned subject, they determine the issues or skills of special concern.

Such buzz groups offer an excellent instrument for probing the feelings of learners about their achievements in reaching course objectives. In this context, the groups meet after the program is well underway to recommend courses of action for the remaining time together.

Here are two examples: In an Effective Business Writing program, participants form small teams for twenty minutes to compile a list of questions they want answered and key issues they wish to discuss. A typical list would include things such as "Getting it through the boss without heartbreaking changes," "Can you use a preposition to end a sentence with?" and "How to get rid of gobbledygook." The second example is from a workshop for experienced instructors. They might develop two lists. One is for "Things we already know for sure about teaching." The other is for "Questions that come up to haunt us about our teaching."

Lists so generated usually generate lively class discussions. At the same time, they effectively let instructors know where the trainees "are really coming from" and where they truly want to go—and how they feel about getting there.

Role-Plays. Role-plays permit learners to reenact the situations they face on the job, or they will face in the future, or they perceive to be job-like. Through such reenactment they can reexamine previous behavior, try out behaviors they have just acquired, or experiment with behaviors that strike them as potentially useful.

Since there is some pressure associated with role playing, adult participants (even some trainers!) may resist this learning method. This seems unfortunate, so instructors frequently employ these methods:

- Use the "multiple role-play" format with many small role-plays going on simultaneously in various parts of the room.
- Keep the cast of characters quite small when using the multiple formats.
- Reinforce the experimental behaviors of the role players—never their "theatrical effectiveness."
- Keep the physical facilities, or "stage setting," to a minimum. Attention focuses on the content, or processes, of the situation being enacted, not on the theatrical aspects of the play or the players.
- Move into initial role-plays with a minimum of fanfare. For example, a trainee might comment, "I have this problem with an employee who keeps evading the issue." The instructor then asks a question that will encourage the trainee to "play" the employee. The question might be, "What was the last thing they said while evading an issue?" Once the trainee quotes the evader, the role-play has begun. The instructor may soon ask the class, "Who would like to carry on this conversation?" Or the instructor may designate someone to carry on.
- Call the process something else—as "a simulation" in the example above.

Such spontaneous role-plays add involvement, variety, reality, and specificity to the learning experience. When role-plays are more structured, role descriptions are given to participants. These often include not only the characters in the situation but also an "observer's role." When observers are used, the points to watch for are listed in much the same way as those used in any other observation sheet. These are, after all, learning aids that help "imprint" action steps and standards in the minds of the observers.

Each role description should give the character a goal to shoot for in the conversation or situation—and perhaps a motive for that goal. Specific tips about how to play the role should be avoided at all costs. For example, it's probably better to instruct the player thus: "You intend to keep at this supervisor until you get an apology," than to say, "You regard yourself as a hard-headed individual who takes no nonsense from anyone—and you don't intend to give this supervisor any satisfaction whatsoever while the two of you are talking." That locks the players in and prevents any real growth as they experiment with behaviors in reaching a role-played understanding.

Specific time limits can be assigned. This helps the role-players focus on reaching their objectives and cuts down on the occasional horseplay. When time is up, the instructor can merely clap hands to refocus attention and launch the next step. It is not important that the situation be "resolved" as in a novel or a play—only that critical moments be re-enacted. If role-players fail to reach their objectives in allotted times, they may very well be learning something! Indeed, they almost certainly are learning something about which behaviors are nonproductive. This can be a very rich learning if they have another opportunity to replay the situation by using different behaviors.

The processes and the learners' perceptions of those processes are likely to be the appropriate focus on role-plays. This indicates the vital importance of a feedback, or debriefing, session after the role-plays. Such feedback may very well deal with the feelings as much as it deals with the intellectual content of the transactions. When the instructor wishes to focus on content, a checklist such as those given to observers is useful.

For example, in a role-play teaching the use of open, directive, and reflective questions, the situation might very well call for reenacting an oral proposal to a client manager. Checklists for observers and post-role-play feedback might consider such questions as these:

- What objections were raised to the proposal?
- Which type of question did the proposer use when this happened?
- List examples of "loaded" questions that slipped into the conversation.

- Check each time the proposer used an open question.
- How many reflective questions did the proposer use?
- How many of each type did the manager use?
- List examples of the open questions used by the proposer.
- List examples of effective reflective questions.

If the role-play is designed not to focus on such specific techniques as questions but rather on feelings and perceptions, then the checklist for the observer's sheet might ask questions similar to these:

- What nonverbal symptoms appeared when there were differences of opinion?
- What did the participants say to share their feelings?
- When feelings were openly shared, how did the other people react?
- In what ways did the participants handle conflict?
- How did the participants show their regard (or nonregard) for the feelings of other participants?
- How did the participants show their regard (or nonregard) for the opinions of other participants?

To make the role-plays relevant and realistic, instructors sometimes ask participants to write their own role-plays. The very exercise of describing a problem situation or a problem employee often creates new insights into the troublesome situation. Enacting the role-play with peer learners playing familiar roles often gives trainees an entirely new perspective on the situation. More poignant learnings can result when the creators of the situation take an active role—even to "being" their own problem personalities.

Reverse Role-Plays. Reverse role-plays are helpful methods for understanding another person's viewpoint. It works equally well when the objective is to see how others perceive oneself. As the title implies, at a critical moment in the role-play, participants switch roles. Thus the "supervisor" becomes the "supervised"—and may acquire brand new insights into what it feels like. Interviewers, playing an interviewee in class, can better empathize with the penetratingly personal questions they asked just a moment ago—or that they ask every day on the job.

Reverse role playing requires sensitive monitoring by the instructors. First they must know just when to switch the roles. Next, they need to make certain that during the debriefing or feedback session, all participants have the chance to share the feelings they experienced during the enactment.

Doubling Role-Plays. Doubling role-plays lets observers of the role-plays get into the action when they feel moved to do so. They simply step behind the current player and become another "body and voice" for that character. If their reactions to the dynamics and interplay differ sharply, then the role-play is indeed exposing varied perceptions to a single stimulus.

There are several reasons why observers might want to take an active part in the role-play. Perhaps they want to help a current player out of a distressing situation. Perhaps they feel that a current player is missing an opportunity. Perhaps they think a current player is being unrealistic. Perhaps they just want to offer another solution to a problem.

When doubling is used to encourage examination of alternative ways to handle a situation, it constitutes a kind of brainstorm at the application level. If we look at the methods on a kind of continuum, we can see that doubling is an enacted brainstorm, just as role-playing is an enacted case study.

Rotation Role-Plays. Rotation during role-plays is just a slight variation on doubling. Instead of several people ending up as one character, one learner replaces another participant in the role-play. The replacement can be spontaneous and is similar to that of the "tag dances" at the senior prom. In rotation, the learners are in greater control of the content and processes. The instructor, who quietly asks an observer to enter into the role-play as a designated character, can also manage the rotations.

An obvious advantage of rotation is that the participative base can be spread throughout the class. More subtly, this form of role playing permits added dimensions to the analysis of the situation or to the motivation of the characters.

Finding Metaphors. When humans become emotional, they call things by the wrong names. Out of anger, we call someone a beast; out of love, we call the same person a baby doll! This is metaphor, and the search for metaphors can be a growing experience.

To come up with the right image, we must analyze and synthesize; above all, we must use that creative right brain of ours. Many searches for metaphor occur in adult training:

- The T-shirt exercise: You inscribe a T-shirt with a saying that captures my character or behavior; I do the same for you.
- The Library Exercise does the same thing with book titles.
- The Movie Marquee does it with film titles.
- Collages are pictorial metaphors from photos in old newspapers and magazines assembled by a person or a team to capture the spirit of an

idea, a movement, an event, or an organization—or whatever else instructors or students wish to symbolize to express their feelings or ideas.

As the instructions for one metaphoric search explain: "All of us seek ways to understand, interpret, and synthesize our experience. We now call this 'Putting it all together.' Ancients did so with poetry; they sought synonyms, comparisons, images, metaphors." So do adults in T&D settings seek meaning by finding metaphors for their projects and problems, their loved ones, their organizations, or one another, even for "this training program."

Simulations.   Simulations are somewhat like action mazes being role-played. Usually, they are extensive designs with carefully programmed decision points. Working with a mythical firm, participants may serve as the board of directors or members of a consulting team. They are given data about various external conditions, internal situations, and critical decisions.

Their roles may be "generalized" ("You are all members of") or specified. For the latter, one person is specified as Chairman of the Board, another as Vice President of Finance, another as T&D Manager, and so on until all critical viewpoints are represented in the simulation.

In either format, the participants discuss the critical situations and make their decisions. When that step takes place, they receive feedback about the consequences of those decisions. The programs are sometimes printed for instructors to distribute, sometimes put onto a computer as a form of computer-assisted instruction.

Typically, simulations involve teams of learners working together. They are thus effective in team-building programs, or in providing a "laboratory" of group dynamics. In-baskets are actually simple, one-person simulations.

Games.   Games result when simulations are made competitive and teams compete to see who makes the more effective decisions. Some T&D specialists feel that the gamed simulations increase the energy and commitment of the participants and add motivation to the learning.

Simpler games are used in a variety of ways. Tinker-Toy® projects can be used as a medium for learning team processes. Some games can be used to make didactic points. Even simpler didactic games can challenge individual learners. One of these is the common puzzle about connecting nine dots into four interconnected straight lines. Because the instructions prohibit lifting the pencil from the paper, the puzzle cannot be solved without exceeding the implied boundary of the dots. Thus it teaches the wisdom of "going outside the problem in order to solve the problem."

When people participate in games, many behaviors manifest themselves. Some of these behaviors may be identified as either contributive or counter-productive to group goals. Thus games are sometimes used in organization-development programs as both diagnostic and training tools.

Of course, games can be used to develop specific skills; for example, to develop spontaneity and thinking on one's feet. The "Long Tale" helps with these goals. Someone launches a fictitious story, develops it to a critical point, and then points to another member to take over. This game can also help develop active listening skills; if you aren't listening, you can't possibly pick up the narrative with a relevant "next chapter." Self-disclosure can be encouraged by a kind of "Fruit Basket Upset" game in which people must change places when leaders (or fellow participants) call out such challenges as "Do you find your present work assignment challenging?" or "Do you feel that you are getting something out of this training?" or "Do you feel that your ideas are being heard by the group?" or "Do you feel uncomfortable revealing how you feel about these questions?" All who say yes must hurriedly exchange places.

Whether the instructor uses new games or traditional games, the motives are to encourage greater involvement. Thus, light games sometimes appear right after lunch when some competition—even some physical activity—can help regenerate the body functions.

Clinics.   Clinics, in learning designs, are sessions in which learners devote their energy to solving a given problem. Clinics thus use the discussion format. They are helpful in developing problem-solving, decisionmaking, or team membership skills. If the clinic is to be truly useful, participants must view the problem as real or relevant to their own jobs. It should provide for inputs from all students so that it meets the andragogic or facilitative criterion of using learners' experience and valued skill to expanding their capabilities. A clinic might address a real-world situation, come up with a real solution—and still be a learning experience. That can happen, of course, only if the problem-solving processes are examined concurrent to and as part of the clinic.

Critical Incident.   Critical incident method also identifies and analyzes actual participant experiences as a basis for better understanding real problems, or for expanding insights by analyzing the "critical incidents" in the careers of the participants.

The rationale is that all experience can be a source of learning—but that some moments are of such critical impact that they significantly mold future behavior. Concentration on these incidents permits a generalization about a far greater sampling of relevant experience than instructors can supply.

The critical-incident method varies slightly from the clinic or from just having participants write up their own case studies. It doesn't ask them to identify problem situations for class analysis—but rather to describe the details of an incident that "changed their lives." Sometimes known as the "peak-experience" approach, this method is used extensively in upper management or executive development programs. The critical-incident approach enhances the validity and perceived relevance of the course content because the incidents come from the learners themselves—and are perceived to have great value.

Fishbowls. "Fishbowls" constitute another special kind of discussion. The title comes from the structuring, where at certain phases some of the discussants sit in the center (the fishbowl) to discuss the issue. Other members observe this fishbowl and eventually take a place in it themselves.

Fishbowls may be used as instruments for analysis of group processes, or as instruments to control the content of a topical discussion. Technically, the method works about like this:

1. Choose a vital subject.
2. Prepare from six to eight catalytic questions for the moderator.
3. Assign or draw numbers for all participants.
4. Arrange chairs into an inner ring and an outer ring.
5. Place participants with the odd numbers in the inner ring.
6. Even-numbered participants take seats in the outer ring.
7. Designate one inner-ring moderator to use the questions in arousing and maintaining the discussion.
8. Tell others in the fishbowl (inner ring) that their role is to keep the discussion going—but to limit their inputs to no more than one minute per input.
9. Appoint the outer-ring members (even numbers) to different roles; assign people specifically to observe:

   - the number of times each person speaks
   - the number of times the discussion drifts to other topics
   - who interrupts, and who is interrupted
   - facial and other nonverbal communications
   - disagreements—with and by whom?
   - any conclusions about the subject or the processes

10. At the appointed time, stop the fishbowl and feed back the data gathered in step 9.

Repeat steps 7, 8, 9, and 10, but with the even-numbered people in the fishbowl and those with the odd numbers assuming the observers' roles.

Used in the manner described there, the fishbowl is clearly more concerned with group process than with course content. If instructors wish content to be the focus, they can divide the group into small buzz groups, each of which discusses all the catalytic questions. Each group also designates the sequence in which its members will participate in the fishbowl. At the appointed time, the first fishbowl starts. Only fishbowlers may speak, but if they misrepresent their group, a "caucus" can call them back for short re-instructions or for a change of representative.

When fishbowls take this form, participants can acquire the content of the discussion and skill in reflecting group opinions. To ensure this last learning for all trainees, the instructor must watch time limits carefully to make sure that all students serve as representatives in the fishbowl for a useful period of time.

Hot Role-Plays.   Hot role-plays are used to resolve issues that arise in the dynamics of classroom processes. This type of role playing differs from structured role-plays in that no instructions are given to participants; it is a spontaneous outgrowth of the classroom dynamics. Thus, hostilities between members, characteristic behaviors of students, deep misunderstandings, or blockages of group processes can become the content of a spontaneous "hot" role-play. The only instructions are those that come extemporaneously from the instructor, who decides that the best way to get the issue out into the open is to use a hot role-play.

Words such as "Alter-Egoing" or "Magic Shop" or "Magic Wand" appear as titles of forms in hot role playing. The Magic Wand might work when a participant says, "If I could just tell that so-and-so what I really think!" The instructor hands the participant a pencil or a pointer and says, "Okay. This magic wand gives you the power to do just that. I'm So-and-So. Tell me off!" Magic Shops are similar: "You're in this magic shop and you have enough money to buy anything you see. What can I get for you today?" Or there are Empty Chairs. The role-player fills them imaginatively with someone with whom communication comes hard—and starts communicating.

These applications tend to be therapeutic, but not all hot role-plays have therapy as their objective. Keener insights into how one appears to others can result from Alter-Egoing. For example, during class activities, one participant might rather consistently "put down" others in the group. The process observer, after such an overstatement, might try to let the overstater see the impact of that behavior by saying, "We're all really pretty damn stupid, aren't we?" Or again, "old-timers" may repeatedly preface their remarks with "In my twenty-seven years with this outfit . . ." If the observer feels this is causing others to resist the old-timer, the observer might say, as a kind of echo, "I see you telling us that without your seniority, we can't make proper judgments." These examples may be crude, but they explain why this method is known as "hot" role playing. When participants Alter-Ego each other as a structured exercise in sharing perceptions, the heat can get down-right tropical!

OD Data Gathering. Organization development (OD) data gathering uses a great many "hot" interventions if feelings are impeding the collection of "cooler" data. Feelings may be so deeply suppressed that the consultant feels lesser methods will never uncover them. A common technique is Organizational Mapping, in which people take a position reflecting such things as their relative influence or their relative comfort with other members of the group.

Another method is "Polling," in which a paper-and-pencil instrument is used so that members can indicate whom they perceive as most and least influential, or most and least helpful, or most and least cooperative—or most and least anything else the consultant feels would be helpful data for their renewal effort.

"T-Shirting" or "The Library" also reveals perceptions about how members of the group relate to group goals and to one another. In T-Shirting, they decide what the inscription should be on each other's T-shirts. Typical products of this exercise are "There Must Be A Better Way," or "I Am So Smart I Make Myself Sick," or "Tomorrow Has Been Canceled Due To Lack of Interest." In The Library, book titles are assigned to each member: *In Cold Blood, Once Is Not Enough,* or *The High and the Mighty* were products of one such intervention.

Another form of data gathering is to compile "Do More/Do Less" lists. Every member prepares a list for every member, headed with two titles: "I wish you would do more of this" and "I wish you would do less of this."

These polling activities are really searches for metaphors to get at the truth of perceptions. The metaphor can also be physical, as in "physical representations."

Neurolinguistic Programming (NLP) observes eye movement and other unconscious physical behaviors to identify patterns of thought and feeling. This highly technical data gathering and analysis requires the services of a trained specialist.

"Maps" require people to position themselves in a row (and agree that they are properly sequenced!) in relation to things such as relative influence, power, flexibility—any issue requiring clarification and resolution. A tougher map reflects working relationships: In a room without furniture, you are to stand near people with whom you enjoy working, away from those with whom you feel friction. This process itself is revealing. Explanations about why you are where you are can lead to open the identification of problems and action planning to overcome them.

By their very titles, these methods declare that they are unusual . . . not a part of the ordinary instructor's repertoire. They assuredly do not come up very often in day-to-day classroom situations. But they are there, available for that small percent of learning situations where the new behavior is highly threatening. Such methods become especially useful when personal blockages in group dynamics make it impossible for the learner to take initial or significant steps toward new insights and new behavior.

Summary

Asking which method to use for a training program is like asking a physician which instrument to use for surgery. It all depends on the nature of the operation! Fortunately, the contemporary T&D specialist, whether a designer or an instructor, has a vast range of instruments from which to choose. The well-rounded lesson plan in T&D programs will undoubtedly involve more than just one method. Variety is an important ingredient in adult learning experiences.

Teaching Technique

In *The Imperial Animal,* Tiger and Fox (1971) make a wonderful comment about the nature of teaching: "We have a propensity to learn. We also have a propensity to teach. These combine to make the teacher-student relationship a very satisfying one. That it often is not may very well be that what is primarily a social relationship has become a technical transaction" (152).

If the instructor-learner relationship is reduced to nothing more than a technical interchange, that is indeed sad.

Nonetheless, anybody who teaches or leads conferences knows that there are "little things" you can do to make the experience more successful. Those "little things" are called technique.

In a sense, the instructor manages a series of stimulus-response (SR) patterns. These SR dynamics involve several relationships: interaction between the learner and the program content; interaction between one learner and other learners; interaction between the learner and the instructor.

The Instructor's Use of Objectives

A most useful instrument in the instructor's professional toolkit is the list of learning objectives. We might look at it this way: Instructors need some way to focus the attention of all learners on a single concept. What better focus can you have than the goals of the learning? How do instructors bring this about? At the very first class session, people sit down with a list of the course objectives. They discuss the meaning, the impact, and the importance of applying each one. Some instructors go further and emphasize the objectives through visual aids. Such visual statements may:

1. Help control discussions. When students see the printed words, they tend to filter their comments by asking, "Is it appropriate?" A visual reminder by the learning objectives helps them make a good decision.

2. Help smooth transitions from one segment to another by providing a "road map" of the total course design.
3. Increase the value of "process" sessions by causing learners to ask themselves what they have achieved and what remains for them to learn.
4. Give new focus and emphasis to the goals, reminding learners why they are in the training.

If there have been pre-training conversations between students and their immediate "boss" about the learning objectives, the instructor can: (1) mention that, or (2) refer back to written notices about the program, which ought always to feature the learning objectives prominently.

The objectives are useful in other ways as the program continues. They can serve as a reasonable control when students wander from the subject. A discreet inquiry about how the comment or activity contributes toward the goal will either bring learners back to a profitable path—or show the instructor some exciting new dimension of the learning experience. When learners cannot see the relevance of class activity, instructors can help establish that relevance by analysis of the objectives. When giving themselves feedback about their own progress, the only real reference point learners have is comparing their present ability to the ultimate objectives.

At the end of the program, a list of objectives is most useful. In quiet, introspective moments, all learners can evaluate their own achievements for each objective. A group discussion can refocus on the desired behaviors and how they can be applied on the job. Action planning that relates to learning objectives has sharper direction than mere general resolutions to "do good things."

Let's summarize: Because the objectives are so useful, professional instructors use them as a technical instrument. They insist on pre-training communications at which learners (and, one hopes, their bosses) set expectations by analyzing the objectives. They hold early discussions and use the objectives to refine expectations and to clarify questions; they revisit the objectives at intermediate "Quaker Meetings," open discussions in which learners can explain how they feel about the program and their progress. They summarize at the end by looking at the objectives as a way to check the learners' sense of achievement, to double-check that all material has been covered and all goals met, and as a way to focus on on-the-job application.

Ongoing Measurement

Instructors use periodic feedback as an effective way to motivate their learners.

Whenever possible, they provide some early "pre-test" activity that lets all the learners discover where they are in relation to the ultimate goals. Experienced instructors tend to avoid the word "tests." They point out that this is really a "diagnosis," or a way to "find out what we already know and what we already can do." In this sense, the pre-test may be called a "baseline" or an "index" of the learner's beginning "inventory."

If the same pre-test instrument is used again later in the program, learners receive an ongoing sense of their accomplishments.

If parallel instruments are used for a final (or "terminal") examination, learners have concrete evidence that they have indeed met their learning objectives. The point is that the instructor must always key the measurement and feedback in with the objectives.

There are instruments for affective as well as cognitive goals. Agree/Disagree questionnaires can show how people have changed their positions on issues central to the program. There are, of course, no "right or wrong" answers in measuring feelings. For example, look at these samples from a questionnaire on womanhood:

Indicate whether you Agree Strongly, Tend to Agree, Have No Opinion, Tend to Disagree, or Disagree Strongly with these statements:

- Marriage is an institution that primarily benefits males.
- Job vacancy notices should not mention gender.
- Women should receive preferential treatment right now as an indemnity for past discrimination.
- The charge that women are over-emotional is a male smokescreen.

These are not used in feminists' programs about Women's Liberation; rather, they are used when the learning objectives involve values, communication styles, or mental flexibility—what the American Society for Training and Development (ASTD) Competence Study calls "Intellectual Versatility."

Ongoing measurement need not use paper-and-pencil formats. They can be performance tryouts, such as assembling or repairing an instrument, troubleshooting a machine, or performing a mental regimen—such as successive steps in an assertiveness model or a rational problem-solving process. Again, the important thing is to relate the measurement to one of the learning objectives. Thus there is great value in check-sheets on which learners score their own performance on details of the task they are learning to master.

Questioning Techniques

Questions are an important instrument for professional instructors. They employ questions as routine devices for maintaining communication; they may even use questions as a control device for "troublesome" students. Let's examine the use of questions in greater detail.

Directive questions can review factual material and help learners discover new insights. Examples: "What is the square root of 144?" "Give an example of horizontal loading as opposed to real job enrichment."

Reflective questions can double-check feelings, can consolidate issues and insights. Example: "You feel, then, that your own job is confining?" "Am I correct in sensing that you feel we've explored this topic more than enough?"

Open questions cannot be answered with a yes or a no or with facts. They are thus useful in probing for feelings and in testing a learner's inventory. "How do you feel about the Equal Rights Amendment?" "What do you know for sure about how adults learn?" When good instructors sense latent apathy or hostility, they tend to use open questions. In one-on-one as well as in group sessions, open questions can communicate a concern that allows apathetic or negative learners to redirect their psychic energies.

Besides knowing when to use each type of question, professional instructors master other questioning techniques.

First, they avoid the "Any questions?" trap. To ask a class "Are there any questions?" rarely produces anything at all—much less cogent interrogation! Therefore, professional instructors stimulate with carefully planned provocative questions that:

- Elicit specific opinions or feelings
- Require an examination of all sides of an issue
- Permit a learner to share a relevant valued experience
- Arouse sufficient interest that the answers trigger related questions from the class

Maybe after instructors positively reinforce student-initiated questions, the "Any questions?" question will produce a flurry of questions. But usually students ask questions when (1) the class activity stimulates them to do so, (2) they feel reinforced for asking, or (3) they are stimulated to ask another question because the instructor asked a good question in the first place.

Professional instructors have learned not to interrupt pondering students with follow-up questions. They wait for the student to respond. The follow-up (or "tandem") question usually stems from the instructor's desire to help the student. It rarely works. If the initial question has been well-conceived, students will need a few seconds to think. Let them do so. Asking another question, or rephrasing the old one, just gives them two things to think about at once. One was enough! This is especially true when learners are having trouble formulating their answers. Instructors just add frustration by rephrasing or changing the question. A wonderful cartoon captures the learner's viewpoint on this; the exasperated student exclaims, "Just when I thought I had the answer, I forgot the question!"

Experience also teaches instructors to ask the question before naming the respondent. Why is this important? Because it permits *all* the students to decide how they would answer. If not called upon, they can check their intended response with the one given—and be ready to participate if it is incorrect or incomplete. Such covert involvement keeps them "attending" during the entire session; this technique avoids the daydreaming potential that comes when they have been excused from answering a question by an instructor who asked someone else before even asking the question. Because all students "attend" all the time, they are more likely to enliven and enrich the discussion by comments or questions of their own.

Experienced instructors call on students in an irregular, unpredictable sequence. They don't go around the room in clockwise or counterclockwise patterns. They don't go down the alphabetical roster. Students who do not know when they will be called upon tend to answer every question in their own minds.

When students ask questions, professional instructors usually give the asker the first chance to answer. Why? Because the instructor may feel this will allow the learner to grow in self-confidence. Or because it will let askers discover the answers they are capable of giving but may be ignoring for the moment.

As a second choice, instructors like to redirect a student's question to other class members. This keeps attention on the content rather than on a dominant instructor. It provides a helpful way for adults to invest their existing inventory in the learning process. It gives the instructor useful feedback about where the students are in their progress toward learning goals.

A poor third choice is for the instructor to answer the student question. There are, to be sure, times when this is appropriate, but only if:

1. The question deals with course logistics (only the instructor knows those answers), or
2. The questioner specifically asked for the instructor's opinion (and then it's "maybe"), or
3. It is appropriate or necessary to color the discussion by revealing the instructor's opinion, or
4. The class has been totally unable to come up with a right answer, and
5. The search elsewhere would delay processes beyond the value of the question.

That seems like a lot of times when instructors may legitimately give answers, but those "iffy" cases don't come up very often!

Professional instructors use questions to "get a discussion going." In *Teaching Tips*, W. J. McKeachie warns against asking questions that obviously have only one right answer. Discussion questions, he says, "need to get at relationships, applications or analysis of facts and materials." He also identifies a need to frame the questions at a level of abstraction appropriate to the class. "Students are most likely to participate in discussion when they feel they have an experience or an idea that will contribute" (1969, 54). Directive questions (those having one right answer) are useful for review—not for stimulation.

Getting Attention Versus Getting Involvement

Instructors who seek dominance and attention rather than learning would do well to seek employment in the lecture hall, the pulpit, the theatre, or the nightclub rather than in the classroom.

The issue for instructors is, "Do I want to cause learning, or do I want to make a great impression?" Although the two are not incompatible, they are by no means synonymous.

Another way of looking at it goes like this: "Do I want to do all the work myself—or would I like the learners to do some of their own work by getting busy in learning activities?" Real trainers and real instructors want to stimulate, not to overpower; they want to facilitate, not to deprive or smother.

That being so, questions that elicit thought and activities that involve learners replace startling statements and flamboyant stimuli.

Yet "centering" or "polarizing" techniques are necessary. They change attention from the previous topics of concentration to the reality of the learning. We have previously mentioned two ways to "center": reviewing objectives, and questions. Andragogic designs stress the importance of learners' involvement in any centering method.

A traditional method has been to have the class "get acquainted with one another." This is especially common when participants come from various parts of the organization and are assumed to be strangers to one another. It's hard to know precisely what such introductions accomplish unless the class activity uses a great deal of interrelationships between learners. Since andragogic designs *do* depend upon this interrelating, the method of introducing is a technical activity deserving some attention.

A typical get-acquainted activity has each person stand up and share something biographical: name, position, seniority, family data, hobbies.

The goal behind all these introductions is for every participant to get acquainted with everyone else. That objective needs to be made very clear when the activity is announced and launched. If the introductions are purely ritual-istic, they become sterile. It is useful for the instructor to explain convincingly that getting to know one another at the beginning helps a lot in achieving learning goals.

Use of Repetition

There is a mistaken notion that sheer repetition assists learning. Sheer repeti-tion may assist memorization—but that means it's useful only in achieving knowledge. Repetition doesn't help comprehension much, nor does it help the other more advanced cognitive and affective objectives. Repeating a psychomo-tor behavior can provide the "practice that makes perfect," but even as we say that we should discover something else about the principle of repetition: It's repetition by the learner that pays off—not repetition by the instructor!

Repetition by the learner helps the "imprinting" process, memorizing key words, or perfecting psychomotor skills through drill. For other types of skill, repetition is most valuable when it's "repetition with a difference." That ex-plains the value of having learners themselves put ideas into their own words and of hearing other learners express the ideas in varying phrases. Each per-son's phrasing is original, and gives learners "ownership" of the idea. It lets them personally adapt a stimulus so they are comfortable with it; it allows them to hear the same concept different ways from different people.

When drill takes the form of problems or simple case studies, it also offers repetition with a difference. Principles are applied repeatedly, but in different contexts or with different ingredients. Such drill permits repetition at the "appli-cation level" and reduces mere repetition of theory to a practical, useful activity.

For example, merely repeating "two times two is four" again and again is a sterile exercise. Asking how many children there are in a house with two fami-lies, each of which has two children, improves the experience accompanying the drill—and the ability to retain and apply the formula. There is real value in educational use of the literary device of "incremental repetition," or "repetition with a difference."

Relating to Students

Carl Rogers (1969) stresses that instructors should be just as concerned about their relationship with students as they are about their course content or ex-pertise. This doesn't mean that they stand up in front of the class and immedi-ately seek affection.

Unskilled ego-centered instructors do that. Nor does it mean that instructors win popularity contests—or that they confuse comradeship with a useful instructor-learner relationship. It does mean that they *care* about the relationship. That, in turn, probably means that they care about the learners enough to make certain that every one of them achieves all the desired learning objectives.

In a somewhat oversimplified way, this means that instructors consistently look for student behaviors to reinforce positively. Why? Because instructors know that people tend to repeat behaviors for which they feel "rewarded." Thus when a student gets part (but not all) of an answer correct, the instructor commends the correct part—then follows with a question that encourages the learner to improve what's wrong or to add what's missing. The essential technique? To form the habit of doing this; to develop skill in locating "what's right"; to find out the private, unique personal "rewards" each person cherishes.

Beyond—or better, *before*—positive reinforcement comes letting students know that the program means business—that they are accountable for learning. This can be implied in the initial discussion about objectives. However, it's likely that this important message should not be implicit: It's wise to make a statement that when one is in training, the organization expects that learning will occur "just as our organization would expect you to complete your regular tasks if you were on the job today instead of here." Above all, the message that learning is a serious business is communicated by instructors who themselves are businesslike and professional.

There is always a temptation to "do as the Romans do." In modern organizations, the Romans nowadays are using lots of words that only a few years ago were considered to be in bad taste. No definitive studies prove this next point; but it does seem that when the instructor's language becomes too informal or profane, students lose respect for the learning experience. Conversely, stilted formal language can impede learning. Students may not know what those big words mean. An instructor's display of an extensive vocabulary can discourage and even humiliate learners. Yet some technical words are big words, and they are absolutely necessary. Instructors need not apologize for using jargon; it's the only correct word, and professionalism must involve a concrete, specialized vocabulary. Similarly, some earthy words are the only ones, and they precisely convey feelings. Perhaps the moral is just this: Use technical jargon and slang when it is accurate, necessary, and comfortable—but don't use either too much! The excesses, not the words themselves, are what may impede learning.

Humor is another thing. Like language, it involves the issue of taste. Since taste is an individual thing, humor isn't universal in the learning world. The danger is that when one is "being funny," nobody laughs. That silence can make an instructor mightily lonely! Nobody can really define humor; only a few ground rules are of much help to instructors. One vital criterion: The humor must be relevant to the topic or the immediate situation. Jokes seldom work if brought in just to let the instructor say something funny. Another important point: The joke should be kind, not scornful. It should not ridicule a person or a group. Next, the joke should be new to the listeners. It's difficult (if not impossible) to be sure that a relevant story hasn't made the rounds. So smart instructors follow this rule: If there's even a glimmer that this is an "old clinker," forget it. Finally, the joke should be short. It need not be a one-liner, but nothing kills humor so much as embellishment. Added details belabor the point; adapting a story to local conditions is often painful; pretending that it happened to someone in the room seldom adds to the hilarity—it usually just makes the situation awkward and amateurish.

If instructors focus on learners' needs, classroom dynamics make for pleasant, exciting relationships. However, there are such things as problem students. What does the instructor do when trainees refuse to invest energy in learning or when a trainee consistently distracts others?

Sometimes this problem takes peculiar twists. Maybe a student talks a great deal, consuming valuable class time and distracting other learners with irrelevant ideas. What's the "desired behavior"? Longer periods of silence, right? Reinforcement theory would urge the instructor to listen for significantly long periods of quiet. After such silence, the instructor should give the student a chance to do something pleasant—even if that "something" is to talk!

There's a general rule: "Never interrupt a talking student." Well, the case of the excessive talker may be one exception. Instructors may have to remind such "chatterers" that time is limited—just to protect other learners. If instructors can send such messages in private counseling sessions, or at breaks, so much the better. That strategy avoids calling the entire group's attention to the problem. But as a last resort, an instructor may need to be a timekeeper.

What about "the mouse," the student who talks too little or not at all? The instructor may get mice to "attend" by trying these techniques:

- Open questions, seeking opinions or feelings, produce answers that are easy to reinforce.
- One-on-one conversation, at breaks or over-the-shoulder, may establish rapport and allow the instructor to reinforce private comments so that the student will want to talk to the entire class.
- Small groups may be more comfortable for "the mouse" and make it easier for the instructor to "eavesdrop" and commend something about input from the quiet one.

Then there is "the parrot," who talks an appropriate amount, but always quotes someone else, goes the party line, or avoids expressing an original idea.

Instructors need to listen for the first trace (or "successive approximation") of originality, praise it, and call the attention of the class to the uniqueness of that idea. Special techniques include these:

- Probing with open questions.
- Asking learners to give Pro/Con analysis of a cliched opinion.
- Having learners imagine what opponents would say in rebuttal to a statement they've just expressed.
- Having them work with others (and eventually alone) to find metaphors for the views they parrot or the theories, models, or processes the class is studying. For example, a computer might be "Otto" because it's so automatic; in one factory they call their robot "Clyde the Claw." Parrots are troublesome to convert to creative contributors, but they are less disruptive to the group processes than "the contradictors," who take exception to everything said by instructors and anyone else.
- Again, Pro/Con analysis helps because it makes sure that contradictors are required to contribute to both sides and are reinforced for the "both-sidedness" of their analyses.
- Paying very little attention to their negativism eventually helps mules who seek only attention.

Confrontation is probably a "No-No!" because the attention it involves may be perceived as positive reinforcement by the class. If it must happen, the confrontation should probably occur privately, and must focus on the negative behavior—not degenerate into a debate about one of the issues raised by the "problem" participant.

In all these situations, reinforcement theory helps. If instructors can find no behavior to reinforce positively, then neutral reinforcement at least prevents the situation from worsening.

What does that mean? Merely doing nothing to encourage the undesirable behavior. For example, during discussions, one trainee consistently wanders from the subject. The instructor merely says, "I see" or "Yes. Who else would like to comment?" or "Oh." There should be no further inquiry, no insistence upon an explanation. Or again, a trainee takes exception to many key principles. Rather than argue or draw attention to this, the instructor gives a minimum response: "This may become clear later," or maybe the instructor says nothing at all. The less attention to the behavior, the more likely it is that it will disappear.

But that can be a slow process, and it isn't always easy to accomplish. Furthermore, ignoring troublesome trainees may destroy the businesslike atmosphere that supports other learners. How much heckling can you tolerate from a satanic "devil's advocate"? How long can noisy splinter conversations be allowed to distract? What is your obligation to see some activity from those who refuse to participate—even to take part in the performance tryouts?

At such times, private counseling is probably necessary. Away from the classroom pressures, instructors may discover mistaken expectations or hidden reasons for the poor performance. They may help learners discover that the two can have a profitable relationship in reaching behavioral objectives. Some confrontation, gentle or forceful, may be necessary. There may even be occasions when the instructor must request the trainee to drop the program.

We need to distinguish between two behaviors: ongoing appropriate reinforcement and discipline. The first process is inevitable; the second is only rarely necessary in organizational classes or conferences.

When do adult instructors need to discipline adult students? Very, very rarely. Professionals agree that discipline is necessary only when their authority is being challenged. Now, this doesn't mean that discipline is applied each time the learner questions the correctness of data, or the tasks, or the processes. It's only applied when there is open defiance, when the gauntlet has been thrown down so clearly and so persistently that the instructor can no longer function effectively with other learners. Instructors must deal with such an impasse, and discipline is one way of doing so.

Discipline in organizational training does not mean punishment. There is no authority for (and less sense in) making them "stay after school" or stand in the corner. Instructors can't give forty lashes or draw-and-quarter their trainees. Verbal tongue-lashings are about all most instructors think of as available disciplinary action.

Discipline often results only in defiance by the employees. Since instructors will never be able to please all their students on every issue, failure to deal with defiance means that the defiance will recur. In organizational T&D, trainees who do not invest a minimum effort in the learning process are not doing their assigned work. Why not return them to their regular workplaces and send explanations through regular channels?

If policy prohibits such expulsion, then isolation of the problem students as much as possible may minimize their ravages on other learners. When there are early signs of defiance, instructors may schedule individual (or "small team") activity. This method gives the defiant one less visibility, and therefore less reinforcement for the defiant behaviors. It also provides a chance to observe individual behaviors; instructors who do that often find the cause of the defiance, or the "private reinforcer" to use on the belligerent learner. Above all, the instructor has closer contact because of the smaller group—and thus has a better chance of discovering something to reinforce, some successive approximation of constructive participation in class activities.

On rare occasions, several problem students appear in the same session. Isolation is probably the most effective strategy after positive and neutral reinforcement have failed. Because instructors don't want the negative ones to infect the more positive learners, they seat troublemakers at the same table and assign them to the same buzz groups. This doesn't solve the real problem, but it limits the scope of the damage such students can inflict.

Another solution that doesn't solve anything is direct eye contact with the troublemakers. It doesn't reinforce their negativism, and it makes their behavior less public—but it probably throttles their energy, encouraging later, more active insurrection. Direct eye contact is useful only as a stopgap before private consultation when the instructor can get at the real root of the problem.

Incidentally, when people talk inappropriately, instructors might well use more directive questions: Specific people are asked to reply to factual inquires. These questions offer more containment and are appropriate when control rather than facilitation is necessary. But it's wise to remember that control is necessary only when other techniques have failed—and that it rarely becomes the central need in organizational T&D systems that have communicated and maintained a businesslike policy about learning. It is even less necessary in classes and conferences where teachers are facilitative and andragogical.

Summary

Sheer technique will not produce great instruction. Truly great instruction will not be fatally impeded by clumsy technique.

However, an instructor's attention to little details can sharpen and intensify the dynamics of the learning activity. This means that the stimuli applied by the instructor will be sharper and more productive. That sharper stimulation in turn permits a greater interaction between the learner and the course content, between peer learners, and between learners and instructors.

In professional instruction, an instructor's awkwardness or amateurism does not blur learning processes. The stimuli are adapted more quickly and more productively if the instructor is a professional. That professionalism is often based on the mastery of a few teaching techniques.

Training Facilities

The Influence of the T&D Manager

Should we perhaps call them "learning rooms" instead of training rooms? Or should we stress the word "environment?" That is an increasingly popular word, and the more we learn about learning, the more the environment seems to be a significant factor in bringing about behavior change.

Besides, it may seem that architects make all the decisions about the rooms we use for our training programs. Things such as the modularity of the structure, costs, and building codes determine such key decisions as dimensions and ceiling height. T&D managers may easily feel "out of it" when it comes to these key decisions.

However, T&D managers can influence architectural decisions when buildings are in the planning stage; instructors can do a great deal to adjust the physical environment during training; and everybody in the T&D function can observe key criteria when selecting hotels, motels, and conference sites.

Criteria for Learning Rooms

Different kinds of learnings require different environments. For example, if contemplation and introspection are involved, calm and quiet seem necessary. If the learning requires movement, lots of open space is a must. Even so, there are general criteria. This chapter focuses on traditional training classrooms. Designers of classrooms for technology-mediated learning (computer-based learning, distance learning, etc.) should consult specialized texts or other experts for optimal design characteristics for those rooms.

Experienced instructors will tell you they want flexibility, isolation, lighting control, capacity to accommodate computer equipment, and ventilation. Each of them is important enough to rate individual discussion.

Flexibility

If instructors or course designers had to settle for just one quality in learning rooms, chances are they'd opt for flexibility.

Flexibility is an understandable criterion if you just stop to think about the wide variety of methods professional T&D specialists currently employ. Within one room—probably within one afternoon—class activities may vary from watching a video to fish bowling; from using a computer to appearing on a video camera; from taking part in a discussion to role playing or to doing a bit of meditating. Naturally, the instructor wants a room that can quickly and easily be rearranged.

Flexibility has several dimensions. A major element of flexibility is size. Cramped quarters don't give the needed flexibility or that sense of growth potential needed for the learning experience. One way to estimate the adequacy of a room is to calculate the square feet needed for each participant. Such calculations need to allow for chairs, tables, access, and capacity for course equipment. For "theater-type" sessions, 9 or 10 square feet per person is about right. Of course, this arrangement limits one to "tell-and-show" presentational methods. Classroom set-ups (rows of chairs, probably with arm-tablets) require from 15 to 17 square feet per participant. Conference arrangements place learners at tables, and require from 23 to 25 square feet per person. The table should allow at least 30 linear inches per person. It should also provide from 18 to 24 inches of depth. This permits learners to spread their papers and learning materials during workshop activities.

For that reason, tables that are 60 inches long are excellent: They offer the minimum working dimensions for participants, but they can be easily shifted to new arrangements. Such flexibility doesn't apply to the 6-foot tables often ordered for training rooms. The 6-foot table offers an additional hazard: the temptation to crowd three people onto each side! It follows that tables 60 inches by 36 inches permit two people to sit at each side and provide adequate table-top space and face-to-face seating for two-way communication during discussion and team task activities.

Plenty of space is a "must" if buzz groups are to work simultaneously in a learning center—and there's much to be said for their visible proximity to one another. The synergism produced by such nearness vanishes quickly (as do lots of precious minutes!) if the groups must commute to nearby breakout rooms. Besides, how often are these rooms truly "nearby"?

Square rooms can be changed on a functional or daily basis. The wall that is "front" today can be the side or rear wall tomorrow. In fact, any wall can be "the front" except the one with the door by which people come and go—and even that can be the focus of a small buzz group when the class is divided into teams, which tend to create their own "environment." Of course, when learners concentrate on what they are doing, the whole idea of "front" becomes passé and meaningless.

Rectangular rooms should not be so deep that participants have to strain to talk to other participants at the front of the room, or to hear them. Generally, the bigger the room and the more cavernous the feel, the less discussion and interaction will occur. There is actually greater risk in getting a room too big than one too small. If a room is a bit small, participants may trip over each other a little bit, but the learning still occurs effectively. If the room is too big or the ceiling too high, learning may be inhibited because little interaction occurs.

In any event, astute instructors of multiday training "reorient" the classroom every day or so, allowing students a new perspective and causing them to take seats in different positions and beside different people. That is often healthy action: Those with impaired sight or hearing can privately solve their problems, and everyone becomes acquainted with more members of the class.

At sessions with no visual presentation, tables and chairs can face a different direction. This shift gives a "different feeling" and subtly underlines the theme that during training, change is the name of the game.

Ceiling height is important. Anything under ten feet may pose problems for instructors and conference leaders. The screen should be high enough so that learners in the rear can see it "above" and not "around" the heads of people in front of them. Experts urge that the top of the screen be as high as possible. But don't have the ceiling too high, either, if lots of interaction is desired. Acoustical engineering is a special technology, beyond the range of most T&D managers. However, anyone can check a few things. Carpets should be low pile and nonabsorptive. T&D managers can influence such details when designing new training centers; T&D specialists can check these features when selecting rooms in rented or leased facilities.

Students' chairs should receive careful consideration. Participants just don't learn well if they are uncomfortable! This is one place not to scrimp on the budget. Chairs should be well padded, the backs slightly curved, and provide major support in the lumbar area. Parts that contact the learner (seat and frame) should be constructed of material that does not conduct heat or cold. If desks, or tablet arms, are included, the writing surfaces should be slightly inclined and about twenty-seven inches above the floor.

Isolation

Isolation is another criterion. Isolation implies that the room is sufficiently removed from the workplace—physically or psychologically—so that the learners know they are in training. If the proper policies prevail, such isolation can take place within a few feet of the workplace. Bosses of trainees should understand that when their employees are in training, the instructor is "the boss" and every effort should be made to minimize interrupting trainees. Isolation can also be achieved by policy. Many organizations establish and enforce the "Work equals Learn" philosophy, which simply means that while employees are enrolled in training, the company expects them to acquire the behaviors outlined in the learning objectives.

Effective isolation is further achieved by a policy communicated before reporting to training: Instead of performing regular duties, for the period of the training trainees are expected to achieve the objectives of the program. "Learning" is their work.

Thus isolation is both physical and psychological. Considerations in achieving isolation range from getting far away from highways, airports, and loud plumbing to getting away from the boss.

Lighting Control

Lighting control is a prime criterion for visual presentations. Although total darkness is undesirable, excess sunlight can dampen the sensory impact of even the most colorful presentations. One dimension of lighting control is the ability to eliminate light; another is the ability to diminish it by degrees. The advantages of rheostat controls are obvious—especially if there are several. In some designs, different learners will be doing different things simultaneously. Thus, if the instructor can have bright light in one portion of the room and dim light in another, multimethod designs are easily executed. When the screen must be placed near permanent light fixtures, there's trouble. If there aren't rheostats to dim them, or switches to eliminate the light, then a ladder and a quick twist become the instructor's problem-solving tools.

All learning rooms have the potential problem of glare. Removing naked lamps and glossy surfaces can best prevent glare. Trainers who inherit rooms with glaring lamps and windows should install shades and drapes. Trainers who rent public rooms filled with glossy tables should insist upon tablecloths. (By the way, here's a tip: When arranging to rent rooms, be sure to insist that there be a tablecloth for each table. Otherwise, when you go to move the tables to fit the changing activities of the design, you'll find that the cloths don't come out evenly and you will waste lots of time adjusting the water glasses and pitchers.)

Lighting control involves more than merely dimming and directing illumination. The computer has become an essential tool of the interrogative mind.

Electrical wiring that will accommodate computer equipment is thus imperative in the contemporary learning room.

Ventilation

Ventilation is another criterion for learning rooms. An additional argument for high ceilings is that when the temperature goes up, so does the heat. But high ceilings will not guarantee good ventilation. Experienced instructors will tell you that ventilation is a "lose-lose" situation. "You can't please all the people any of the time—or any of the people for more than about fifteen minutes at a time!" These old-timers say they prefer to keep things a little on the cool side; they'd rather have people alert than asleep!

Let's emphasize that point about keeping the air moving. T&D managers who are acquiring new learning rooms would be wise to see that there is proper equipment to provide the minimum air velocity of from twelve to fifteen feet per minute.

In summary, by checking rooms for compliance with those four criteria—flexibility, isolation, lighting control, and ventilation—the T&D specialist is more likely to be in quarters where learning can easily happen. Beyond the room itself, instructors and conference leaders can do some things to make room arrangements suitable to the participation planned for each module of the training.

Room Arrangement

Flexibility is a vital criterion for the training room because instructors will need to rearrange the furniture so that it fits the variety of methods they will be using. The more andragogical the learning design, the more varied the furniture arrangements. This statement implies that the furniture will be moved—and quite often.

Even if the functional activities of the learning design don't demand a rearrangement, there are several reasons for changing the furniture from time to time:

- Individuals are given a new perspective on the activity by sitting in different parts of the room.
- Individuals get better acquainted with more of their peer-participants when they move around from time to time.
- Disabled individuals are not consistently and permanently punished by being great distances from the screen or from the speakers.

- Small cliques do not arise. (There's nothing wrong with cliques, but sometimes they can become problems by forcing their norms or their agenda upon the entire group.)

The various functional arrangements often found in T&D learning rooms may be analyzed according to their facilitation of two-way communication. In this analysis, we will look at them on that basis, starting with the least encumbering arrangements and proceeding to the more formal plans that control rather than encourage free-and-easy communication between participants and communications between participants and the instructor. Finally, we'll consider arrangements that "deformalize" those rigid arrangements.

The un-furnitured circle in Figure 12.1 is probably the most democratic and unencumbered of all arrangements. There is no status symbol denoting a leader, and every participant has direct sight lines to every other participant. Since there is no table between participants, each person is, in a sense, "totally revealed." Subtle nonverbal communications are possible. This arrangement is typical for groups and team building and for data gathering sessions in organization-development programs.

This circle (Figure 12.2) is uncluttered, but there is a clear-cut leader. Consider this as a grouping for a brainstorming session. One person is in control, partly because of the standing position and partly because of a "scepter of authority": the pencil and the flipchart or chalkboard.

When the circular table is used (Figure 12.3), participants still have direct access to each other, including facial nonverbal communications. Remember the Paris peace talks? Remember when the nations argued relentlessly about the shape of the table? It apparently *does* make a difference! Informal studies show that there will be more conversation and shorter inputs and that more members will participate when the same people sit at round tables rather than at square ones!

Instructors can always arrange rectangular tables into various rectangular patterns. The square arrangement (Figure 12.4) produces several noteworthy effects. Participants are now seated in rows, the first step toward formality. In rows (as opposed to arcs), nobody can see the faces of all the other participants. Depending upon where visual aids are placed, one side or another may become the "head" of the table. An interesting sidelight: Informal studies show that a gap in the center, as shown here, retards participation. A solid table (Figure 12.5) seems to encourage conversation. When there is a "hole in the middle," some people don't speak at all, and those who do speak tend to talk for longer periods. It would thus seem that when instructors want more control, they should arrange the tables around a central "void." For more democratic conversation, the tables should be joined to form a solid unit. This holds true with any rectangular arrangement.

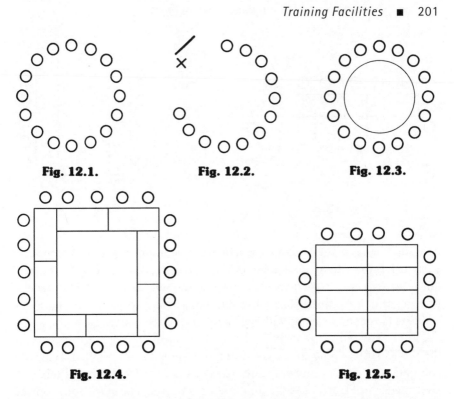

Fig. 12.1. **Fig. 12.2.** **Fig. 12.3.**

Fig. 12.4. **Fig. 12.5.**

If the rectangle becomes long and narrow (Figure 12.6), there are longer lines. Thus, even fewer people can communicate face-to-face with their peers. The positions on the short dimension of the table are often identified as "leadership seats." Could this be because the father sat at the head of the table? Indeed, even when no leader is appointed, members along the sides tend to look to the end positions and expect people seated there to dominate.

You'd probably win the bet if you wagered that more management development conferences use the "U" (Figure 12.7) than any other arrangement. It has a sense of the "senate" with equality of membership—but there is no doubt about who is presiding. It is frequently effective, even though it does have a formality and imposes a constraint on participants. Since there are just three rows of people, a great many participants are blocked from viewing the faces of their peers. Although some clutter results from placing people on the inside of the "U," as in Figure 12.8, such placement does open up more visual contact and bring the entire group into close physical proximity. That proximity cannot be ignored; the farther apart members are from one another, the more reserved their behavior—and the greater the control.

Whenever rectangles are used, the participants should be encouraged (or forced by the nature of the activity) to take distinctly different positions every

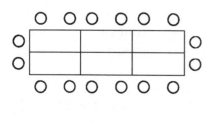

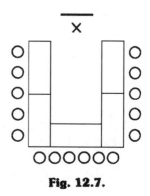

Fig. 12.6.   **Fig. 12.7.**

now and then. If name cards are used, they can be shifted regularly. When such a practice is to be used, it's a good idea to start it at the first break or the first lunch break. This lets participants know that mobility is the norm for the entire program. Most instructors encourage participants to move voluntarily in addition to the moves made with the name cards or the varying activity.

Simply "softening" the shape of the "U" can make considerable difference in the participants' ability to see and communicate with one another. With the conventional "U," there are only three rows of students. By placing the tables at an angle, as in Figure 12.9, the long rows are broken into numerous shorter rows and participants' mutual sight lines are improved.

Tables can also be arranged in circular or semicircular patterns (Figure 12.10). An advantage is the return to the "arc." More people are able to see the faces of more peers than they can in some rectangular arrangements.

Cabaret arrangements, such as the one in Figure 12.11, facilitate the establishment of buzz groups for team tasks, games, and individual study. A cabaret setting is especially useful during workshop or programmed instruction modules within longer programs. Each table can be designated for a particular activity. At the same time, sight lines and the proximity of learners encourage a free exchange of ideas. Discussions involving the entire group can occur as easily in this arrangement as in any other. The instructors can easily assume a position of authority, yet can just as easily move among individuals or teams when they are working at tables. The cabaret plan reflects an informal, flexible type of learning environment.

The scattershot method (Figure 12.12) may appear extremely haphazard. It actually permits the quick change of a learner's focus and produces tremendous investments of a learner's energy. It works very well in multiple role-plays, two-person team tasks, and highly synergistic action training. When necessary, participants can quickly form larger groups. The scattershot arrangement produces high interpersonal and intergroup communication. It's

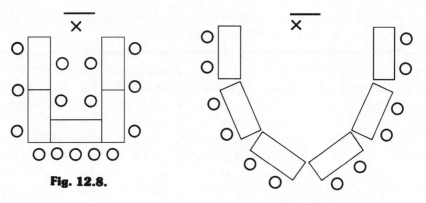

Fig. 12.8.

Fig. 12.9.

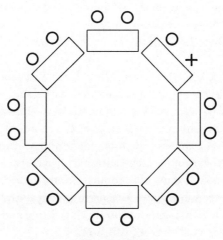

Fig. 12.10.

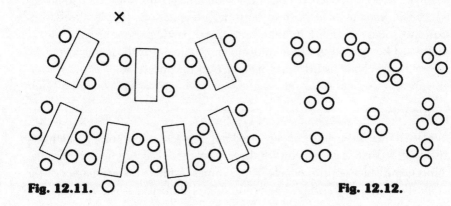

Fig. 12.11.

Fig. 12.12.

bad for note taking, but the scattershot grouping is designed for experiential training in which notes are rarely necessary.

The "classroom" set-up is almost the opposite. As shown in Figure 12.13, it reminds us of academic classrooms—and is somewhat undesirable. When students occupy chairs with arm tablets, the arrangement does have great flexibility. It's easy to shift to scattershot groupings and to break up the "military" rows of seats found in most "schools."

Organizational "classroom" arrangements (Figure 12.14) usually feature rows of tables. These indicate that the instructor will have considerable control. The rows limit face-to-face communication by participants—unless they twist a lot; it's hard to talk to anyone save the instructor or to one's neighbor. Unless there is ample room between the rows of tables, instructors cannot easily reach individual learners to review their progress. There is a barrier against forming natural groups for team tasks. There is no easy way for instructors to provide private or semiprivate counseling.

An antidote for these limitations is a wide aisle between each row (Figure 12.15).

If seating is restricted to the recommended two-at-a-table, instructors can have access to every learner without the undue "nearness" of other participants.

Converting the rows to arcs, as in Figure 12.16, will enhance the learners' ability to communicate with one another. They can more easily see each others' faces, and the lines are bent—so the total environment seems less structured and less rigid. This "chevron," or arched arrangement, isn't seen very often, but it's a useful plan in square rooms or in rooms with the recommended 3:4 ratio.

The modified chevron in Figure 12.17 permits a great deal of cross communication among participants without too much twisting and turning. Instructors are still able to access all parts of the room.

It goes without saying (but probably should be said anyway) that whenever possible the more formal arrangement should be set up so that the main entrance is *behind* the learners. In such formal, presentation-type situations, control and focus are hard to maintain when participants are periodically stimulated by the arrival of the mid-morning coffee—or those outsiders who ignore the "Do Not Disturb" sign hanging over the doorknob!

Summary

A "place to make learning happen" need not be a grand room, elaborately furnished. It needn't be equipped with the latest electronic equipment, media machinery, and fancy control panels. Those things facilitate the mechanics of the support systems of learning. They shouldn't be ridiculed—but in themselves they don't guarantee learning.

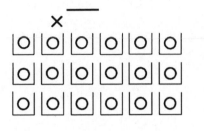

Fig. 12.13.

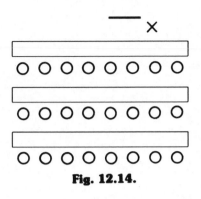

Fig. 12.14.

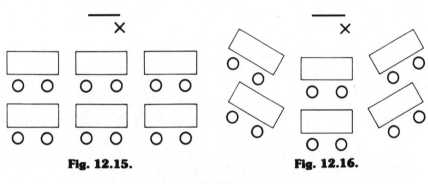

Fig. 12.15.

Fig. 12.16.

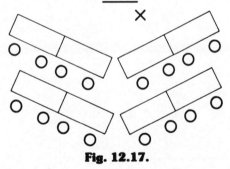

Fig. 12.17.

A room in which learning can happen is flexible—quickly responsive to the group's need for a new arrangement. Because it is isolated, learners never doubt that their mission is to learn. Lighting and ventilation are not obstacles to maintaining that focus on learning.

But above all, the room permits the creativity of the instructor to put things where trainee-participants can quickly use them as tools for their learning processes.

13

Enhancing Transfer of Learning

Training Transfer

This chapter focuses on transfer of learning. Although there are multiple definitions of transfer, it is generally agreed that the transfer of learning involves the application, generalization, and maintenance of new knowledge and skills (Ford and Weissbein 1997). Training and development professionals have traditionally focused on learning as an outcome, and mostly on learning design as their way to influence outcomes. Performance-oriented training and development fundamentally changes this. In fact, we endorse the following statements:

- The transfer of learning into job performance is just as important, if not more important, than learning.
- Without attention to transfer, good learning often results in no return to the organization.
- Transfer can be managed and improved, but it requires T&D professionals to influence organizational factors that may be out of their direct control.
- Without transfer, training fails.

Consider these examples. An accountant returns from a training program and reports to his colleagues that there is no way this new system will work in their culture. A woman applies the model of leadership she recently learned at a training session and her supervisor criticizes her "new way of doing things." A plant operator reports that the training was excellent but didn't fit the realities of their production unit. In these examples, neither training program produced positive job performance changes, but these employees were not struggling with or complaining about the training they had attended. Rather, the challenges they faced arose when they turned their attention to transferring their new learning to on-the-job performance. The outcome for all three of these employees was most likely frustration, confusion, and a diminished opportunity to apply improved ways of doing their work.

This scope of the problem is magnified when one analyzes recent statistics that indicate investment in training activities aimed at improving employees' job performance represents a huge financial expenditure in the United States. In 2001, organizations having more than one hundred employees were estimated to have spent over $68 billion in direct costs on formal training (*Training Magazine* 2002). With the inclusion of indirect costs, informal on-the-job training, and costs incurred by smaller organizations, total training expenditures could easily reach $200 billion or more annually. Of this expenditure, as little as 10 percent is estimated to pay off in performance improvements resulting from the transfer of learned knowledge, skills, and abilities to the job (Baldwin and Ford 1988). Our experience in workshops is that most managers estimate that about 25 percent of training transfers into job performance. Although the exact amount of transfer is unknown, the transfer problem is believed to be so pervasive that there is rarely a learning-performance situation in which such a problem does not exist (Broad and Newstrom 1992). The cost to organizations is huge. If only 25 percent transfers, then $51 billion are wasted! Even if 50 percent transfers, that still leaves $34 billion down the drain.

Learning Transfer Systems

Organizations wishing to enhance the return on investment from learning/training investments must understand all the factors that affect the transfer of learning and then intervene to improve factors inhibiting transfer. Traditionally, "transfer climate" was used to describe factors affecting transfer. We prefer to use "transfer system," which we define as all factors in the person, training, and organization that influence the transfer of learning to job performance. Thus, the transfer system is a broader construct than transfer climate but includes all factors traditionally referred to as transfer climate. For example, the validity of the training content is part of the system of influences that affects transfer, but is not a climate construct. Transfer can be completely understood and predicted only by examining the entire system of influences.

The big leap for most training and development professionals is the realization that the transfer system includes not only things under their control such as the learning design but also the work environment into which the employees take the learning and try to use it. "But we can't make managers do things," object many T&D professionals. They are right. But here's the problem. If the training doesn't result in job performance, who will be blamed? Training! Even if it is a work environment problem, training takes the blame, so your only choice is to try to influence the work environment actively so that your training will lead to on-the-job performance improvement. You can ignore it and make excuses all day, but in the end you will only lose. T&D professionals have to get out of their comfort zone of learning and become savvy about turning their learning into job performance. That means working to change the transfer environment.

Learning and transfer of learning are critical outcomes in Human Resource Development (HRD). Research during the last ten years has demonstrated that the transfer of learning is complex and involves multiple factors and influences. Several studies have established that transfer climate can significantly affect an individual's ability and motivation to transfer learning to job performance. Although many authors support the importance of transfer climate, some stating that it may be even as important as training itself, until recently there was not a clear understanding of what constitutes an organizational transfer climate.

Diagnosing Learning Transfer System Problems

The first step in improving transfer is an accurate diagnosis of the factors inhibiting transfer. Holton, Bates, and Ruona (2000) have developed a diagnostic tool to help organizations identify these so that they can be "fixed." Their tool is the Learning Transfer System Inventory (LTSI), a well-validated and psychometrically sound instrument that assesses sixteen factors in the learning transfer system. It is designed to be as useful for practitioners as it is for researchers. Designed as a diagnostic tool, this instrument pinpoints which elements in the transfer system serve as leverage points for change (Holton 2000).

The LTSI is based on the HRD Research and Evaluation Model (Holton 1996) theoretical framework. The macrostructure of that model hypothesizes that HRD outcomes are a function of ability, motivation, and environmental influences (Noe and Schmitt 1986) at three outcome levels: learning, individual performance, and organizational performance. Secondary influences such as attitudes and personality are also included, particularly ones that impact motivation. The sixteen factors measured by the LTSI are grouped by the macrostructure of the HRD Research and Evaluation Model:

- *Ability* can be a barrier on the job or in the learning event. Two factors focus on ability to use learning on the job: the lack of opportunity to use learning, or a lack of personal capacity to try out learning. Two other factors deal with elements of the learning event that enable learners to transfer the learning. The learning content may have little perceived content validity, making it difficult for learners to understand how it relates to their jobs. Finally, it may be taught with low transfer design so that learners have little chance of turning knowledge into workplace expertise.

- *Motivation* factors comprise the second group. Workers need to have the ability to apply knowledge and the motivation to do so. Motivation has two components: (1) workers have to believe that the expended effort will change performance and (2) that changed performance leads to valued outcomes.
- *Work environment* factors comprise the third group. Research consistently shows that the work environment can be a tremendous barrier to workers' use of knowledge and expertise. Three factors deal with the worker/supervisor relationship: feedback/performance coaching about learning use; the amount of support for learning use; and the extent to which supervisors actively oppose using new knowledge and expertise. Two factors deal with the work group: peer support for using new approaches and the extent to which the group norm is openness to change. Two factors deal with the reward systems: the extent to which the outcomes for the person are either positive or negative.
- *Secondary influences* include two factors influencing motivation. Learner readiness addresses the need to prepare learners to participate meaningfully in training. Workers also need to have high performance self-efficacy, or the general belief that they *can* use learning to change their performance.

What follows is a brief description of the sixteen factors, including questions that might be used in an interview of focus group format to obtain information about each of the sixteen factors (Swanson and Holton 1999). Readers are cautioned that such data is not scientifically valid, but may be useful for initial investigations.

Ability to Use Learning

The first group is comprised of four factors that deal with the ability of the worker to use their learning on the job (Table 13.1).

TABLE 13.1. Ability to Use Learning

Potential Barrier	Definition	Audit Questions
Opportunity to use learning	The extent to which workers are provided with or obtain resources and tasks on the job enabling them to use their knowledge and expertise.	❏ Do workers have opportunities on the job to apply their knowledge and expertise? ❏ Do they have the resources needed to use their learning (equipment, information, materials, and supplies)? ❏ Are there enough funds to utilize learning? ❏ Are there enough supporting people to allow workers to implement their learning?
Personal capacity for transfer	The extent to which individuals have the time, energy and mental space in their work lives to make changes required to use learning on the job.	❏ Are workers' workloads adjusted to practice their expertise? ❏ Do workers have the personal energy to devote to new methods? ❏ Are workers' stress-levels already so high they cannot cope with more change?
Perceived content validity	The extent to which the participants judge the learning content to reflect job requirements accurately.	❏ Are the skills and knowledge taught similarly enough to performance expectations to be viewed as credible? ❏ Are they what the individual needs in order to perform more effectively? ❏ Are the instructional methods, aids, and equipment used similar to those used in the work environment?
Transfer design	The extent to which learning has been designed to match job requirements and give participants the ability to transfer learning to job application.	❏ Is the learning designed to clearly link it to on-the-job performance? ❏ Do examples, activities and exercises clearly demonstrate how to apply new knowledge and skills? ❏ Are the teaching methods used similar to the work environment?
Learner readiness	The extent to which individuals are prepared to enter and participate in learning.	❏ Did individuals have the opportunity to provide input prior to the learning intervention? ❏ Did they know what to expect? ❏ Did they understand how training was related to job-related development and work performance?

Motivation to Use Learning

Motivational factors comprise the second group (see Table 13.2). Workers, in viewing their own learning, need to have the ability to apply knowledge and the motivation to do so. Motivation has two components: First, workers have to believe that the expended effort will change performance. Then, workers have to believe that changed performance leads to outcomes they value. Workers

TABLE 13.2. Motivation to Use Learning

Potential Barrier	Definition	Audit Questions
Motivation to transfer learning	Are workers motivated to utilize their knowledge and expertise in their work?	❑ Do learners feel better able to perform? ❑ Do they plan to use their knowledge and expertise? ❑ Do workers believe their learning will help them to perform on-the-job more effectively?
Performance self-efficacy	Workers' general belief that they are able to change their performance when they want to.	❑ Do workers feel confident and self-assured about applying their abilities in their jobs? ❑ Can they overcome obstacles that hinder the use of their knowledge and skills?
Transfer effort— performance expectations	The expectation that effort devoted to use learning will lead to changes in job performance.	❑ Do workers believe that applying their knowledge and expertise will improve their performance? ❑ Do workers believe that investing effort to utilize new learning has made a difference in the past? ❑ Do workers believe that doing so will affect future productivity and effectiveness?
Performance— outcomes expectations	The expectation that changes in job performance will lead to outcomes valued by the individual.	❑ Do workers believe the application of knowledge and expertise learned will lead to personal recognition that they value? ❑ Does the organization demonstrate the link between development, performance, and recognition? ❑ Does the organization clearly articulate performance expectations and recognize individuals when they do well? ❑ Are individuals rewarded for effective and improved performance? ❑ Does the organization create an environment in which individuals feel positive about performing well?

also need to have high performance self-efficacy, which is the general belief that they *can* use learning to change their performance.

Work Environments Designed to Use Learning

The third group consists of work environment factors—system designs and rewards. Research consistently shows that the work environment can be a tremendous barrier to workers using their knowledge and expertise. Table 13.3 illustrates these factors.

Intervening to Improve Learning Transfer Systems

Mary Broad (Broad and Newstrom 1992; Broad in press) has been a leader in translating transfer research into actionable strategies. She recognized that

TABLE 13.3. Work Environment Designed to Be a Catalyst for Learning Transfer

Potential Barrier	Definition	Audit Questions
Supervisor feedback/ performance coaching	Formal and informal indicators from an organization about an individual's job performance	❏ Do individuals receive constructive input and assistance when applying new abilities or attempting to improve work performance? ❏ Do they receive informal and formal feedback from people in their work environment (peers, employees, colleagues)?
Supervisor/ manager support	The extent to which managers support and reinforce learning on-the-job.	❏ Do managers clarify performance expectations after HRD experiences? ❏ Do they identify opportunities to apply knowledge and expertise? ❏ Do they set realistic goals based on new learning? ❏ Do they work with individuals on problems encountered while applying new learning? ❏ Do they provide recognition when individuals successfully apply new learning?
Supervisor/ manager opposition	The extent to which individuals perceive negative responses from managers when applying new learning.	❏ Do managers oppose the use of new knowledge and expertise? ❏ Do managers use techniques different from those learned by workers? ❏ Do they provide negative feedback when individuals successfully apply new learning on-the-job?
Work group support	The extent to which peers reinforce and support use of learning on-the-job.	❏ Do peers mutually identify and implement opportunities to apply new knowledge and expertise? ❏ Do peers encourage the use of or expect the application of new learning? ❏ Do peers display patience with difficulties associated with applying new learning? ❏ Do peers demonstrate appreciation for the use of new expertise?
Openness to change	Are work groups perceived by individuals to resist or discourage the use of new knowledge and expertise?	❏ Do work groups actively resist change? ❏ Are they willing to invest energy to change? ❏ Do they support individuals who use new techniques?
Positive personal rewards	The degree to which applying learning on the job leads to outcomes that are positive for the individual.	❏ Does use of new learning lead to rewards such as increased productivity and work effectiveness, increased personal satisfaction, additional respect, a salary increase or reward, the opportunity to further career development plans, or the opportunity to advance in the organization?
Personal outcomes— negative.	The extent to which individuals believe that applying their knowledge and expertise will lead to negative outcomes.	❏ Does use of new learning lead to negative outcomes such as reprimands, penalties, peer resentment, too much new work, or the likelihood of not getting a raise if newly acquired expertise is used?

most of the transfer research was *not* action-oriented. She and her colleagues have devoted themselves to developing strategies to improve learning transfer systems (Broad and Newstrom 1992). Most recently, she developed a transfer system improvement process that guides practitioners through critical steps to improve transfer. (Broad in press). Figure 13.1 below shows the complete process.

They make the case that learning professionals must become *learning transfer managers* to ensure that the emphasis on transfer is shared and implemented by all stakeholders. Learning transfer (LT) managers must help all stakeholders learn the six factors supporting learning transfer. LT managers must include, as part of their management responsibilities, the education of stakeholders (managers, performers, coworkers, others) about the factors affecting performance and the oversight and tracking of those stakeholders' transfer strategies (Broad, M.L., in press).

Broad suggests that learning transfer managers are responsible for managing the steps in the process shown in Figure 13.1. Although the process often cannot be applied exactly as shown, it provides a nice framework to plan learning transfer with stakeholders and a checklist to see that "messier" processes cover all the necessary steps. Each of the steps is described below (from Broad in press).

1. Develop/Maintain Expertise As LT Manager

The LT manager needs three main areas of expertise:

- Detailed information on the industry and the organization, including:
  Major lines of business
  Market share and competition
  Regulatory/legislative climate
  Industry issues and trends

- Human Performance Technology (HPT) skills, with emphasis on performance and transfer concepts and best practices:
  Performance analysis, to identify *current performance* and compare it to *desired performance*
  Gap and cause analysis, to analyze the *gap* between current and desired performance and to identify *root causes* for the gap
  Intervention selection and design, to identify and design *appropriate learning interventions* to close the gap
  Transfer concepts and stakeholder roles, to identify effective *transfer strategies* by stakeholders

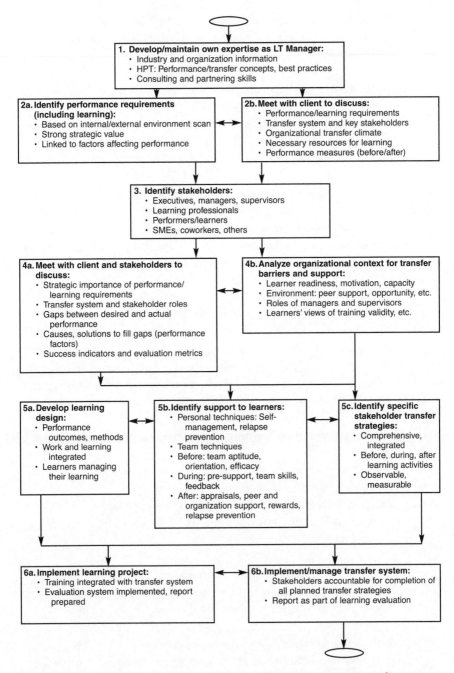

Fig. 13.1. A model for managing the organizational learning/transfer system.

NOTE: The LT manager shares steps 2a–6b with client and other stakeholders.

SOURCE: Broad in press.

Project implementation, to *manage* the entire learning intervention
Evaluation, to determine the extent to which the intervention is
successful

- Consulting and partnering skills:
  Networking
  Identifying and gaining clients
  Communication
  Consultation process

2A. IDENTIFY PERFORMANCE REQUIREMENTS (INCLUDING LEARNING)

Stakeholders can help identify which factors affecting performance may be
present or missing, including learning. Strategically important learning requirements (and other interventions) are then discussed with potential clients
(step 2b).

2B. MEET WITH CLIENT

The LT manager meets with a client who has a real stake in the strategic
learning requirement. When learning is required, the LT manager emphasizes
to the client that cohesive support by all major stakeholders is essential to ensure learning, transfer of new skills to job performance, and desired organizational results. This discussion should include:

- Performance and related learning requirements with strong strategic
  value
- Transfer process and key stakeholders
- Organizational transfer climate
- Necessary resources to support a learning/transfer project
- Measures of successful performance after learning, and baseline per-
  formance data before learning

3. IDENTIFY STAKEHOLDERS

The LT manager and client identify major stakeholders concerned about
strategic goals and performance required to achieve them, including:

- Executives, managers, and performers' supervisors
- Performance consultants and other learning professionals (including
  the LT manager)

- Performers who are potential learners
- Subject matter experts (SMEs) and performers' coworkers
- Internal or external suppliers and customers
- Other interested parties (e.g., union representatives, quality control specialists)

4A. MEET WITH CLIENT AND STAKEHOLDERS

The client and LT manager meet with all major stakeholders to discuss the importance of transfer in accomplishing strategic goals, including:

- Strategic importance of performance and learning requirements
- The transfer system and stakeholders' roles
- Gaps between desired and actual performance
- Causes and solutions to fill gaps
- Success indicators and evaluation metrics

These discussions provide information for step 4b.

4B. ANALYZE ORGANIZATIONAL CONTEXT FOR TRANSFER BARRIERS AND SUPPORT

The LT manager and client explore the organizational context for the desired performance. This includes all of the sixteen factors discussed above. The questions presented are ideal for leading these discussions. All analytical information is shared among LT manager, client, and stakeholders to gain agreement on the intervention and necessary transfer support. (This information is also useful in step 4a.)

5A. DEVELOP LEARNING DESIGN

Based on the previous steps, the LT manager develops the learning design:

- Desired performance outcomes and learners' methods for achievement
- Real work incorporated into learning exercises and practice
- Learning activities integrated into the workplace
- Learners managing their learning

5B. IDENTIFY SUPPORT FOR LEARNERS

The LT manager and learner representatives identify useful learning transfer strategies before, during, and after learning activities. Strategies include:

- Personal techniques such as self-management and relapse prevention
- Team techniques, including:
    Before: assessments of team aptitude, orientation to transfer, efficacy in transfer
    During: advance organizers, team skills training, feedback on training performance
    After: performance appraisals, support from peers and organization, rewards, relapse prevention

5C. IDENTIFY SPECIFIC STAKEHOLDER TRANSFER STRATEGIES

The LT manager helps each stakeholder identify strategies to support learning transfer before, during, and after learning activities. These are integrated with the learning design (5a) and other support for learners (5b), and give learners resources, opportunities for application, incentives, and rewards. The strategies chosen:

- Are comprehensive and integrated
- Occur before, during, and after learning activities
- Are observable and measurable

Broad and Newstrom (1992) is an excellent compilation of a wide variety of very specific and practical strategies that can be used before, during, and after learning with trainers, trainees, and managers in this step.

6A. IMPLEMENT LEARNING PROJECT

The LT manager begins delivery of learning activities and implements the evaluation process.

- Training delivery is integrated with the transfer system (6b) including before/during/after stakeholder strategies.
- Evaluation data are gathered and a report prepared for all stakeholders, including descriptions of all transfer strategies and assessments of their effectiveness.

6B. IMPLEMENT/MANAGE TRANSFER SYSTEM

The LT manager and stakeholders implement all planned transfer strategies (before, during, and after learning activities) and monitor their effectiveness.

- Stakeholders are accountable for the completion of all planned transfer strategies.
- The LT manager prepares a report on the use and effectiveness of transfer strategies that is included in the evaluation report (6a).

The final report, with evaluation data, becomes an effective "marketing tool" to demonstrate the effectiveness of collaborative stakeholder strategies to support transfer.

Completion of steps 6a and 6b can be considered the end of the learning transfer project. However, in an actual complex organizational system, improved performance in one area usually leads to requests for improved performance—and transfer support—in other areas.

Closing the Transfer Gap

Holton and Baldwin (in press) introduced a new concept in the transfer literature called *transfer distance*. Figure 13.2 below illustrates this new concept. At the far left (step 1), you can see the basic type of learning—acquiring knowledge. At the far right (step 6), you see the maximum level of transfer, called far transfer. Far transfer occurs when an employee applies new learning not only to the immediate task the training was designed for but generalizes the learning to new or different tasks. Near transfer occurs when an employee applies the learning only to the immediate tasks focused upon in training. In between these two ends of the process are intermediate steps.

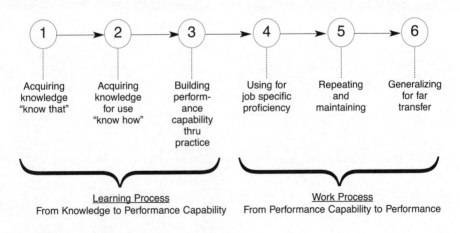

Fig. 13.2. Transfer distance model.

SOURCE: **Holton and Baldwin in press.**

Summary

Fundamentally, all transfer improvement strategies are concerned with bridging the gap. Some do it through learning design that makes learning more realistic and job-like so that steps 1, 2, and 3 are all incorporated into the learning. The traditional education model of training included only step 1 and left trainees on their own to learn how to apply the material. The newest learning methods, such as action learning, are an effort to prepare learners fully for job application. Some even make learning and the job occur simultaneously to close the gap even further.

The point of this is found in the following questions to ask yourself:

- How big is the transfer "gap" in your organization?
- When trainees leave your training, are they at step 1, or step 2, or step 3?
- What type of transfer are you expecting—step 4, step 5, or all the way to step 6?
- Are your training designs consistent with your transfer expectations?
- Is bridging the transfer gap being left to chance, or are you managing the bridge building?

The bigger the gap, the more urgent should be your efforts to put transfer management processes in place. Remember that the transfer gap will cost you "real" money if unbridged.

14

Training and Development Budgets

Training and development managers prepare budgets about the same way as any other manager prepares budgets—with a few special considerations.

Of course, the items T&D managers include in the budget are training-related—and there is always the issue of trainees' salaries. Do they show up in the T&D budget or in the budgets for the trainees' regular departments? Then there is the ambiguity of forecasting performance problems that haven't yet happened. How can anybody possibly forecast the cost of solving a problem that hasn't yet revealed itself, much less been scoped? Then, finally, there is the sensitive issue of trying to assign dollar values to human performance, a process that frightens many people and usually angers humanists.

This urge to demonstrate a return on the training investment is not new—but it is certainly growing in intensity. More and more T&D managers are learning that their job security (to say nothing of their own satisfaction with their achievements) depends heavily upon their ability to calculate the cost of performance deficiencies and the cost of correcting them.

In short, good T&D budgeting puts the T&D dollar where the organization will find the biggest return on its investment.

To some degree, this implies a change in the way T&D managers talk to top management about the T&D function in the way they "sell" their services. Management doesn't care about test results. They care about the results employees achieve by using their training; that's the only way to "sell" training to management.

Therefore, in this chapter we will look at some general "rules of thumb" for planning the volume of T&D activity. Next, we will consider a process for computing the cost of performance problems. Then, to determine whether training is or is not a cost-effective activity, we will finally look at formulae for computing the cost of training.

By doing these things, we will have answered our question, "What's special about Training and Development budgets?"

General Estimating Policies

How much of the organization's total budget should be invested in T&D activities?

For normal operations, most organizations allocate between about 2 and 4 percent of their total employee salary cost to T&D. World class organizations and those heavily dependent on human expertise (e.g., consulting, software development) allocate as much as 5 to 6 percent of their total employee salary cost. Of course, there are some exceptional circumstances. New plants will need much higher allocations for their first six months. When a totally new product or service is introduced, the allocation may double for anywhere from three to six months.

Then there are unusual circumstances in which offices or entire plants may shut down for training. Plant start-ups, retooling, new product lines, installation of totally new processes or procedures, a new management team; all these might require training as a precursor to production. Shutdowns mean extremely high costs—100 percent during the training period. However, budgets are usually annualized, so the ultimate costs are more normal, though somewhat swollen.

The same thing happens when a distressed department uses organizational development (OD). The T&D manager should budget (or counsel the client to budget) at least five times the usual training allocation. After all, the major energy of the top-salaried people will be devoted to analysis of their mission, structures, processes, and relationships. It's quite probable that eventually *all* employees will become involved, so there are periods where redeveloping the organization, not production, is the focus. In this sense, the OD intervention is different from a shutdown only to the degree to which normal work continues.

Another unusual condition arises when an organization discovers almost too late that it has been neglecting its management development. It is not terribly rare for an organization or a department to discover that huge percentages of its management will be retiring within a very few years. The ensuing extra effort to train replacements demands extra budget allocations. The actual amount will depend upon the numbers to be educated and developed. It is not unusual, however, for such crises to require from five to six times the normal management development expenditures.

T&D Staff Size

To answer that, we must look at the total organization and determine the numbers of people whose major contribution is training or developing others. We will (1) make no effort to determine whether they are T&D Department employees or line employees doing T&D work, and (2) consider the total manpower posts devoted to T&D, even though they may involve several people working part-time to fill up one post.

The best strategy is to obtain benchmarking data for companies similar to yours. Many industry trade associations collect and distribute such data. The American Society for Training and Development (ASTD) *(www.astd.org)* produces several annual reports and offers a free benchmarking service to companies that provide data for their database. The Saratoga Institute *(www.saratogainstitute.com)* also publishes a great deal of statistical data on training and development.

Such data are useful only as "benchmarks" and must be augmented with reliable signals from the top of the organization. This is just one more reason why the T&D manager needs to be—and actually is—increasingly close to the people who make the major planning decisions. By both physical and organizational proximity, the T&D or the Human Resource Director is indeed one of the strategic planners.

But broad, sweeping plans and policies are ultimately validated and carried out through details, one step at a time. The discovery of a performance problem, current or imminent because of new programs, is the first moment the T&D manager is certain about the volume of work the T&D specialists will face. As a result, flexibility in staff size is highly desirable.

The variation between "highs" and "lows" isn't devastating. There is more than one way for the T&D staff to absorb the fluctuation:

- Since the T&D department needs more than normal allocations for educating its own staff, sometimes that can be slowed down to take care of unexpected peak workloads.
- People with T&D experience can be rotated into other managerial positions as part of their own education and development. When the peak occurs, they can be temporarily reassigned to the T&D project.
- Outside resources (consultants, contract instructors, or graduate students studying T&D in nearby universities) can temporarily augment the staff during heavy workloads.
- Temporary staff members, employed for one project only or for a limited number of projects, can lighten a heavy workload. These people also learn a great deal about when to train and how to do it well; they are thus rich resources as strong allies in other parts of the organization.

Each of these is a useful option—but the best way to avoid unexpected peaks in workload is (repeat!) for the T&D manager to be in constant communication with the chief executives of the organization. This permits an early warning system that not only protects the T&D department against surprises but also allows the T&D manager to counsel the executives about the real human resource costs of contemplated policy changes and programs.

The initial question from most T&D managers is, "What will it cost to run the department?" That can't be answered until an estimate is made about how many performance problems deserve solving. Not always, but usually, the basis for deciding whether a performance problem is worth solving is the cost-effectiveness. For this reason, the most pervasive budgeting question the T&D manager asks is, "What will it cost this organization to keep employees performing at standard?"

A good specific question is this: "What is this performance problem costing us?" The answers to that question are not always easy to discover—but they are usually there. Let's look at the process for getting the answers.

Computing the Cost of Performance Deficiencies

As we've noted, every employee performs a certain number of tasks. The successful completion of each task represents one accomplishment every time it's done. The unit may be a letter written, a shipment packed, a grievance handled, a decision made, a customer order taken, or an unhappy client mollified. When a performance problem arises, those accomplishments are either missing or substandard: The unit of satisfactory accomplishment is not there as an "output."

The formula for costing out performance deficiencies is first to determine the unit. The second step is to determine the cost of that unit. The third step is to multiply the cost-per-unit by the number of defective units.

Let's take a simple example. Sales agents consistently make errors in listing product categories at the cash register. Twenty percent of their daily total of 160 slips must be returned. That means we have 32 defective units each day, 160 per week, or 8,000 in a fifty-week year. Our study shows that it takes an auditor fifteen minutes to correct each error. Then supervisors are expected to follow up, spending an average of ten minutes making sure the clerks use the proper code next time. If the clerks earn $10 per hour, and if auditors and supervisors average $20 per hour, what are the salary costs to the organization?

Well, we can calculate the cost by adding three elements:

Fifteen minutes of auditor time costs one-fourth of $20, or $5.00.
Ten minutes of supervisory time costs one-sixth of $2, or $3.33.
Ten minutes of clerk time costs one-sixth of $10, or $1.67.

In making this estimate, we will ignore the time the clerk spent making the wrong entry. Nor will we try to compute the consequences, which are probably bad data in inventory control systems. We'll stick to the salary costs of the deficiency. We add the three amounts:

$$\$5.00 + 3.33 + 1.67 = \$10 \text{ per unit.}$$

We know that on our staff we have 8,000 defective units per year, so we multiply 8,000 times $10. This tells us that the performance problem is costing $80,000 dollars annually. We won't know whether it's worth correcting until we estimate the cost of the training. It may be that it's better to install some sort of job aid for the clerks to check.

Not all units of performance are equally easy to cost out. For one reason, there are hidden costs. This means that the computation and analysis just to get the unit cost is more complex. For another reason, some units don't immediately reveal their costs. How do you put a price tag on the loss of a valued customer due to a rude employee? On the loss of morale due to a flagrant misuse of discipline? On the confusion resulting from a distorted or lost message from management?

T&D managers who *want* to cost out these apparently ambiguous deficiencies can do so.

"Wanting to do so" is the most important element. For that lost customer, it's possible to use standard figures: What's the profit from the average customer? How many do we estimate we have lost due to rudeness last year? It's easy to multiply the two figures. Or the lost message: What are some typical deficiencies that grew out of the loss? Maybe it's using an obsolete price list; maybe it's the overtime we had to pay because the swing shift didn't show up on time. The point is that where there is a will, there are data! In these days of computer-generated data, most management information systems provide more printout than people really want to have! Somewhere in that jungle of figures is the precise fact needed to put a price tag on a defective unit of performance that is just waiting for the T&D manager who *wants* to track it down!

There are two significant notes of caution in this process:

1. The figures used in computing the cost of performance deficiencies must be seen as valid by the manager who "owns" the problem.
2. The data should generally be available through normal reporting channels rather than produced by channels designed only for this study.

Nonetheless, when analyzing the cost of performance problems, one element appears in nearly all the problems: the *time* wasted by the bad performance. It's a simple step to tie behaviors into time, and time into salary. From those data, one can compute dollars-and-cents salary costs. Material costs also tend to be available in other management reporting systems. When these two factors have been accounted for, the cost-per-unit is usually pretty well established.

Both the "flagrant misuse of discipline" and the "lost message" situation can be costed out by figuring a typical amount of time lost per incident—and then estimating the number of incidents. In bad discipline, time is spent in complaining, grieving, regretting, "getting even." Similar events can be traced, as we have already done, with the lost or distorted message problems.

Granted, the *real* loss may be neither time nor money. It may be esteem and trust and loyalty and job satisfaction. Nobody denies that these are as valid as the real costs. But astute T&D managers don't try to put price tags on these human values. Rather, they make their point on what they *can* prove with the price tags that go along with the greater psychic costs.

The cost-effectiveness activity doesn't take away a thing from the humanistic enthusiasts; it merely permits the T&D manager to justify training and development as an economic investment. In doing that, the cost-effectiveness activity also gives the data needed to make effective dollars-and-cents decisions about whether solving the problem is a sound investment—and if so, which problems are most damaging.

The point is that when T&D managers genuinely wish to do cost-effectiveness studies, they can do so. The data are usually there. The technology exists. To review, let's go through the steps of the process:

1. Identify a single unit of defective performance.
2. Calculate (or make the best possible estimate) the cost of one unit.
3. Count or calculate the number of defective units—usually for one year.
4. Multiply the unit cost by the number of defective units. This will give the annual cost of the performance problem.

Once the T&D manager, acting as consultant to the organization, has computed the cost of the deficiency, the next step is to compute the cost of the program.

Computing the Cost of Training

Training is really a relatively expensive solution for performance problems. It contrasts sharply with the cost of other solutions:

1. *Feedback* is often a low-cost solution because the implementation mechanisms are so simple. They can frequently be installed even in

large organizations for just a few cents per worker and following only a few days of design.

2. *Job aids,* once the task analysis is complete, can be printed for a few pennies or dollars. Once installed at the workplace, they can guide the performer as a substitute for training. (For very complex tasks or operations, they often supplement training as an effective post-training "handout" or follow-up.)

3. *Job engineering* takes longer and is more expensive to install because it requires thorough task analysis and involves enlisting management and worker support for the new distribution of tasks and responsibilities. However, it is still often less costly to do this than to design, conduct, and evaluate the recurring training programs made necessary by "undoable" jobs that cause friction, stress, and/or boredom.

4. *Contingency management* is time consuming, and may require much greater expenditure during the analysis. However, new contingencies can be installed with relatively low costs—if the positive reinforcers selected for contingencies are integral to the work itself and not expensive external incentives.

5. *Organizational development,* as we have noted, is costly in management time, but it requires relatively few materials. Furthermore, it often involves relatively small, albeit "costly," numbers of participants who represent the top of the salary scale. However, if it succeeds, the OD intervention should prevent many future performance problems.

Training is expensive because to budget for the *total* training program the T&D manager must include such items as program production, trainee costs, conducting the program, evaluation costs, and follow-up activities.

Salary and material costs during the design phase of a training program add up fast. Trainee costs (travel, materials, and salary) add up even faster; after all, there are far more trainees than there are instructional designers. In fact, trainee costs are really the most significant cost of training, not the direct cost of running a program.

The T&D manager is concerned about controlling costs wherever and whenever possible. On one level, this means that the monies that are actually spent are consistent with the monies budgeted for that purpose. On another level, there is concern to keep each expenditure appropriate to its contribution to the entire T&D effort.

Production costs can be divided into two categories: Staff and Materials. Staff costs must include time spent in "front-end" analysis; this means the consultation about the real cause of the performance problem and the appropriate solutions. It also includes the staff time spent in developing the materials used in the solution.

How much does "analysis" cost? What does it involve? Joe Harless, a major performance technologist, has pointed out that "An ounce of analysis is worth a pound of objectives." Other authorities have said that the analysis activity looks like this:

Planning	5%
Task analysis (defining the standard)	30%
Developing objectives	5%
Developing evaluation (criterion test)	10%
Validating test	10%
Developing materials	15%
Trying out the program	10%
Revising and retesting	10%
Publishing (or overseeing it)	5%

You may wonder at the low percentage of time given to "developing objectives." Consider, though, that this means merely casting the task analysis (or standards) into useful phraseology. The total time devoted to defining the desired learning really comes to 45 percent. It includes task analysis, developing objectives, and developing the criterion test. All those activities aid the process of pinpointing the desired outcomes of the training.

The "front-end analysis" detailed in that list includes some items which do not apply to non-training solutions. Nor does the list reveal how much of the *total* training cost goes to analysis.

A checklist documenting all the costs of training might look like this:

TABLE 14.1. A Formula for Computing Training Production Costs

	Item	Formula	Total
Staff Costs:			
Salaries:	Consulting Designing Conducting Evaluating	Number of people times median salary times number of hours on the project _____	
Fees:	Outside designers and consultants	Total fees and expenses paid out	_____
Travel:	Tickets	Total from expense reports	_____
	Other expenses	Total from expense reports, per diem times number of days	_____
Overhead:		Use standard organization figures; if none exist, use 100 percent of base salary	_____

(continued on next page)

TABLE 14.1. *(continued)*

Item	Formula	Total
Materials:		
Audiovisuals	Actual costs to purchase or produce	_____
Manuals and materials	Local figures; public or in-house printshop quotations	_____
Announcements	Local figures needed here	_____
Special equipment	Total purchase price; normally amoritized over 10 years	_____
	Total cost to produce the training program:	_____

Development time depends heavily upon the format in which the training is presented. A convenient rule of thumb uses this formula to estimate the ratio between production costs and class time:

TABLE 14.2. Guidelines for Estimating Course Development Time

If the format is	Then figure this many hours of production for each hour of presentation
Technical formal courses	5 to 15
Self-contained for hand-off to other instructors	50 to 100
Conventional management development	20 to 30
Programmed instruction	80 to 120
Technical on-site	1 to 3
Computer-assisted instruction	Up to 350

Production costs are not limited to design. Instructors must also prepare to teach. This doesn't mean those minutes or hours spent the day before class— moving the furniture, setting up projectors, or putting paper and pencils at each learner position. This refers to the instructors' activity in preparing themselves to teach the program. In other words, it refers to eliminating their own DKs (deficiency of knowledge) about the particular program. They go like this:

TABLE 14.3. Guidelines for Estimating Instructor Preparation Time Based on Course Length

Does the course last	Then for each class hour, budget this many preparation hours
5 days or less?	3 hours preparation for 1 hour of teaching
Between 5 and 10 days?	2.5 hours preparation for 1 teaching hour
Over 10 days?	2 hours preparation per hour of teaching

Another approach to the instructor-preparation estimating involves the methods used in the program rather than the length of the course. When methods are considered, the estimates might be more like this:

TABLE 14.4. Guidelines for Estimating Instructor Preparation Time Based on Instructional Method

If the methods are	Then for each class hour, budget this many preparation hours
A tell-and-show by instructor	5 to 10
Mediated tell-and-show	1 (to preview the program)
Group discussion	Less than 1
Action or experiential	1.5 (The instructor should *do* the role-plays, games, or whatever; then analyze the probable dynamics.)

When the program requires or permits a formal tryout period, there may be unusual costs for travel and facilities. They are probably a good investment. Few training programs can be expected to move from the mind of the designer to the classroom without some revision and improvement. The same may be said when feedback mechanisms, contingency management, or job engineering are the solutions to the performance problem.

Such tryouts bring another cost: the salary of the "test" or "control" population. T&D managers with "button-down" budgets want to charge those salaries to the production costs of the program.

That raises the entire issue of trainees' salaries. Should salary costs be considered part of the cost of training? This issue takes us to the budget for "conducting the training."

If T&D managers want rigorous proof that their programs pay their own way, they usually insist on including trainees' salaries as part of the program costs. Even if there is no formal paper transfer of these funds, they want to know exactly what total amount of human resources must be invested to improve those resources. Some include fringe benefits; others include the downtime—production lost because the participant was off the job. A thorough cost estimate for conducting training looks like this:

TABLE 14.5. A Formula for Computing the Costs of Conducting Training

Trainee Costs:	Total
Number of trainees (by paygroup) x median salary x training hours	_____
Number of trainees x hourly fringe benefit charges x hours	_____

(continued on next page)

Table 14.5. *(continued)*

Trainee Costs:	Total
Travel costs: Total from expense reports, or median cost x number of trainees	———
Per diem: Total from expense reports, or median allowance x the number of trainees x number of days	———
Student materials: Unit costs x number of trainees	———
Trainee replacement costs: Number of hours x median salary	———
Lost production: Value-per-unit x the number of lost units, or value-per-unit x the reduced production	———
Faculty costs:	
Number of trainers x number of hours x median salary	———
Travel costs: Total tickets, or median x number of trainers	———
Per diem: Total from expense reports, or median allowance x number of trainers x number of days	———
Special equipment or services:	
Rental of equipment: Total charges. If purchased, amortize over 10 years	———

The cost of evaluating training may be considered as a distinct phase, or as items in the earlier phases. The important thing is to make the budget reflect the cost of evaluation. Documenting the costs further increases the probability that evaluation will be done—and that the total training budget will honestly reflect the total cost of training.

A document for estimating evaluation costs would probably look like this:

TABLE 14.6. Cost of Evaluating Training

Item	Formula	Total
Salaries:		
Design:		
Selecting criteria		
Creating instruments	Number of hours x median salary	———
Data sources:	Number of hours x median salary	———
Graduates and managers		
Interviewers (if applicable)	Number of hours x median salary	———
Data analysis	Number of hours x median salary	———
Materials:		
Printing	Actual local costs	———
Mailing	Units x two-way postage	———

(continued on next page)

TABLE 14.6. *(continued)*

Item	Formula	Total
Salaries:		
Travel (if interviews are used):		
Tickets	Actual totals	_____
Expenses	Actual totals or allowance x number of days	_____
	Total cost of evaluating the training:	_____

The total cost of the program is, of course, computed by adding the production costs, conducting costs, and evaluation costs. As the next summary chart shows, it is also possible to compare and contrast programs by computing the cost per trainee, the cost per hour, and the cost per trainee hour:

TABLE 14.7. Total Training Costs

Cost Items	Dollars	Cost Per Trainee	Cost Per Hour	Cost Per Trainee Hour
		Divide $ by number of trainees	*Divide $ by number of hours*	*Divide $ by (number of trainees) x (number of hours)*
Production costs:				
Staff	_____	_____	_____	_____
Material	_____	_____	_____	_____
Total training costs				
Cost Items	Dollars	Cost Per Trainee: Divide $ by number of trainees	Cost Per Hour: Divide $ by number of hours	Cost Per Trainee Hour: Divide $ by (number of trainees) x (number of hours)
Course conduct costs:				
Trainee	_____	_____	_____	_____
Faculty	_____	_____	_____	_____
Equipment/services	_____	_____	_____	_____
Evaluation costs:				
Salaries	_____	_____	_____	_____
Materials	_____	_____	_____	_____
Travel	_____	_____	_____	_____
Totals:	_____	_____	_____	_____

How Budgeting Helps the "Go/No Go" Decision

By now it should be quite apparent that the budgeting process is another decisionmaking instrument for the T&D manager. To decide whether to pursue a solution to a recognized performance problem to find more economical solutions—these questions can be answered by good budgeting practice.

For every performance problem, the T&D manager asks, "Is this problem costing a significant amount of dollars?" If the answer is a yes, the next inquiry should be, "Can we solve the problem by investing fewer dollars than the problem is costing us?" That answer sometimes dictates a decision either to live with the problem or to consider less costly alternative solutions.

Schematically, the process looks something like Figure 14.1. As the chart indicates, not all performance problems should be solved. The T&D manager has a major consultative responsibility to help management recognize this condition when it is true to help invest the T&D dollars and energy in problems with the highest payoff.

It doesn't necessarily follow that all decisions rest on cost-effectiveness. Sometimes the emotional strain of an unsolved problem is just too great to bear. The human beings involved with the problem cannot go on living with it—even though there is no economic loss from the problem. There may also be legal reasons for proceeding with training which is not cost-effective.

Summary

In any event, the T&D manager must be concerned with the dollars-and-cents dimension of human resource development; those who ignore the economic impact of performance problems build their entire T&D operation on a shaky foundation. Continued refusal to confront the cost-effectiveness issue can jeopardize entire T&D departments—and even worse, entire careers. This is especially true during hard times, when we hear the lament "Training is the first thing to go around here!"

However, when T&D managers insist upon rigorous economic analysis of performance deficiencies, such budget cuts are minimized or eliminated. In organizations where T&D managers perform a solid, accurate cost analysis, training budgets tend to remain stable, and even to grow when profits sag. Why?

If the T&D manager insists upon a cost-effective operation of programs that enhance productivity (and probably the quality of work life while doing that!) then chief executives will probably consider T&D dollars as investments, not expenses. The prevailing philosophy is that dollars invested in human productivity will ultimately produce a more cost-effective operation, and therefore greater security for all the "human resources" in the organization.

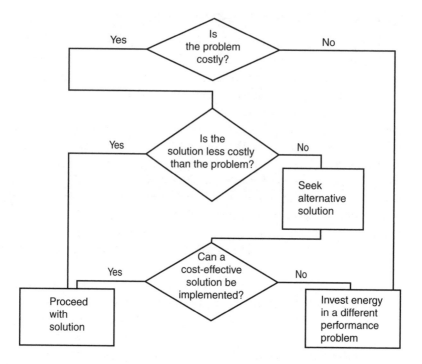

Fig. 14.1.

The go/no go decision process.

Measuring Training and Development

At least four people have good reasons for measuring T&D activities. Learners certainly want to know about their progress toward objectives. Instructors can intelligently modify and improve their own performance only by measuring learners' progress. T&D managers, knowing that learning is the product of their subsystem, have compelling reasons to measure. And finally, client-managers need measurement as an indication that they're solving or eliminating performance problems and getting something back on the training investment.

What Is Measurement?

First, let's distinguish between measurement and evaluation. Measurement is the process of gathering data; evaluation is the process of making judgments about those data.

Stated formally, measurement is the act of assigning numerals to processes or events or items by using some consistent set of rules. To evaluate, it is not necessary to measure; that is, we can make judgments about the beauty of a landscape without measuring the distance between trees and clouds. However, if we wish to make sound judgments about an organizational operation, hard data are necessary. We must count some objective evidence of conditions. Thus, evaluation based on measurement has definite advantages:

- It reduces the possibility of disagreement between evaluators.
- It provides concrete feedback about what the program has achieved. If appropriately used throughout the training, it also provides continuous data about how the learning is progressing.
- It permits positive comparison of pre- and postproblem status.

Evaluation involves making judgments about ideas, works, solutions, methods, or materials. It involves the use of criteria. When applied to determining the effectiveness of training, evaluation therefore would depend upon measuring the conditions caused by the problem, the progress made by learners in acquiring behaviors to solve the problem, the application of new behavior, and the impact of that application upon the problem.

Let's identify measurement and evaluation in a typical T&D program. Suppose the Manager of Collections comes to the T&D manager, saying that the collection letters are pretty bad. "How bad are they?" asks the T&D manager.

"Here's how bad!" comes the reply. "We write one hundred twenty collection letters every day. We get some kind of payment from only eighteen. That's intolerable!" In this scenario, there has been measurement. Someone determined the daily output; someone counted the responses. That's measurement. But the Manager of Collections commented, "Here's how bad!" and "That's intolerable!" These are evaluations.

The process of measuring should be integral to all T&D functions. Without measurement, there is no positive assurance that the ensuing judgments are accurate. Without data, there is no proof that a real performance problem exists. Without measurement, there is no assurance that T&D efforts have really achieved their objectives or that they have really paid their way by returning to the organization values in excess of the expenditures. Data is essential for the T&D manager to make good decisions. Continued existence and future budgets depend on gathering relevant and accurate data on which to make intelligent decisions.

If we think of the acronym ME for Measurement and Evaluation, we have an appropriate symbol. "ME" is a selfish, first-person word. However, it is wise selfishness to measure and evaluate at all phases of the T&D cycle (Figure 15.1). Let's examine that process in more detail.

Scales of Measurement

Skill in applying statistical methods is a great asset for the T&D manager who wishes to demonstrate beyond all doubt that T&D programs (not coincidence) have caused changes. Larger T&D departments employ such a statistical specialist. Smaller ones access similar experts employed in other parts of the organization. If the organization has nobody qualified to supply this statistical consulting service, outside help is usually available through local colleges and universities.

However, a great deal of effective measurement can be achieved without professional help. Quite clearly, the first step is to determine what you're going to measure. "Units of performance" is the inevitable answer in T&D measurements. The Manager of Collections counted letters written and payments received. A

1. DETERMINATION OF A
   DEFECTIVE BASELINE

BASELINE NUMBER ONE

6. SYSTEM MEASUREMENT
   AND EVALUATION

?

Someone counts on-the-job
performance
and calculates   BASELINE NUMBER TWO
a new baseline.
Hopefully, it's not defective
at all! The ultimate evaluation
is, "Did the situation improve
enough to pay for the training?"

Someone had to count incidents of
performance (by a group or by an individual) to determine for certain that
the situation exists, and that it exists
to a degree that is serious or intolerable.

2. ESTABLISHING LEARNING
   OBJECTIVES

5A. AND FOR BOTH ANSWERS:

Is that good enough? Is
performance at standard?

If there is to be a measurement,
someone must make sure that the
objectives involve observable actions and *measurable* criteria. Only
then can anybody count the learning
accomplishments.

5. ON THE JOB MEASUREMENT

	For the
For	*trained*
individuals:	*population:*
"How often and	"How often and
how well did I?"	how well did
	they?"

3. CONDUCTING THE LEARNING
   (CHANGE) PROGRAM

There are both measurement and
evaluation during training. Both
learners and instructors measure
the number of correct units to
answer the question, "How am I doing?" They examine their feelings to
answer questions like, "How am I
feeling?" and "Are my feelings aiding
or impeding my learning?"

4. TERMINAL TESTING

This is a job tryout, so both
learners and instructors can
test the ability to perform all
the objectives to all the
criteria. Learners can answer the question, "Can I?"
Instructors get answers to
the question, "Can they?"

Fig. 15.1.

The ME cycle—measurement and evaluation.

shop operation might count and classify such things as defective units, accidents, and time lost due to accidents. Sales departments can count sales made, calls completed, volume of orders. In measuring management performance, there are such things as grievances, decisions, counseling sessions, turnover, budgets planned, budgets adhered to—and, above all, total production.

The next step is to select the scale to be used in the measurement.

Nominal scales are often seen in T&D measurement. They offer a simple "classify-and-count" process. Nominal scales permit the measurer to classify "satisfactory" and "defective" units. Such a simple scale permits only a limited analysis—but those limits are broad enough to tell T&D specialists and client/managers what they want to know.

From nominal scales we legitimately arrive at totals, modes, and medians.

Nobody needs a lesson in how to compute totals, but modes and medians are technical terms. Let's define them: The mode is, as the name implies, the most frequent occurrence; the median is the center number in a series.

Thus if we measure the seniority of a group of trainees, our tally might look like this:

TABLE 15.1. Example of a Simple Nominal Scale

In Service	Number of Occurrences (f = frequency)	
Less than 1 year	⊬⊬	5
Between 1 and 2 years	///	3
Between 2 and 3 years	//	2
Between 3 and 4 years	////	4
Between 4 and 5 years	/	1
5 years or more	⊬⊬ ////	9

The mode is quite clearly, "five years or more of service," because more people fall into that group than into any other group in the tally. The median seniority is "between three and four years." Why? Because that group is the midpoint; there are as many trainees with less seniority (ten) as there are with more seniority—also ten. That is, the same number of people is on each side of the "median" category.

In nominal scales, when measuring the situation before and after a T&D effort, the mode and the median represent legitimate indices. An average, or mean, is not a valid index when using a nominal scale.

Ordinal scales are more useful in measuring such "invisible" elements as perceptions or values. Ordinal scales put items into a rank order. They tell who has more or less of something, or which values rank highest. For example, in determining training needs, T&D managers sometimes hand line managers a list of behavioral objectives with instructions to rank them from first to last in "importance for your subordinates."

Or one might ask students in a Leadership Workshop to rank these five skills by putting a number 1 by the most vital, a 2 by the next most vital, and so on until you have placed a 5 by the least important skill:

Clear communications _____
Counseling _____
Delegating _____
Time management _____
Problem solving _____

Ordinal scales are extremely useful in post-training feedback. Graduates can indicate which of the acquired skills they value most, and so on down to where they designate "no value" in their on-the-job application. In such feedback, ordinal and nominal scales can be effectively combined. Graduates can also indicate how often they have used each of the new behaviors. This can be done in one of two ways: feedback forms that are tallied at short intervals, or perceptual to the best of your memory estimates.

In the feedback sheet, a typical form merely lists the objectives of the training. Graduates check off each time they use the behavior. Such forms are submitted to the immediate "boss" rather than to the T&D department. After the boss has analyzed the on-the-job application, two things happen. First comes positive reinforcement and counseling. Second, the sheets are forwarded to the T&D department, where organizational trends can be established and analyzed.

To review: The tallies represent nominal scales; the rank ordering is an ordinal scale activity. Ordinal scales also provide data, which may legitimately provide medians and modes but not means.

Interval scales are used on such measurement tools as yardsticks and thermometers. As the title implies, they measure distances between phenomena; they measure intervals. Accurate interval scales follow one important principle: The interval between checkpoints is always exactly equal to the interval between other checkpoints. If the distance between the 11 and the 12 on your ruler isn't precisely the same distance as the interval between the 10 and the 11, your ruler is faulty. One degree of temperature on the thermometer must be exactly the same as another degree. If it isn't, you may be sicker than you think!

A major problem with past T&D measurement has been the frequent use of interval scales on which the intervals were not defined—much less equal. The typical end-of-training form measures accurately when it asks for opinions; it is only pretending to measure legitimately when it asks for numbers on a scale posing as an interval scale—but it isn't. To compound the confusion, many T&D managers take the data from non-equal interval scales and average it. Remember the hypothetical case we examined about the two sessions of the same course with the same average score!

When using legitimate interval scales, what legitimate mathematical functions may we properly perform? Modes, percentiles, and deviations are legitimate. So are means, *if* the intervals are fixed and equal. Since that list includes two new terms, let's examine the concept of percentiles and deviations.

Parents may have been told that their child is in the second quartile on a given achievement test. What does that mean? It means that of all the students taking the test, 50 percent were in lower quartiles—and 25 percent were in the higher or top quartile. Quartiles divide a population into four groups of equal size. *Percentiles* are more precise. If a child is in the 99th percentile, 99 out of every 100 children earned a lower test score. Percentiles simply show a person's position in a population of 100.

More useful is the concept of *deviation*. It merely shows how far one unit deviates from the average unit. Deviations are not generally meaningful in themselves—only in comparison to other deviations. They cannot be calculated unless there is a legitimate average, or mean, from which to operate.

Let's take an example to illustrate their importance. Assume that you have just become the T&D manager and are looking over the ratings given two recent sessions of an introductory management program. The previous T&D manager used a five-point scale to measure satisfaction with the course. You note that each session scored an average, or mean rating, of 3.15. This strikes you as unusual, so you compile a distribution tally of all the ratings for each session. Here is what your tally reveals:

TABLE 15.2. Why Frequencies Tell More Than Just Reporting the Mean

Rated as	Session 1 (f)		Session 2 (f)	
5	// ###	7		0
4	////	4	////	4
3	/	1	### ### ###	15
2	/	1	/	1
1	// ###	7		0
		N = 20		N = 20

One look at the raw data shows that the two sessions were remarkably different in perceived experiences—yet the averaging shows them to be identical.

In statistical terms, the standard deviation of session 1 is much larger than session 2, indicating wider disparity in opinion.

Finally, there are *ratio scales*. They can tell variability from an absolute condition. This implies the necessity of an absolute zero—a condition we don't see in developmental operations. Who can conceive of a person with zero intelligence, or zero achievement? However, unless one is using a legitimate ratio scale, with an absolute zero, it is really improper to make evaluations such as "Eve did twice as well on that as anyone else," or "Mary is picking this up beautifully. She did three times better today than she did yesterday!"

Baselines: What They Are and Why They Are Important

When you're taking an automobile trip, it's nice to know where you are, how far you've come, and how far it is to your destination. Does that explain the reasons for pre-, post-, and intermediate-measurement activities?

Enlightened learning systems consider such measurement, accompanied by the appropriate feedback, as integral to every growth or change process.

To measure progress toward a destination or objective, you must know where you started. "Where you start" is a baseline.

Baselines are imperative in premeasurement and postmeasurement. Somebody needs to count the number of imperfect performance units. Probably someone should place a price tag on each defective unit. There need to be figures about such things as rejects, grievances, undecided grievances, customers lost—whichever key indicator can be identified as a reliable index of the problem performance. The process for establishing baselines is simple enough—but it isn't always easy to find that key indicator. In finding indicators, acceptance by the client management is essential.

The three steps to baseline measurement involve:

1. Defining in the most precise terms possible the object to be measured. This is that key indicator: tasks accomplished; faulty accomplishments; dollars spent; dollars wasted; time wasted; numbers of students.
2. Defining the numerical scale from which the number or measurements will be assigned.
3. Making sure that the measurement procedure is analogous to reality, and that it won't be contaminated by uncontrollable variables such as strikes, floods, depressions, new policies, or new procedures.

Baselines can be established for individuals as well as for organizations. Perhaps one manager is giving a decision in only three of ten grievances per year. Maybe in a population of thirty managers, only 63 of 256 grievances per year are settled; the rest are "kicked upstairs." The T&D manager wants pre- and postbaselines to justify and evaluate the program. Instructors and learners want individual baselines so that they can set personal priorities and measure their successes. This is just a practical application of the $D = M - I$ formula. To measure deficiencies (what a trainee still needs to learn) one repeatedly measures the "I" (what the trainee now knows).

Instruments

A highway map and a mileage table help tourists measure their progress. In T&D, the tools of measurement are called "instruments."

Instruments for measuring learning usually involve some form of test, either by paper and pencil or by performance.

One obvious way to find out where an individual "is coming from" is to give a test on what that individual already knows. This is commonly called a pretest. A popular way of doing this is to administer the criterion (or final) test, or its equivalent, at the first session. If this test is explained properly, given in a goal-setting and diagnostic atmosphere, it need not be threatening. Actually, it can do more than measure; it can set expectations.

Such pre-testing assuredly lets learners and instructors form a clear picture of what they don't need to stress—because people already know it. It tells what they do need to emphasize—because so few knew the correct answer. But above all, it gives *individual* diagnostic data. Learners can pinpoint the areas they must concentrate on; instructors know how each trainee performed and where extra individual counseling will be needed. The pre-test is, in a sense, a practical application of andragogy: The experience (inventory) of learners is examined and becomes an early ingredient in the learning process.

If there are feelings about the content, or if the objectives are in the affective domain, the instrument must uncover the affective inventory; for this, several instruments are useful.

Agree/disagree tests are easy for data gathering, and they can focus the learner on key concepts. Such a test presents crucial statements to students, who then indicate how they feel about them. It's a nominal scale because the intervals are unequal. For example, a workshop for new instructors might use the instrument in Figure 15.2.

Items in agree/disagree instruments should be controversial enough to elicit a range of opinion. Eliminating the "No Opinion" option gives an even number of columns and forces respondents to "fish or cut bait" without sharp "Agree/Disagree" decisions. The use of several columns permits: (1) a measure of intensity of opinion; and (2) the possibility to graciously change an opinion as the learning proceeds.

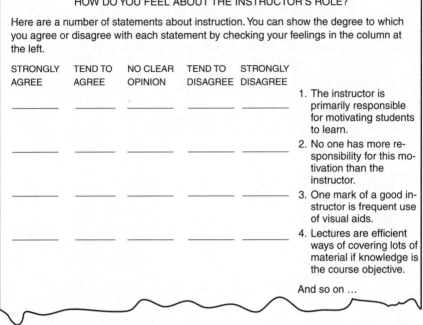

Fig. 15.2. Sample ADA test.

Another instrument for probing feelings is a variation of this instrument. Two very different opinions are presented, the students sharing their feelings on a nominal scale shown between them. Figure 15.3 presents an example.

Another way to get at opinions is a "pro-rata" scale, in which students assign portions of an established number to reflect relative preferences. For example, you want to determine how managers feel about Occupational Safety and Health laws. The question might read:

> Considering all the legislation with which you are familiar, what percent has had a GOOD effect and what percent has had a BAD effect on society. You *must* assign a total of 100 percent.

GOOD_____   BAD_____

Now assign 100 percent again, but this time answer the question to show how you feel about the impact upon this organization.

GOOD EFFECT_____   BAD EFFECT_____

HOW DO YOU FEEL ABOUT THE INSTRUCTOR'S ROLE?

Here are some opposing viewpoints about what instructors should do. You can indicate whether you agree strongly (AS), tend to agree (TA), have no opinion (NO), tend to disagree (TD), or strongly disagree (SD) by a check mark in the appropriate column.

	AS	TA	NO	TD	SD	
Instructors have prime responsibility for motivating students.	—	—	—	—	—	Immediate bosses have prime responsibility for motivating students.
Instructors should be far above average in emotional control.	—	—	—	—	—	Instructors have as much right to be human and lose control as anyone else.
Student questions should be answered by the instructor.	—	—	—	—	—	Student questions should be referred to the class for answers.
Student questions should be answered with another question.	—	—	—	—	—	Student questions should be reinforced with answers, not with other questions.
And so on ...						And so on ...

Fig. 15.3.   Variation of ADA test.

Another version of the pro-rata instrument might look like this:

BOX 15.1.   Using a Pro-Rata Scale for Performance Appraisal

Assume that you are using a numerical scale to appraise your subordinates. You want to indicate *the relative importance* of performance elements. You have exactly 100 points to assign to the elements listed below, and to two other factors if you wish to add elements that are missing. Remember, the numbers you assign must total 100.

Relationship with others	_____
Dependability	_____
Quality of work	_____
Quantity of work	_____
Personality	_____
_____	_____
_____	_____
_____	Total: 100

This form uses a nominal scale, and data from it can legitimately be used to calculate modes, medians, and totals; such data reveal nothing about averages.

A Thematic Apperception Test (TAT) is really a psychological measurement tool. A modified form can measure learners' affective inventory. In TATs, students write a story about a picture. Their stories reveal their feelings. The TAT has some interesting applications in T&D measurements. For example, learners might look at a picture of people entering a room. A sign by the door carries the name of the training program. By telling a story about the situation or the people, or by capturing the conversation of the people in the picture, trainees reveal their own feelings.

By classifying the trainees' statements, instructors can learn a great deal about how participants feel. Do they mention course content? Or do they show social concerns, mentioning the other students and what instructors will be like? Do they reveal organizational anxieties? Things such as "Why am I here?" or "My boss is the one who needs this!" or "Who ever heard of these instructors?" Instructors can also classify the data as "Approach" (comments showing inquiry, eagerness, anticipation, affirmation) or "Aversive" (reluctance, dread, fear, resignation). By repeating the same picture later, instructors can change the description to elicit interim or end-of-training data.

Many instructors like a "Team Effectiveness" instrument. Such devices come in several forms. The TAT version can ask trainees to discuss the way the people work together, and thus can reveal feelings that don't come out in open discussion. Another very simple method is to ask all participants to write down three adjectives to describe their feelings about the group. Usually, they put just one word on a small sheet of paper. The papers are shuffled and read aloud. During this reading, other members and instructors can comment, or explain how they feel about the words—their appropriateness, their causes, and the implications. It's often useful to tally these words so that trends can be identified and acted upon.

More formal instruments can deal with specific dimensions of the group dynamics and learning activity. At periodic intervals, members respond anonymously and then collectively discuss issues like those shown on the form in Figure 15.4. (Incidentally, if the need for anonymity persists, there's evidence the group isn't maturing.) Note that there are seven positions. Generally, instruments that use a numeric scale should use at least five positions and no more than seven. The odd number permits the participant to take any position on a continuum, including the neutral (center) position. Research suggests that scales bigger than seven are usually beyond the ability of most people to discriminate between the response points.

When trainers want a definite commitment, or pro/con data, they should use an even number of choices. That is, the trainee who selects "1" or "2" instead of

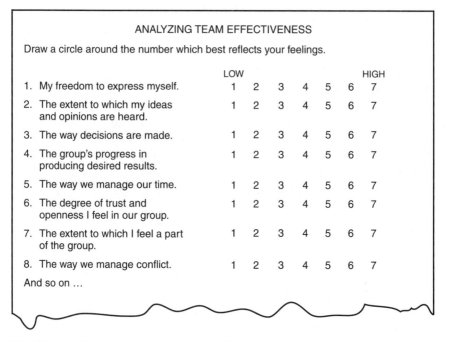

Fig. 15.4.   Form for analyzing team effectiveness.

"3" or "4" is making a statement of dissatisfaction: On a four-point scale, there is no middle number on which participants can express neutrality.

Instruments such as the TAT or Team Effectiveness scale sometimes reveal feelings that don't come out in open discussions seeking to acquire the same data. This doesn't mean that Process Analysis Sessions are not effective. They are—and they should be used as ongoing, noninstrumented measurement activity. They help measure participants' feelings about their own participation, about their own progress, and about the program and the instructors. There is just one problem with instrument-less sessions: Trainers have neither an instrument nor assurance that they've created an atmosphere in which participants freely express themselves.

Such feedback during the learning offers a most dynamic form of measurement. It provides data for decisions in dealing with people, with the group, and with course content. Because it involves the learners in that process, it motivates them to make a conscious investment of their energy in constructive ways.

Instruments or activities such as Process Analysis or TAT would obviously be no help in measuring progress toward psychomotor skills or cognitive acquisitions—but they might help explain and correct sluggish group dynamics in a program designed to reach such objectives.

The point is this: The instrument may fit either the objective of the program or the objective of the measurement. To measure learning, the instrument should be appropriate to the domain of the learning objective. There are no precise guidelines, but the guidelines shown in Figure 15.5 are useful.

In the cognitive domain, paper-and-pencil instruments seem to prevail. They deserve a few comments. Adults are people who went to school—and as students in academic systems they took a lot of tests. They didn't like them very much, but they're accustomed to them. They are especially familiar with some of the quick-scoring formats such as True/False and Multiple Choice.

Now, if feedback is motivating, yet people don't like these tests, there's an interesting conflict of conclusions! It can be easily explained by the way in which the paper-and-pencil tests were conceived and administered. Schoolteachers so often devised "trick" questions, or used so-called objective tests to enforce subjective opinions. The entire testing process became a destructive game—not a legitimate vehicle for receiving honest feedback. Example: "There is no Fourth of July in Great Britain." True or False? Of course there is; they just don't have a celebration. Another example: "The instructor is the most important person in the classroom." True or False? Well, that depends, doesn't it?

Not only were the tests tricky and arbitrary, they were often fed back in highly competitive forms: you got an A, or you got an F, or you were "in the lower quartile on a bell-shaped curve"!

In organizational settings, we are rarely interested in "normal distributions" or the competitive positioning of students. Nor are we primarily interested in the retention of information. We want to know that knowledge is there only to be sure that learners possess a proper inventory before they begin to apply the knowledge. In test-writing language, the tests in training should be "criterion referenced" instead of "norm referenced."

Criterion referenced means that the test is constructed according to the job-related knowledge required. It is the trainer's job to try to get EVERYONE to learn EVERYTHING. Instead of seeking a normal distribution of test scores, the goal is for every trainee to score a "100." To accomplish that, trainers should test what is needed on the job, and then teach what is needed on the job. In effect, the trainer teaches to the test! In education that is a "no-no," but in training it is precisely what happens in well-designed training.

Thus "factual recall" forms such as True/False, Multiple Choice, and Matching have to be carefully designed for T&D measurement. You want to avoid the game in which testers try to outwit students and learners try to outguess the testers! Generally True/False tests should be avoided because they encourage guessing (a 50 percent chance of being right). Multiple Choice questions should focus on application of knowledge, not just rote memorization. Factual recall can also be tested through short-answer recall questions.

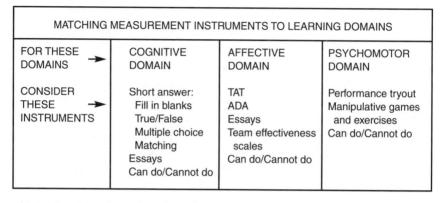

Fig. 15.5. Matching measurement to learning domains.

It is beyond the scope of this book to teach test writing, but suffice it to say that every trainer should receive training in how to write criterion-referenced tests. Much of the angst among adult learners about tests is caused by years of taking poorly written tests. Good criterion-referenced tests appear fair to learners, help them learn, and see few objections because they are so clearly closely linked to the job. Two excellent resources are Norman Gronlund, *Assessment of Student Achievement,* 7th ed. (Boston: Allyn & Bacon, 2002); S. Shrock, W. Coscarelli, and P. Eyres, *Criterion-Referenced Test Development,* 2d ed. (Alexandria, Va.: International Society for Performance Improvement, 2000).

Post-Training Measurement

At the End of Training. When the training ends and the learners are ready to return to their work posts, the really appropriate measurement is a "terminal test" of their skill in performing all the course objectives. Such performance testing would undoubtedly enhance most T&D programs and better ensure effective results. Thus, the final sessions may use simulations, try-outs of the desired performance, role-plays, or paper-and-pencil tests as measurement as well as regular learning activities. If these activities are truly measurement tools, they probably should call attention to the achievement (or nonachievement) of each objective and each criterion. Such checklists become effective nominal scales. Learners can count their own achievements to measure and reinforce the learnings—and to redefine goals and skills not yet "mastered."

What happens too often is that students are asked to evaluate the training program at the very end of the program. This is unfortunate at a time when measurement is what is needed and students are asked to make evaluations. Besides, the timing is bad. The data should have been part of ongoing measurement and evaluation throughout the program. Now, at closing, most participants just want to go home! If an evaluation can be made meaningful at such a moment, it is probably the learners' estimates of how much they have acquired (I can/I cannot), or how much they think they will apply the new learnings on the job. Thus, the most effective instruments tend to present these types of questions:

1. As a result of this training, I plan to make these changes in the way I do my work:
2. As evidence that these changes are producing results, I will be looking for these indices and/or symptoms of improved operations:
3. To feel completely confident in performing the new skills, I would like further help in . . .
4. This training has shown me that I need future training in . . .
5. When my boss "debriefs" me on this training, I will ask for special help in . . .
6. The best feedback I can give myself about how well I am applying my new knowledge/skill is . . .
7. If my peers or bosses hassle me about doing things in a different way, I will counter that by . . .
8. In the future, when my peers are scheduled to attend this program I have just completed, I intend to help them get the most out of it by . . .

What aren't useful are so-called happy sheets or smile sheets. Such measures have consistently shown very low correlation with learning and performance. Thus, they really don't measure anything of long-term importance to trainers. Experienced trainers will tell you that it is relatively easy to make people happy. Persuading them to learn something that they can use on the job is not always what will make them happy. The smile-sheet trap is admittedly a seductive one, but avoid it. You know how it goes: Make them like you and it feels like job security. Wrong! In the long run, you will succeed only by offering training that makes a *real* difference on the job. Unfortunately, such learning may sometimes be confusing, hard work, challenging, intimidating, or scary—not the kind of learning that makes people happy in the short run.

Another end-of-training instrument that provides meaningful quantitative information for the learner, the instructor, the T&D manager, and the client-management ties intended use directly into course objectives. A typical form is shown in Figure 15.6.

It is significant that the instrument uses the behavioral objectives of the learning program, thus reminding graduates of their learnings and linking those objectives with the world of work by equating them to performance standards.

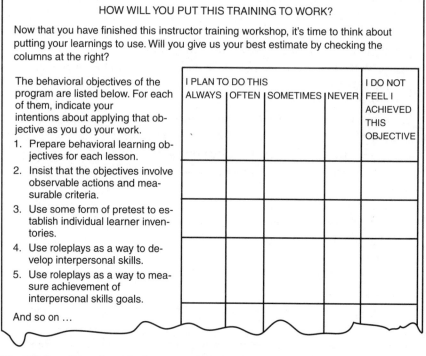

Fig. 15.6. Sample end-of-training instrument.

On-the-Job Measurement. The ultimate impact of a T&D program can be determined only by measurement, which occurs some time after the training itself. Such measurement needs to reach the individual and the organization. For the individual, the concern is the perseverance of the new behavior; for the organization, the focus is the impact of the accumulated behaviors upon the operation.

One effective way to measure the perseverance of the new behaviors in graduates is to ask all graduates (at an appropriate interval after the program) how often they are using the new skills. If the form leaves room for added comments, some affective data can be collected right along with the quantitative measurements.

One instrument for doing this is a mere tally on which the graduates make a checkmark each time they perform the new skill. There is obviously great value in asking graduates to do just that: The tally provides inherent motivation to use the new skill and triggers effective follow-up conversations between graduates and "the boss." It gives the latter a great chance to reinforce the new behavior before routing the tallies to the T&D department for quantitative measurement of the program's impact.

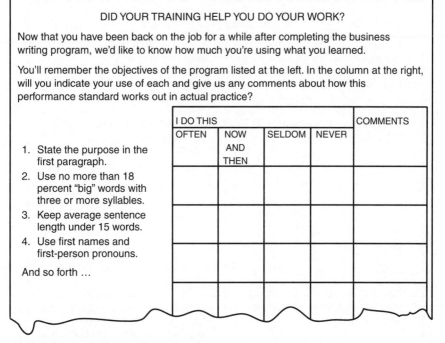

Fig. 15.7. Collecting affective data.

A more sophisticated instrument is shown in Figure 15.7, with its right-hand column for perceptual data.

Obviously the captions for the vertical columns can be given different headings in the instruments shown in both Figures 15.6 and 15.7. A more specific version uses time-based terms such as "HOURLY," "DAILY," "WEEKLY," "MONTHLY," or "NEVER."

The right hand "COMMENTS" column elicits more frequent and more specific data if phrased "WITH THESE RESULTS." Another version asks for an appraisal with headings that read:

I DO THIS ONCE EVERY	AND THE RESULTS ARE
HOUR/DAY/WEEK/MONTH	AWFUL/BAD/SO-SO/GOOD/GREAT

A totally different approach is to avoid "cueing" by mentioning the training objectives, *yet* to focus on the on-the-job application of the learning. Figure15.8 shows how this can be done in a relatively simple way.

Mail the forms to the superior, with instructions for the local manager to give them to the graduates and to collect them from the graduates. There are several important advantages to such a routine:

POST-TRAINING FEEDBACK

Now that you have had a chance to apply what you learned in the effective counseling skills workshop, how is it going? We'd value your opinion. After you've filled
in this form, will you talk it over with your immediate superior; then have it forwarded with the superior's comments to the T&D department? Thanks for helping
us find out what happens when you use the training on the job.

I'VE DONE THESE THINGS THAT I FEEL GOOD ABOUT:	AND THIS IS WHAT HAPPENED TO MAKE ME GLAD THAT I USED THE NEW SKILL:
I'VE DONE THESE THINGS THAT I WISH I HADN'T:	THIS IS WHAT HAPPENED TO MAKE ME FEEL THAT THE NEW BEHAVIOR DIDN'T WORK OUT VERY WELL:

IF I WERE TO GET THE TRAINING NOW, I WOULD
ALSO LIKE TO LEARN HOW TO:

Fig. 15.8. Sample form for self-selecting behavioral objectives being used.

1. Graduates tend to put more importance on the measurement form
   when they receive it from their own "boss."
2. There is a greater return of the forms when the feedback is accomplished through regular reporting channels.

3. The conversation between the graduate and the immediate superior is stimulated.
4. Over time, and after repeated circulation of such measurement forms, the philosophy that training is supposed to produce a change in on-the-job behaviors is communicated and underlined.

Some T&D directors like to validate the perceptions of the graduate with parallel inquiry directed to the superiors themselves. When this is the goal, some simple changes of wording can provide a double check. Forms such as the one we just examined (Figure 15.7) can be sent to *both* parties: the graduates and the superior. The form for the superior then reads something like Figure 15.8. You will note the extra question on the form for the boss. Some T&D managers like to route these inquiries to the boss's boss to send the message through more of the organization, and to increase the number of returns.

How do you persuade people to return these post-training instruments? There are several approaches:

1. Route them "from" and back "to" a top executive in the client/user department. (That executive can reroute them to T&D.)
2. Keep all the instruments as simple and timesaving as you possibly can.
3. As part of the "contract" for offering the training, insist upon agreement that the using department will distribute the instruments and then follow up on them.
4. Use Web-based surveys when possible so that they are quick and easy to complete.
5. Arrange some contingencies:

   - Letters of thanks to random respondents.
   - A personal "Thank you" to respondents you happen to meet in the halls or on your next visit to their area.
   - Explanations that you will (or why you cannot) use a graduate's suggested changes in programs.
   - Incentives to managers who consistently forward the completed instruments to you: golf balls; pen-and-pencil sets; desk calendars; a new text on management technique, theory, or philosophy.
   - A raffle of rather elegant gifts in which every completed response entitles the respondent and the boss who forwards the instrument to one token. A few organizations find such lotteries unacceptable; others regard them as standard events. Sponsors of lotteries point to increased returns and to increased enrollments in training programs!
   - An award to the "Measurement Manager of the Year."

Measurement has some other effects, too. The very process of measuring tends to increase the use of the new behaviors. There is an old adage that says, "In organizations, what is important gets measured" and its corollary, "What's measured, becomes important." Thus, measuring outcomes puts the focus on the behaviors that lead to those outcomes and signals the organization that you are really serious about outcomes from the training you are conducting.

The feedback tells the T&D departments how well they are succeeding and where they are falling short. It also tells them whether the things they are teaching people to do are indeed reinforced in the "real-world" environment. In a sense, this measurement provides data that continuously validate and evaluate the legitimacy of training objectives.

But something else should happen, too. The sum of the individual measurements should be used to determine a new baseline for each performance deficiency that caused the training. Then that sum should be validated against key indices. If the program was born because accidents in the Pocahontas Plant were too high, then the postprogram feedback should reveal that individuals are practicing good safety behaviors. Finally, the post-training baseline should show that accidents are no longer a problem at the Pocahontas Plant. The ME cycle measurement should uncover new baselines for programs that have impact. One hopes the second baseline will differ from the pre-program baseline in desired directions.

Summary

If any one element is more important than others in effective measurement, it is selecting the proper thing to count.

There's a significant dilemma there. If measurement doesn't count, if it isn't quantitative, then it isn't really measurement. If it counts the wrong things, it is an inappropriate measurement.

First, when we measure T&D achievements, the things we count should represent what we are seeking. That's true whether we measure perceptions, learning, or performance units. Next, those things should be inherently valuable. Finally, the search itself should develop an increasingly satisfactory performance of those inherently valuable units.

Assessing the Results of
the Training Programs

16

The good news today is that Human Resource Development (HRD) and Training and Development (T&D) have not been so highly valued since World War II as they are today. In a service- and information-driven economy, employee expertise becomes the primary source of competitive advantage. The not-so-good news is that with that has come a sharply increased demand that HRD and training demonstrate that they are achieving the outcomes their host organizations need. Because training has become a vital strategic component, organizations are demanding that it work!

The Traditional Approach: The Kirkpatrick Model

The Kirkpatrick model (1998) of training evaluation has dominated training evaluation discussion since it was first published forty years ago (Kirkpatrick 1959a, 1959b, 1960a, 1960b). It suggests that training should be evaluated at four "levels": 1—participant reactions, 2—learning, 3—on-the-job behaviors, and 4—results from behavior change. The American Society for Training and Development (ASTD) has embraced this framework in its learning outcomes report (Bassi and Ahlstrand 2000). As part of its benchmarking service, participants provided data on standardized measures of Level 1 and Level 3 outcomes.

Despite its popularity with practitioners, in recent years the four-level taxonomy has come under increasingly intense criticism (Alliger, Tannenbaum, Bennett, Traver, and Shotland 1997; Alliger and Janak, 1989; Holton 1996; Swanson and Holton 1999). The chief criticisms are:

- *Not supported by research.* Research has consistently shown that the levels within the taxonomy are not related, or only correlated at a low level.

- *Emphasis on reaction measures.* Research has shown that reaction measures have a nearly zero correlation with learning or performance outcome measures.
- *Failure to update the model.* The model has remained the same for the last forty years with little effort to update or revise it.
- *Not used.* As will be discussed in the next section, the model is not widely used. Despite forty years of urging people to use it, most do not find it a useful approach.
- *Can lead to incorrect decisions.* The model leaves out so many important variables that four-level data alone is insufficient to make correct and informed decisions about training program effectiveness.

To What Extent Is Program Evaluation Conducted in Practice?

One stream of research in training evaluation has been to document the extent to which methods are used in practice. This research is important because it shows to what extent prescriptive models and methods are actually used in practice, which in turn should inform the development of new models and methods. Despite efforts to build new evaluation models, most surveys of evaluation practices use the Kirkpatrick framework because it is the most widely recognized.

The data is too voluminous to include here (interested readers should see Swanson and Holton 2001; and Twitchell, Holton, and Trott 2000 for a review of surveys). However, the overall conclusions from these surveys are (a) many organizations use Levels 1 and 2 evaluation for at least some programs; (b) fewer than half the organizations even try Level 4; and (c) only a small percentage of programs receive Level 3 and 4 evaluation. Overall, these findings present a very disappointing view of evaluation practices.

Furthermore, when following the literature back to the development of the four levels forty years ago, there seems to have been little change in the amount of evaluation conducted within business and industry. As early as 1953 (Wallace and Twitchell 1953), researchers were discussing the lack of training evaluation and the need for it. Today's literature contains parallel comments and the lack of training evaluation still exists. The trend they suggest is striking: Only modest gains have been made in the number of organizations using these evaluation practices. More specifically, it would appear that modest gains were made in Levels 1 and 2 from 1968 to 1989, but little gain in the last twelve years. Even more troubling is that very little gain has occurred at Levels 3 and 4, which are the most important levels for demonstrating training's effect on organizational performance.

The main reason training is not evaluated is usually the same for *all* levels—it is not required by the organization. The usual interpretation of this is that it continues to raise serious questions about whether training is valued by organizations as a core business process.

The second most important reason for not doing Levels 3 and 4 is usually lack of time, with lack of training close behind. Evaluation continues to be seen harder to accomplish than it should be.

If forty years of promoting evaluation has not changed the overall picture, something else must be needed. Clearly the Kirkpatrick model of training evaluation has *not* been effective in making evaluation an integral part of Human Resource Development (HRD) practice. It does not matter if you examine practitioners more highly trained in evaluation (instructional designers), those that have more well-defined outcomes (technical trainers, health care), those in more sophisticated organizations (American Society for Training and Development [ASTD] benchmarking group), or simply average training practitioners, the level of evaluation use is about the same and is not changing much.

A New Approach: The Results Assessment System

Swanson and Holton (1999) introduced the Results Assessment System (RAS) as a practical but theoretically sound approach to assessing results from training programs. Readers will feel initial comfort with the *Results Assessment System* relative to the familiar *4-Level Evaluation Model*. At first glance, they are not radically different from one another. A second glance reveals fundamental, substantial differences in (1) their evaluation and assessment priorities, and (2) the completeness of the practical research-based process and tools offered in the *Results Assessment System*. The material in this chapter is based on Swanson and Holton's 1999 book.

First, notice the name doesn't include "evaluation." Go to any bookshelf of management or organizational books and look up the word "evaluation" in the index. How often do you think the word is mentioned? We can't find it. Yet, members of the HRD profession consistently talk about evaluation but rarely practice it in the field. What is going on here? One clue is in the terms found in the indexes of most business books—words such as performance, assessment, and measurement. In contrast, evaluation professionals tend to be consultants who study educational and government programs rather than focus on core organizational performance and processes. We have come to realize that the word "evaluation" evokes a negative schoolhouse picture and the idea of assigning grades to ill-defined activities.

In contrast, the *Results Assessment System* is about assessing results, which is different from evaluation. *Assessment* of results is a core organizational process. HRD is a means to achieve some larger result in an organization. It is for this reason that results assessment is not optional, for it is the results that impact the organization and ultimately provide outputs desired by customers. For HRD to be a core organizational process, it then follows that results must be assessed.

Results assessment can be defined *as determining whether desired outputs have been achieved by the HRD interventions.* In their book, Swanson and Holton present a system for assessing results from HRD interventions that has four basic components: *a process, results domains, a plan,* and *tools.*

The process

The core process of the *Results Assessment System* is illustrated in Figure 16.1. This five-step process view of assessing results provides a simple and direct journey from analysis inputs to decision outputs.

Several aspects of this process are worth noting here:

1. To be most effective, results assessment requires strong front-end analysis. It is hard to assess outcomes if the goals are not well defined.
2. This process has an action orientation in that the final outcome is presumed to be decisions about HRD interventions and actions taken to maintain, change, or eliminate programs. The purpose is not research.
3. The five steps present a simple and logical progression of activities essential to effective results assessment.
4. Considerable emphasis is placed on defining expected results and properly interpreting them, in addition to the issues of developing good measures.
5. These five steps describe the steps you will take within your organization to put these tools to work.

Results Domains

The promise we have for you is that you will learn how to measure results within three domains: *performance, learning,* and *perceptions.* Each domain has two options within it. These domains and options within *the Results Assessment System* are defined as follows:

Performance Results are defined as:

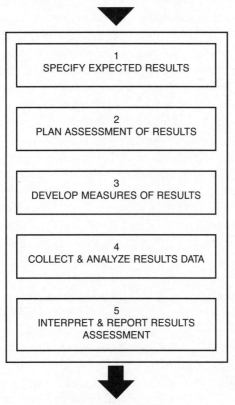

FRONT-END ANALYSIS INPUTS

1
SPECIFY EXPECTED RESULTS

2
PLAN ASSESSMENT OF RESULTS

3
DEVELOP MEASURES OF RESULTS

4
COLLECT & ANALYZE RESULTS DATA

5
INTERPRET & REPORT RESULTS
ASSESSMENT

DECISION OUTPUTS

Fig. 16.1. Results assessment process.

SOURCE: **Swanson and Holton 1999.**

System: The units of mission-related outputs in the form of goods and/or services having value to the customer and that are related to the core organizational, work processes, and group/individual contributors in the organization.

Financial: the conversion of the output units of goods and/or services attributable to the intervention into money and financial interpretation.

The assessment of system, mission-related outputs are bottom-line talk. Things such as 50,000 cars made; the patient lived; or 5,000 service contracts sold. Those pursuing improvements in an organization face a key dilemma—mission-related outputs. Although the focal point is the output goal, the means, or driver, of that goal may look very different. A simple analogy would be a sporting event in which the goal is to win by throwing the ball through the hoop more times than the opponent—scoring points.

T&D officers who are determined to be relevant to the main thrust of their organizations will opt for evaluation by contribution to goals. They see themselves as members of the problem-solving team. They are specifically concerned with the organization's performance problems. They prioritize training needs in direct proportion to organizational urgencies. They therefore want to know whether training has eliminated or alleviated those urgent problems.

A critical element of such evaluation is identifying and selecting the key indicator. The evaluation process involves deciding how many units must be bad to require action—and what improvement must be made for the program to be adjudged successful. Among the indicators considered are:

Units of work per hour	Total days absenteeism
Units of work per worker	Number of absenteeism incidents
Number of sales	Scrap
Dollar value per sale	Rejects
Ratio of sales to calls	Backorders filled
Percent of quota achieved	Dollar value for backorders filled
Total dollar value of sales	Tasks completed
Number of grievances	Percent of tasks completed
Percent of grievances decided	properly
Percent of grievance decisions	Budgets submitted
sustained	Budgets achieved within X percent
Inventory turnover	of forecast
Percent of counseling problems	Employee turnover
solved	Cost of accidents
Machine downtime	Letters and reports completed
Number of disabling accidents	Percent of letters and reports that
Total minutes tardiness	get the desired results

The T&D department evaluating its contribution to the organization must not ignore the standard operating indices already established. The baselines that reveal deficiencies are often the same baselines included in regular management reports. It is not always necessary to identify a new indicator. When a useful indicator is already part of regular reports, it is folly to invent new indicators! T&D officers who can find existing indices can "talk to management in their own language."

So now we see that another dimension of evaluation is the cost-effectiveness of the solution. The formula hardly needs repeating—but we'll repeat it anyhow:

Cost of the performance deficiency
Minus the cost of the improvement program
Equals the cost-effectiveness of the improvement program

To apply this formula to any given program, T&D specialists must wear their very best consultants' hats, identifying not only the key indicators but the cost of each unit. For the collection letters, one might compute the total time spent in writing letters. That would give salary costs. Add to that the cost of materials and facilities. These data are always available somewhere in departmental budgets or records. By adding those totals together, we find the total cost of letter writing. To determine the unit cost, we divide that total by the number of letters. The phone calls would be a bit more difficult to price, but it can be done. The phone bills are easily available, but the time costs could be more elusive. Some observation or work-sampling can give the needed facts: How much of their time do people spend on the telephone?

Similar logic and investigation can be used on those elusive management tasks that "nobody can measure." One can always estimate the time spent on tasks; one can always secure standard overhead figures for departments. And one can always find the "product"—that's how we knew we had a deficiency in the first place!

Thus meetings should produce decisions; grievance hearings should produce findings; counseling should produce changed performance. The way we knew we had a problem in the first place was that these products were too few or too faulty. Our evaluation merely asks, after we've counted and priced the new levels of productivity, "Is the change sufficient? Sufficient to meet the organizational goals? Sufficient to pay for the training?"

When putting price tags on human values, clever T&D consultants quickly point out to client managers that the ultimate price tags may very well be psychic inestimable elements such as morale, human dignity, team spirit. But, they add just as quickly, these can come through programs that justify themselves on purely economic bases.

They are also careful not to jump to superficial indicators of changes in the operation. Things such as "smiling faces" or "infractions reported by supervisors" don't indicate much. Employees can learn to smile even when they're being rude or feeling miserable; supervisors can learn to look the other way.

Finally, clever T&D consultants err on the conservative side when putting price tags on performance deficiencies. After all, this is a process for evaluating the true cost-effectiveness—not for justifying the program. But some hard data on the "plus side" of the ledger or of a key operating index is necessary before one can applaud training programs on the basis of their contribution to organization goals.

Learning Results

Learning Results are defined as:

Knowledge: Mental achievement acquired through study and experience.

Expertise: Human behaviors, having effective results and optimal efficiency, acquired through study and experience within a specialized domain.

Knowledge, an intellectual or cognitive result of learning experiences, is the basic learning result. It is lodged in a person's mind. Measures of knowledge confirm the level of knowledge held by individuals within a particular subject area. For effectiveness and efficiency, paper-and-pencil tests are the primary means of measuring knowledge.

Human expertise is the second category of learning—the more complex learning result category. People with expertise have knowledge and are able to act upon that knowledge. The effective and efficient ability to act upon knowledge generally comes from experience beyond core knowledge. Measuring human expertise requires that an individual demonstrate behavior in a real or simulated setting. When assessing learning results, we generally recommend that both knowledge results and expertise results be measured. And it is logical that knowledge can be measured some time before expertise in that the learner needs time to gain experience. The span of time will vary depending on the complexity of the area of expertise being developed.

What's a reasonable level of accomplishment? Conscientious learners want to demonstrate 100 percent achievement. Problem learners would settle for near zero. Professional instructors will tell you that they "win a few and lose a few," but that they like to shoot for 100 percent. The fact is, you can't change all the people all the time. "You can't make a silk purse out of a sow's ear," as the adage goes. For in-house programs, where learning goals are totally consistent with standards, 100 percent is a reasonable target, but the percentage will vary considerably with different programs in different parts of the organization. It is considerably lower in public seminars, where the goals may not be specific or reinforced by the management of the participants.

This type of evaluation requires that each learner be tested on each learning objective listed for the program. In very thorough T&D systems, it involves post-training measurement of actual on-the-job use of the new behaviors. Such double-checking shows not just that learners "can"—but that they "actually are."

To count the actual learning accomplishments is one step; to match them against predetermined targets is the second. Arranging the data in a visual display helps both the instructor and the ultimate evaluator. It's possible to build a simple matrix. Let's do that for the program on writing collection letters that we gave those clerks:

CHART 16.1. Basic Job Application Assessment

Objective	Trainee							
	1	2	3	4	5	6	7	8
Directly ask for payment	Yes	Yes	Yes	Yes	Yes	Yes	Yes	Yes
Ask in question format	Yes	Yes	No	No	No	No	No	No
Use first-person pronouns	Yes	Yes	No	Yes	Yes	Yes	Yes	Yes
Avoid thanking in advance	Yes	Yes	No	Yes	No	Yes	Yes	Yes
Set specific deadlines	Yes	Yes	No	No	Yes	Yes	Yes	Yes
Use less than 13% long words	Yes	Yes	No	Yes	Yes	Yes	Yes	Yes

Just a quick glance at such a display tells any analyst that something went wrong on the second objective: Six of eight trainees cannot meet it. It also shows that Learner 3 has troubles: Look at all the "No" entries. The chart should also demonstrate the value of periodic feedback and testing during the learning. Those trends could have been detected and corrected—in ways which would have benefited both the instructors and the learners.

Failures such as those shown in the display bring up another evaluation decision: What should we do about the "No" conditions? Retrain? Reappraise the objectives? Redesign the program? Take a look at the selection process? The answer could conceivably be a yes to every one of those options. There are circumstances in which some or all of those might be reasonable decisions to T&D evaluators. Let's look at the options.

Retraining makes some sense. Failure the first time isn't an unusual result for human endeavor. To reapply the original stimulus may produce different results. Maybe the mere repetition will cause different responses. Maybe there is some unidentified variable in the learner's life that will produce the desired learning the second time around. Instructors must be prepared to cope with individual differences. This may even mean reporting to management back on the job that certain "graduates" need special post-training follow-up. For example, a trainee may meet the qualitative criteria, but not the quantitative. Take apprentice machine operators: At the end of training, they may be doing everything properly—but just not doing it fast enough.

Sometimes organizations are too zealous. They expect too much. "Benchmarks" may be necessary, with certain criteria set for the end-of-training and tougher criteria established for later dates. Here's an example: Learners might be expected to complete five units per hour at the end of the training, eight units per hour two weeks later, and twelve units per hour after a month on the job.

If experience proves that nobody can meet these goals, then consider the second option: that the objectives need to be re-appraised. Some might be evaluated as "just plain unreasonable." If most trainees, but not all of them, fail to meet the desired goals, perhaps individual tolerances could be established. If so, the training department must be sure to follow up with the immediate supervisors of all graduates who cannot perform to the expected standard.

When significant numbers fail to achieve a given goal (or set of goals), then a redesign of the program should be considered. When the "outputs" are missing, it's just reasonable to reevaluate the "inputs." Perhaps new methods, more drill, different visual aids will produce the desired learnings.

Finally, people may fail to meet learning objectives because they lack the needed personal or experiential inventory. Personnel departments and managers have been known to put people into jobs for which they were misfit. It follows, too, that people may be assigned to training programs that involve objectives they cannot master. Even capable people may bring "negative affective inventories." These bad attitudes can inhibit or prevent the acquisition of the new behaviors. Good instructors can overcome some apathy and some negativism—but there is considerable question about how much of this responsibility ought to rest on the instructor's shoulders. Learners and their bosses have a responsibility for motivation, too!

Which brings up a brand new option: sometimes accepting defeat. This means that sometimes the best thing to do is to "give up" on certain individuals. It isn't that these people never could reach the goals; it's just that to produce the learning may be more costly than it is worth. That cost can involve energy and psychic pain as well as money.

When T&D specialists use such a display of achievement of learning goals, they may reasonably evaluate (1) the reasonableness of the goals, (2) the effectiveness of the training design, (3) the effectiveness of the teaching, and (4) the trainees' suitability to the learning assignment. (Did they belong in this program?)

A simple formula permits a quantitative analysis:

1. *Compute the potential:* Number of students multiplied by number of goals.
2. *Test individual achievements:* Test each student on each objective.
3. *Compute gross achievements:* Add all the "Yes" achievements.
4. *Compute achievement quota:* Divide step 3 by step 1.

Some T&D officers set achievement quotas for every program. In highly critical skills, 100 percent achievement is mandatory; 90 percent is more typical for most organizational training. (The remaining 10 percent can accrue on the job with proper supervisory follow-up.) Public seminars seldom establish achievement quotas; indeed, they rarely use performance testing at all. Achievement quotas, or performance testing, show what learning was accomplished. The same approach can reveal on-the-job utilization.

Perception Results

Perception Results are defined as:

> *Participant Perceptions:* Perceptions of people with first-hand experience with systems, processes, goods and/or services.
> *Stakeholder Perceptions:* Perceptions of leaders of systems and/or people with a vested interest in the desired results and the means of achieving them.

Of the three domains, perceptions have the lowest cost and the lowest return. They are lowest in cost in the sense that simple, short, and standardized perceptions rating forms can be produced for participants and stakeholders. They are lowest in return because they provide the least valid information about performance outcomes. Research consistently shows that there is little correlation between perceptions and learning or performance, despite the popular myth that they are related.

Perceptions results are perceptual states held by various people in the organization such as trainees and their managers. Measures of perceptions systematically access this information from selected groups of people. The mantra for perception results domain should be (1) acquire the data; (2) do not spend a disproportionate amount of resources to acquire it; and (3) do not overinterpret it. We recommend that you collect this data only as long as it is not used as a substitute for measuring learning results and/or performance results. For example, people self-reporting that they have learned something is not a measure of what they have learned. We also recommend that you collect perceptions results data from the participants and the stakeholders both. Thus, from a general planning perspective, commit to both participant and stakeholder perception results in the *Results Assessment Plan* and check off both boxes.

When you've asked someone for perceptions, you can do several things to evaluate the data. First, you can count the positive and the negative comments.

Next, you can classify the comments into inherent categories: the content, the instruction, the facilities, the appropriateness of the objectives.

Minor trends should not be used as the basis for action; nor should hotly worded comments. T&D officers would be wise to temper such overstated comments as "The worst program I've ever been sent to!" or "Totally irrelevant to this organization," or "The instructor is an egotist—out to get the students." Such reactions need to be treated as some judgments are at international skating and swimming competition—the highest and the lowest ratings are thrown out in the final computations.

Whenever one seeks perceptual data, there is an eventual "balancing phenomenon" in which comments contradict each other in almost equal numbers. For instance, seventeen people will say the program moved too slowly; eighteen will say it was too rapid.

What does this really tell an evaluator? Probably not that the program was either too slow or too fast, but that the design needs to provide more time for individual activity for one-on-one counseling. That might allow all thirty-five of the commentators to feel comfortably in control of their own scheduling.

It might also tell the instructor that there is too little ongoing process feedback during the class sessions. When as many as 10 percent of any student body mention pacing problems, the instructor is probably not getting feedback soon enough.

This raises an important point: Professional instructors are collecting perceptual data throughout the learning. They establish an atmosphere in which it is more than possible; it is inevitable! Instructors are clearly evaluating on perceptual bases whenever they adjust their instruction as a result of such perceptions.

Another issue is the nature of the question. If the instructor is to be evaluated on delivery, the use of visual aids, personal appearance, and the handling of students' questions, the evaluation should come from a professional. Surgeons don't ask their patients for comments on their scalpel techniques; wide receivers don't ask spectators to evaluate the way they caught that pass. Why, then, do T&D specialists ask learners to evaluate instructional technology? The proper and relevant questions concern learnings, and the learners' perceptions of those learnings.

Then there is the issue of timing. Perceptual data should be gathered at all phases of the learning—not at the end of the program when the real pressures are to go home, go back to the office, or go back to the shop.

The most useful perceptions come during the learning and when the learnings are being applied on the job. At end of learnings, the "I can/I cannot meet the objectives" inquiry is especially useful. Coupled with the actual terminal test data, it gives T&D management cross-validated data on which to make the evaluation. On-the-job perceptions should focus on application of the new learnings.

A useful follow-up instrument asks learners to tally or estimate how often they have used the new skill on the job. Since this is a perceptual approach, they may simply choose between alternatives such as "always" or "often" or "now and then" or "seldom" or "never." When the cumulative totals are presented as the basis for evaluations, modes and medians can be located as the basis for evaluation.

Let's look at such an approach as it is applied to that program for writing collection letters. You have surveyed the perceptions of the perseverance of the acquired skills. The compiled data look like this:

CHART 16.2. Sample Data Analysis Matrix

	Always	Often	Now & Then	Seldom	Never
Directly ask for payment	43	13	1	—	—
Ask in question format	40	10	6	—	1
Use first-person pronouns	50	1	5	1	—
Avoid thanking in advance	51	3	3	—	—
Set specific deadlines	41	12	2	2	—
Use less than 13% long words	35	18	2	1	1

Such a record would produce a favorable evaluation of the program and indicate the general validity of the learning goals and their usefulness—as the graduates perceive them. Such perceptual data, coupled with the hard data about operating results (whether the letters are indeed collecting money!) can give a very rich amount of data on which to base the evaluation of T&D programs.

When post-training perceptions of applications reveal nonuse of the new skills, the T&D consulting follow-up may reveal causes. As we've noted, those causes include such things as unreasonableness of the objective, irrelevance of the objective—and, frequently, failure of the immediate boss to reinforce the new behavior. It is by such evaluation of an existing program that more than one T&D officer learns that the program started one level too low! The indicated action for that evaluative discovery is a training program for the bosses!

Post-training perceptual instruments can also make effective use of open questions. To arrive at perceptions, T&D evaluators like questions such as these:

- If you were attending the same training today, what would you do differently?
- What objectives do feel should be expanded?

- What objectives would you condense?
- What objectives would you drop?
- What objectives would you add?
- What course activities would you expand?
- What course activities would you eliminate?
- What course activities would you condense?
- What would you like to tell us about this course and the way it has influenced you or the way you do your work?

A Results Assessment Plan

Each of the assessment planning decisions is recorded on the *Results Assessment Plan*. Figure 16.2 shows the complete planning sheet. Completing this planning sheet leads you through the five core decisions you need to make about each results option in the *Results Assessment*. These core decisions are in response to the following questions:

1. In terms of results, which of the three domains and six options will be measured?
2. When will the results data be collected (before, during, and after the intervention)?
3. Will the results be compared to: another cycle, a standard, or a norm?
4. How will the data be analyzed?
5. What measurement tools and details are needed to execute the assessment plan?

The horizontal rows (A–F) of the *Results Assessment Plan* represent the three result domains and the six results described above. The vertical columns represent the five core decisions the planner makes in relation to each of the results domains and options. They are numbered 1–5. The next section reviews each of these decisions.

The Core Dimensions

Decision 1: Which of the three result domains and six results options will be measured? It is not always appropriate or necessary to choose all three domains or all six options. For example, when we were consulting with two separate divisions in a large corporation that were located in two states, it was just as if we were working with two different organizations. In one division, HRD had established itself as a major process and we could almost automatically think of

Program
Title: _____
Prepared
by: _____
Approved
by: _____ Date _____

1
Expected Results
(Choose from 3 results 2 options for each)

2
Data Collection Time Line
(Select data collection points pertaining to the program or intervention)

3
Compare
(Use option 7-Cycle, 8-Standard or 9-Norm if pre-post assessments are not used)

4
Data Analysis Plan
(Specify data to be compared to answer the assessment for each domain row A–F; e.g. D3<->D11)

5
Execution Details
(Highlight measures, timing, implementation, etc.)

	check	Before 1 2	During 3 4	After 5 6	7 8 9		
Performance Results							
A. System							
B. Financial							
Learning Results							
C. Knowledge							
D. Expertise							
Perception Results							
E. Participants							
F. Stakeholders							

Fig. 16.2. Results assessment plan.
SOURCE: Swanson and Holton 1999.

all six results options (A–F) as being appropriate: system performance, financial performance, knowledge outcomes, expertise outcomes, participant perceptions, and stakeholder perceptions.

In contrast, the HRD department in the other division had never established itself as a major business process. For example, it never engaged in fundamental performance analysis (the discovery of performance requirements and solutions). Worse yet, the HRD department didn't even have a track record of assessing learning results from any of its programs. As a result, the idea of promising performance results was administratively outside the reach of the HRD workgroup. Their challenge was first to gain credibility through assessing and reporting the knowledge and expertise results (options C and D) from their programs and then grow into performance.

Decision 2: When will results data be collected (before, during, and after the intervention)? Data pertaining to the program, or intervention, will be collected within a *data collection timeline* and recorded in column 2 of the worksheet. Each result option selected can potentially be measured *before, during,* and *after* the intervention. For example, it may be possible to assess system performance outcomes before, during, and after an intervention.

In addition, it may be desirable to measure a result option several times before, during, and after the intervention to find an average score or to plot a trend. As you can see by the *Results Assessment Plan* worksheet, this is represented by two intervals of time in the *before* stage (timeline boxes 1–2), two in the *during* stage (timeline boxes 3–4), and two in the *after* stage (timeline boxes 5–6).

When the T&D officer or client/managers wish to prove absolute causality between the training and the improvement, they need to know that the differences between "pre" and "post" are statistically significant. For this level of analysis, a professional statistician should be involved. Only such technicians can answer the central question, "Are these changes well beyond coincidence?" When profound numerical analysis is necessary, the statistical consultant should be involved in the process from the very beginning. It is dangerous, maybe fatal, to wait until the data have been gathered. By then the T&D director may already have "booted" it in one or more of several ways:

- Necessary pretraining data are missing.
- The instruments asked the wrong questions.
- There was contamination in the measurement process.
- Key indicators are missing.

A common example might be giving a knowledge test before the beginning of a training program to see how much participants already know (knowledge timeline box 2) and then again at the end of the program (knowledge timeline box 4). Another example might be taking expertise measures thirty days (expertise timeline box 5) and ninety days (expertise timeline box 6) after training. The idea is that the timeline identifies specific time intervals to collect specific data can be quickly planned and illustrated with this planning sheet.

Decision 3: Will the results be compared to another cycle, a standard, or a norm? All results measures need to be compared to something to judge the quality of outcomes achieved. Comparison *Options* are shown in column three with boxes 7, 8, and 9.

- Box 7 refers to another *cycle* of the same program (e.g., the May group in Executive Development compared to the August group in Executive Development). This could also be a control group that did not participate in the program.
- Box 8 refers to a *standard*—an attainment level is set that has previously verified meaning. For example, having a 90 percent or higher on-time arrival of flights, a sales standard of 4 million dollars per month for the sales region, an average participant satisfaction rating that is positive. These standards should not be arbitrary. They should both be referenced to existing data and information.
- Box 9 is a *norm*. A norm comes from a large database that provides averages used as a point of comparison. For example, industry averages or benchmarks might be used as a norm. At some point norms, if confirmed, can work their way into being standards.

One mechanism upon which statistical experts may insist is a "control group." Even if you don't have a statistician insisting upon such a control group, you have important reasons for establishing one. This simply means that a part of the "defective population" will not immediately receive training, or any other form of change program. They become the control group; those who are in the training are the "experimental group." The reasons for control groups should be obvious. If the change takes place only in the experimental group, there is some reason to credit the change program for the improvement. If, on the other hand, both the control group and the experimental group move in the same direction, evaluators must question the causal effect of the program. If they move in the same direction at the same speed, better drop the program. In situations like these, the professional statistician is a valuable resource for the evaluation process—valuable but not absolutely indispensable.

Decision 4: How will the data be analyzed? Just what data will be collected, compared, and presented as part of the final evaluation report for a specific intervention? The *Data Analysis Plan* allows planners to state what data will be compared for assessing the results for each of the six selected results options.

An example here is participant perceptions at the end of program (Participant 4) compared to a standard of 2.5 or higher on a 1–4 scale (Participant 8). The data analysis plan is a comparison of the two: *Participant 4— Participant 8.* Here are two other examples:

- average expertise before attending program compared to expertise after participating in the program *(Expertise 2 — Expertise 4);* and
- financial return-on-investment of staff-managed performance improvement efforts compared to external consultant managed efforts *(Financial 6 — Financial 7).*

Decision 5: What other information is needed to execute the assessment plan? This fifth column records details about two critical areas of results assessment: (1) measures to be used, and (2) implementation details. Chapter 15 discussed a variety of measures that can be used. Examples include production data, market share data, paper-and-pencil tests, supervisor performance ratings, customer surveys, cost data, and so forth.

Implementation details might include any specifics about the actual measurement steps and their timing. For example, they might include how the measures will be collected, the instruments distributed and collected, and the timing of the data collection. The general timing on the data collection timeline (Part 2) will need to made more specific, such as the day before the intervention, the last hour of the intervention, or sixty days following the intervention, and so forth.

Making Results Assessment Practical and Credible

Does results assessment look hard to you? Look too difficult to complete? Swanson and Holton (1999) also offer some guidelines on how to make results assessments more practical and doable:

Deciding Which Interventions to Measure. It may surprise you to hear us say that it is not worth the effort to assess the results of all interventions. Assessing results takes resources—time, energy, and money. It makes sense to devote your resources only to assessing results that count. Assessment resources should be devoted to programs having a high potential of benefiting from assessment. Consider these *results quality criteria:*

- Is the intervention *really* being conducted for the purpose of improving performance?
  If not, it probably means people don't care about results.

- Is the intervention forecasted to have significant and meaningful results?

    If not, don't waste your measurement resources.
- Are the costs of not getting results high enough to justify the effort?

    If not, then sponsors may not care about your data.
- Are the people who care about the results important organizational partners?

    If not, then what do you gain?
- If the intervention has shown not to produce results, would it be eliminated or changed?

    If not, then results must not really matter or there is as some other reason it has to be done.
- Are the results really in question?

    If you are sure it works, maybe you can postpone measuring results until you have looked at more questionable programs.

If you can't answer "yes" to all the above questions, then consider devoting your assessment resources to other interventions. Or ask yourself why you are doing the intervention in the first place.

More Than One Place to Start

The hard reality is that not every organization is ready to do everything at once. An organization that has never assessed any interventions may be lucky to implement knowledge assessment; another one that has conducted regular testing is ready to move ahead to performance assessment.

The most important thing is to start. It is okay to start where it is comfortable. But it's not okay to settle for just a low level of results assessment. If results are important, measurement systems should continue to improve until they address most of the measurement domains shown in this book and are providing the information for sound decisions. So start where comfortable, and then improve.

Use Existing Measurement Systems

It is always amazing to see the faces of HRD professionals when they realize how much results assessment information they need is already available in other organizational measurement systems. If the intervention is targeted at real performance-related needs that are important, the chances are very good that someone in the organization is already measuring it. Don't reinvent systems.

The closer assessment systems are to established organizational measurement systems, the more likely they are to last.

Don't Buy More Accuracy Than You Need

The purpose of results assessment is to enable the organization to make sound decisions about interventions. The level of accuracy needed for organizational decisions is considerably less than that needed for research. Your task is to find the "sweet spot" on the accuracy continuum so that you are buying enough accuracy to exceed management expectations slightly so that you earn maximum credibility. If you buy more accuracy than that, you are wasting resources.

For example, consider an organization development program that is likely to return the typical financial return of 800 percent in a year or less (Swanson 1998). Will it really matter to management if your measure is off by 50 percentage points—that is, you report 750 percent or 800 percent? Will you make any better decision about the program if you knew for sure the return was 800 percent? If the answer is yes, then pay for that degree of accuracy. If the answer is no, accept less. Often, giving up a modest amount of accuracy will save considerable resources.

Use Fast-Cycle Measurement Processes

Fast-cycle measurement is an iterative process that works in situations where interventions are repeated with some frequency. The idea is simple but powerful. The first time you assess results, do so with a very wide confidence interval; that is, don't buy much accuracy. If the results are overwhelmingly good, then stop. Continuing the above example, if the initial measurement suggests a range of return from 500 percent to 1000 percent, that *might* be close enough.

Many programs will never need measurement past the first step. Resources saved there can be devoted to more accurate measurement on others. This approach works particularly well in organizations that move too fast for complete assessment processes.

Practical Sampling

There is usually little reason to assess results every time an intervention is repeated. The basic principle of sampling is that unless conditions are substantially different, a measurement made on one group is a reasonable estimate of results for another group. So, for example, one class of managers in a company is likely to be similar to another class if it is an open enrollment class. If so, assessing the results from one class may be enough.

There are many ways to sample, including:

periodic cycles (every other month offered)
subset of classes (one of every three classes offered this month)
subset of attendees (one of every four people involved)

It is up to the assessor to be sure that a sample is not biased. Be sure that the people assessed are approximately representative. Remember that when final statistics are reported, they will be used to make general statements, so make sure your sample is not likely to yield unusual or unrepresentative results.

Embed Results in Program Design

The more fully results assessment becomes integrated with the learning process, the more successful it will be. Unfortunately, the tendency is to treat it as a "research" project, often conducted by an outside expert, which takes place either parallel to or outside the learning process. It is not uncommon to see the data "disappear" with analysts, and the results shared with only a select group of people. When you integrate the results assessment, the process makes the training task easier and makes training more meaningful for the participants.

Create Stakeholder Ownership of Results

Assessment is often something done "unto" participants by outside experts. The outcome is often increased resistance and participants who attack the data as invalid simply because they do not own it. Results assessments that work transfer much of the ownership of the results, and the results assessment, to the stakeholders—primarily the participants and their management. As long as results assessment "belongs" to the HRD department, stakeholders have little reason to take it seriously.

Here are some strategies to build stakeholder ownership of results assessment:

1. Expect results to occur.
2. Have stakeholders involved in determining the measures for performance, learning, and perceptions.

3. Make participants accountable for successful performance and learning results.
4. Make management responsible for collecting, monitoring, and reacting to performance results.
5. Make sure all stakeholders receive reports of all results assessment data.
6. Have stakeholders validate results data.
7. Engage stakeholders is problem solving to correct out-of-conformity results.
8. Have participants and managers conduct as much results assessment as is practical.
9. Integrate results assessment into existing assessment systems, such as strategic planning or departmental performance reviews.

Overcoming Resistance to Results Assessment

Unfortunately, results assessment is not a routine component of most HRD practice. Organization development and personnel training and development programs are often carried out with little or no formal plans for assessment or no thoughts regarding follow-up procedures designed to identify measurable outcomes. Because conducting such assessments is not standard within HRD practice, most organizations do not have the *expertise, culture,* or *systems* in place to make it easy to implement.

What has developed in this type of organization is typical of those that have not focused on results and results assessment. Over the years, HRD activities become increasingly isolated from the systems they are designed to support. And HRD professionals and line managers become less and less closely associated. Eventually, programs take on a life of their own that is separate from the goals and work processes employed to achieve them. A culture of mediocrity, at least as far as learning and performance, takes over.

However, results assessment rarely succeeds in assessing performance outcomes, let alone learning, when assessment is only an occasional event. The most effective strategy is to create a culture in which results assessments become routine and expected. Here are four key strategies for overcoming resistance to change:

Overcoming Resistance Strategy #1: Implement only what the culture will allow.
The first hard lesson that results assessment professionals must learn is that many people do not welcome results assessment in organizations. Most likely, one of these typical reactions from implementing results assessment would occur:

- Fear that the results will not be good
- Anxiety about how the data will be used

- Uncertainty about why results assessment is needed
- Doubt about the validity of assessing results from learning
- Discomfort that the program must lead to organizational and individual performance
- Anger because someone is "checking up" on outcomes
- Wishing that self-directed development were sufficient

Ironically, individuals and companies that have the most to gain from results assessment also have the most to lose if the results are not good. Thus, the resistance may actually be greater in organizations that have the most to gain. Thus, introducing results assessment into an organization has to be seen as *both* a *measurement task* with associated technical issues, and a *culture change process.*

Overcoming Resistance Strategy #2: Compromise on measurement issues in the early stages to gain acceptance.

Insisting on rigorous measurement too soon after introducing results assessment is a common mistake. Conducting more lenient measurement initially and increasing the rigor as the culture adjusts is a preferable approach. By doing so, there is a greater likelihood for acceptance. Although the measurement from early efforts will be less accurate, they will also be less threatening. Over time, participants often begin to demand more accurate data, which is exactly what you want them to do. The key is to do what the culture will allow, and perhaps a little more, and then add to it as acceptance is gained. After a few results assessments have taken place, people usually will see their value and realize that they are not something to be feared.

Overcoming Resistance Strategy #3: Sell Results Assessment.

Do not expect everyone to welcome you with open arms when you propose results assessment! Even senior management may need to be sold on the idea of assessing results from HRD activities. Line managers may see it as just another demand on their time, and they may need to be convinced that it will help them in some way. Participants may be afraid that upper management is just checking up on them and may not realize that they will benefit as well.

In short, you must be prepared to sell the process to senior management, line management, and participants. Here are some key benefits that each group is likely to receive from implementing a program of results assessments; they can be used as selling points.

Senior Management:

- Increased productivity as a result of HRD
- Better use of dollars invested in HRD
- More satisfied line management

LINE MANAGEMENT:

- More immediate payoffs from HRD activities
- Increased productivity
- Greater involvement in HRD goals and planning
- Less time wasted on low value interventions

PARTICIPANTS:

- More targeted HRD interventions
- Clearer goals and performance outcomes expected
- Less time wasted
- Increased opportunities for feedback about program outcomes

Overcoming Resistance Strategy #4: Provide incentives and rewards for results assessment.

You can't ask people in organizations to do things they fear without providing some kind of incentives and rewards for doing so. Introducing results assessment in organizations is no different, particularly when it is an optional rather than mandatory activity. Incentives and rewards serve several purposes, including sending clear signals about the importance of results assessment; encouraging participants to take risks; and gaining support from key opinion leaders.

One frequent response to this suggestion is the statement by HRD managers that they don't have the authority to offer incentives and rewards. We disagree. Consider some of these examples:

- Offering extra assistance to the first groups willing to participate
- Giving preferential access to HRD resources for results assessment participants
- Developing special interventions to address performance improvement needs
- Publicly celebrating accomplishments of participating divisions or groups

Of course, upper management has more power to offer incentives and rewards; for example:

- Extra resources to fund results assessment and subsequent interventions
- Higher "status" to groups using best results assessment practices
- Creating processes to review and act on results assessment recommendations
- Publicly supporting and emphasizing results assessment

Organizations that are serious about results assessment recognize that incentives and rewards act as important signposts on the journey.

Summary

The thrust of effective evaluation is to make responsible judgments about important questions.

If an improved operation is what the T&D department wants to contribute, the inquiry must focus on hard data—and the evaluation must indicate whether or not the problem has been eliminated or significantly diminished. It breaks down into these steps:

1. Identify an unbearably deficient performance.
2. Identify specific units that characterize the problem.
3. Count the number of unacceptable units to establish a baseline.
4. Establish quantitative goals—a postprogram baseline objective.
5. Conduct the change program.
6. Count the satisfactory and unsatisfactory units after the program.
7. Evaluate. Is the number of satisfactory units equal to the objective established in step 4? In other words, did the program produce the desired results?

If the production of new behaviors is the extent of the T&D purpose, the evaluation will focus on the *demonstrated* acquisition and the perseverance of those behaviors. The successive steps are:

1. Establish the performance (learning) objectives.
2. Establish a desired achievement quota (the number of trainees divided into the number of behaviors acquired successfully).
3. Conduct the training or install the change program.
4. Test each trainee over each learning objective.
5. Compute the actual achievement quota.
6. Evaluate. Does the actual achievement quota equal or surpass the desired achievement quota?

When the mere acquisition isn't what the department wants to evaluate, there are additional steps the evaluate the on-the-job application of the new behaviors:

- Wait until a predetermined time and retest the graduates on each of the learning objectives.

- Compute the application quota: Divide the number of successful demonstrations by the number of graduates.
- Evaluate. Do the retentions of the new behavior equal the goals established? (These goals would amount to a step 2a, with quotas established for end-of-training and on-the-job evaluations.)

T&D officers who want to be relevant and accountable seek the hardest possible data from the widest possible range of representative sources.

Selecting and Retaining the T&D Staff

The Barefoot T&D Specialists

You've heard, of course, about the shoemaker's children?

They went barefoot!

Sometimes barefoot employees show up in T&D departments. They work for T&D managers, or for Directors of Human Resources Development, who develop the employees of every department except their own!

We cannot really call these people "neglected professionals" because their lack of expertise prevents them from ever becoming professional. Like the naked feet of the shoemaker's offspring, their missing competencies represent a pathetic and ironic training need: They do not practice T&D effectively because they do not know how to.

This chapter examines methods for putting the right people into the human growth business—and for keeping them growing after selection.

Selecting the T&D Staff

When T&D managers select people for their staffs, they should avoid some of the frequent traps.

Traps to Avoid

The *good-worker* trap is the most common. Because Henry was the best salesman on the force, they made him Sales Trainer in the Northwest Region. Because Eloise was a flawless teller, the bank promoted her to the role of

On-the-Job Trainer. In a few years, Henry and Eloise will be the forgotten "professionals" in the T&D department. Somebody goofed. The selection process was faulty. Demonstrated excellence in one assigned task does not indicate potential excellence in another—especially when that other task is instruction. Doing the task is one thing; teaching others to do it is dramatically different.

When organizations fall into the "good-worker" trap, they usually lose a good worker and gain a bad trainer. The truth is that they also multiply the number of bad workers. Why? Because inept or de-motivating instruction produces new generations who cannot do the job properly, or who have lost interest in doing so.

The *job knowledge* trap is very similar and equally dangerous. It is a particularly common error in selecting trainers. Now, there is nothing wrong with knowing the subject, but since adult growth involves so much more than merely acquiring information, to study under a person who has nothing but subject matter expertise is a cloying and narrowing bore. (It would be unfair to call it an "experience," since sitting and listening is often the fate assigned to students of subject matter experts who pretend to teach.)

An intelligent way to use the resources of subject matter experts (SMEs) is to make them members of the design team for training programs. These SMEs are invaluable: They bring authenticity, reality, and thoroughness to the task analysis or course content. The SMEs contributions are extremely valuable; this technique avoids trying to make communicators out of people who, though highly knowledgeable, may not be articulate enough to explain what they know—much less help others learn it.

Replicating great teachers is a third trap. Here's how it works—to everyone's detriment. The T&D manager recalls with great affection and admiration some great instructor from a private past. Old Smith told great jokes, so the T&D manager decides that a sense of humor is the key ingredient of successful instruction—and proceeds to develop a staff of comedians! Or Miss McGrath was so precise and careful. As a result, some T&D department is populated with an entire staff that thinks like accountants! The T&D manager remembers Professor Horner and the way he told things "like they were." The result? Some T&D staff form a group of abrasive, rabble rousing malcontents; they undercut organizational goals and devastate the organizational image.

Why does this effort to draw analogies with great teachers work so badly? It isn't just that it results in a staff without variety. Another sad effect is that the T&D manager tends to mold the staff into the image of the revered "model." There is no organic growth for staff members.

The fallacy is the one-dimensional nature of the selection and development process. There is no argument about the value of a sense of humor, or care, or precision, or "telling it like it is." But none of these qualities in itself is a sufficient foundation for effective performance as a T&D specialist. The T&D manager must look for several dimensions when populating the T&D staff.

Trap number four is *wants out—not in* candidates. This merely means that some people take T&D assignments not because they want T&D assignments but because they want out of the positions they're in.

This is an especially dangerous trap because it's easy for such applicants to demonstrate great enthusiasm for the training function. They have read (or can easily imagine) all the standard, exciting things to say about how important it is to train and develop others. They grow misty-eyed about the inspiration created by great teachers. Such testimonials are delusive, sweet songs to the ears of T&D managers. But when they select the singers of such sweet songs, they end up with a staff of temporary cheerleaders. That enthusiasm lasts just as long as their new responsibilities dazzle the new T&D specialists. As soon as they tire of it, they start looking. Once again they want out!

The *narrow-role* trap victimizes those who select a candidate who will excel greatly in just one role or very few of the many necessary skills. Such people may have little skill or interest in other facets of the total T&D spectrum. Desire to perform, or competency in just a very areas few raises several potential problems.

First, the job may quickly become impoverished, focusing on such narrow tasks that the occupant becomes bored and disenchanted with the entire T&D process. Second, the T&D manager is unable to achieve the necessary cross-utilization of the staff. If a sudden crisis or a new development requires a consultant's services, the "narrow-role" T&D specialist may be unqualified or uninterested. T&D managers are wise to select people who can grow with the department and into more than one of the four roles that must be fulfilled by someone on the T&D staff.

The *personality* trap is the sixth and final pitfall. It is a two-dimensional snare: (1) the traits are hard to identify, and (2) they distract us from looking for identified skills.

We say we seek a person with "a good personality," whatever that means. We often mean gregarious, extroverted, pleasant, all nice traits. But these traits don't reflect specific, demonstrated competencies. For example, consider these commonly sought characteristics: warmth, indirectness, cognitive organization, and enthusiasm. When we really examine those "traits," they translate into behaviors rather than personality qualities.

"Warmth" boils down to establishing two-way communication and expressing concern for the learners and the learning process.

"Indirectness" involves skill in getting at things obliquely. It means not supplying answers, but answering questions with questions. It means referring the question back to the asker. It means using other learners as a resource for the answers and for the learning.

"Cognitive organization" isn't the same as mastery of the subject, although it implies that. Rather, cognitive organization is skill in retrieving what is known in showing learners where they can find answers in establishing connections between several parts of the learning inquiry.

"Enthusiasm" comes closest to being a trait. Yet even it is defined as "energy for the learner and learning goals." It is clearly distinguished from cheerleading and showmanship.

To understand the real problem encountered from falling into the personality trap, try to make a list of the traits you want in people who join your staff. There's patience, intelligence, flexibility, pleasing appearance, sense of humor, sympathy, and empathy. It begins to sound like a recipe for divinity, doesn't it? Far more to the point are things such as strong legs (to endure through the day) and questioning skills and the ability to count to ten when difficult students become abrasive.

The point is that these personality traits are hard to spot in other people, especially during the limited time available in interviews. Even if we have the aid of written tests, we are unable to match the candidates' inventories with the tasks they will be performing as T&D specialists. At least, we're not able to do so by examining traits. So what do we do instead?

Far better that we look for demonstrated abilities in the form of behaviors, which we can watch for when we interview candidates. What are those skills we seek?

Skills to Look For

The competencies listed in McLagan's (1983) American Society for Training and Development (ASTD) study include skills and "understandings." The skills are:

Career development knowledge	Counseling skill
Data reduction skill	Feedback skill
Industry understanding	Library skills
Model building skills	Negotiation skills
Presentation skill	Questioning skill
Records management skill	Relationship versatility
Objectives preparation skill	Research skill
Delegation skill	Writing skill
Cost-benefit analysis skill	Futuring skill

With all that variety, and with continuous research adding depth to each competency, no one expects to hire a master of all—or probably even to develop one! Yet certain behavioral patterns provide a checklist to use when selecting people for any T&D staff.

These questions get at many of the competencies, with special focus on intellectual and relationship versatility, or counseling and feedback skills. It comes close to combining a search for traits, behaviors, and competencies all at once.

First, *can they listen?* They'll need to do a great deal of it, so it's good technique to give them a chance to listen while being interviewed. This doesn't mean that the interviewer does all the talking. The usual advice is correct: The candidate should do most of the talking. Most—but not all.

Since T&D specialists will need to listen for feelings as well as content, it's also a good idea to see how they handle certain emotional things as well as technical data and intellectual content. Check to see whether applicants pick up the little cues you give them about your feelings; find out how they handle process analysis by sharing some of your feelings about how the interview is going. Reflect upon what they have said, then check their responses to that reflection. Double-check their listening by asking something that requires recall of facts you've already supplied. Find out whether they "pick up on" questions arising out of a topic you've only sketchily described.

Next, do they *probe for feelings?* When they ask you about the work, do they inquire about the human responses associated with performing the tasks? Do they wonder about the qualms their students might feel at learning to do old things in new ways? Do they sense the feelings associated with acquiring brand new behaviors? Listening for feelings represents one essential skill; *probing* for them goes a step beyond (and ahead!) of mere listening. Beyond these, a third level of listening skill is needed.

Do they *respond constructively to feelings?* When you revealed something of your own emotions during the interview, how did the applicant react? Did the applicant change the subject? Blush? Awkward silence? Or did you get a further inquiry? Reflection? As Carl Rogers (1969) points out, the effective facilitator of learning will be as responsive to students' feelings as to their ideas.

Can they *deal with conflict?* For mature ideas to be examined in mature, dynamic ways, T&D specialists will need to handle conflict. When consulting, they will face sharp differences about the nature, causes, and impact of performance problems. As designers, they will experience conflict about the appropriateness of a method, or about the receiving department's readiness for certain learning methodology. Instructors face sharp disagreement about theories, policies, and procedures. Administrators resolve conflict on their staff and they resolve conflicts with and between client-managers.

Can they *change their opinions?* Somewhere between total lack of conviction and plain stubbornness is the degree of flexibility needed in effective T&D specialists. Perhaps it boils down to this for consultants, designers, and instructors:

Does new evidence produce an amendment in their original opinions? For administrators this is a major mental skill. Without it, there is no evidence that the T&D specialist can grow. If T&D specialists cannot grow, they will have great difficulty in stimulating growth in others.

This issue of mental flexibility ("intellectual versatility" in the ASTD Competency Study) again raises the issue of how important subject knowledge is to the instructor's role. The credibility of the instructor is important if the objective of the training is to *expand* the experience of the learner.

It must therefore be apparent that the instructor is more concerned with mental processes than with mental inventory. It must also be apparent that if instructors are selected just because they know the subject they will teach, the training program is headed for trouble. To be master or mistress of a technology is a comforting position—but that very comfort can be the source of failure in the dynamics of the classroom, or when the technology changes. Thus the importance of selecting instructors who can evaluate information and who can change their minds when new information requires new opinions.

Do they *ask a lot of questions?* Questioning skills are important in the repertory of people performing all of the four T&D roles. A propensity to use questions can reveal itself during the interview. Later on, as part of their upgrading, the T&D manager can see that they learn the proper use of open, directive, and reflective types of questions. At the selection stages, one just wants to measure their comfort with the interrogative mode. As good T&D specialists, they'll be there a lot.

Is there a *high energy level* as they communicate? As we have already noted, this is enthusiasm—not showmanship. It is certainly a vastly different thing from public speaking skills. In fact, platform skills can be counterproductive to effective instruction. Why? Ego and speaking skills can tempt the trainer to send signals rather than to indulge in the two-way communication needed to create learning and to test what learners are learning. Speaking skills tempt trainers to feel that the job has been done well if the lesson has been "said" well. The focus is on presentation rather than on learning.

High energy levels, however, are important to the T&D specialist for several reasons:

- Days are long. The analysis of performance problems can mean arduous, taxing efforts that must be plowed through to completion—now. The analysis doesn't end just because the normal workday is over.
- Leadership is hard work. It's physically taxing. At the end of counseling, instructing, or consulting, both the body and the spirit can easily be "all achin' and racked with pain."

- Designing requires creativity—and creation (as many have noted) is part perspiration and part concentration. At any rate, it can be exhausting—and usually is.
- Conference or class leadership requires more than normal vocal and physical outputs. The instructor will need energy in great quantities at moments when the group must be "centered" around a single concept, task, topic, or issue. Group and individual attentions must be redirected every now and then; it requires great concentration, more purposeful movement, and a louder voice.
- Above all, the instructor is always "living the learning" of every person in the group. That demands fantastically high energy levels.

Can the candidates *express themselves effectively?* Verbal skills play a heavy part in success for all four of the T&D roles. This does not mean a big vocabulary or impeccable grammar. Rather, it means a vocabulary that responds to learners' vocabularies. It means a vocabulary that blends the concrete and the abstract so that concepts can become realities—and so immediate realities can lead to insights about principles. It means sentences that make sense the first time learners hear them. It means taking the trouble to communicate the transitions between ideas linking them, contrasting them, showing parallels. It means letting people know when you move up or down the ladder of abstraction on which words and ideas exist. It means checking for clarity and stimulating learners' imagination—simultaneously.

Can the applicant *reinforce?* Be careful of this one. It certainly doesn't mean, "Are they agreeable?" Far from it. All one needs on the T&D staff is a mollycoddle Pollyanna or an obsequious Caspar Milquetoast.

However, the ability to give positive reinforcement is extremely important in probing, in resolving conflict, in teaching. Especially in teaching! Positive reinforcement is vitally helpful in aiding learners as they reach learning goals, particularly difficult learning goals. Effective instructors find the element that is correct or appropriate in each learner-response; then they reinforce that correct element positively. The ability to give this reinforcement can be observed during the initial interview; it can be strengthened as one of the first lessons in the further training of the T&D specialist. (That learning can begin during the interview if the T&D manager effectively reinforces worthwhile behaviors and responses from the candidate.)

There is a long list of things instructors need to do if they are to become growing and growth-creating members of the T&D staff. Let's look at that list, considering first those things needed for classroom instructors and later the list for those who will perform on-the-job training.

If the T&D Specialist Will Do Classroom Teaching and If the T&D Specialist Will Do Conference Leading

Then the initial upgrading should make them able to	*And later follow-up training can make them able to*
Follow lesson plans designed by others	Select media
Comprehend the intent and structure of behaviorally stated learning objectives	Design visual aids for display and/or projection
Write behaviorally stated learning objectives for tasks in all departments that will supply trainees to their classes or conferences	Conduct such special case methods as action mazes, incident process, or critical incidents
Identify complete learning objectives	Design on-the-spot cases and tasks so buzz groups or entire classes can solve identified but unanticipated job-related or learning problems
Develop performance standards	
Use dynamic listening skills	
Comprehend and apply stimulus-response theory	Conduct such special role-playing formats as reversal, rotation, or doubling
Use questioning skills	
Probe for feelings	Create "hot role-plays" for dealing with class dynamics issues
Respond appropriately to feelings	
Lead discussions	Experience T-groups and become able to function as observer for T-groups
Conduct workshops using buzz groups management meetings and team tasks	Function in an open-discussion environment
Administer and review tests and quizzes	Speak before such large groups and professional societies
Administer performance tryouts	
Design performance tryouts	
Conduct Job Instruction Training (JIT)	
Demonstrate how to do specific tasks	
Conduct structured case studies	
Conduct structured games and simulations	
Administer in-baskets	
Reinforce successive approximations of desired behaviors	

That's clearly an extensive list and a big order! All the lists shown here will be like that. Why? Because we want to show the full range of skills the T&D professional will use; and our use of the word "professional" doesn't apply to those who become "stranded" in the T&D Department.

Our professionals are those who can use a wide technology. The list shows the widest technology possible! To do their work well, single-person T&D Departments will need to select carefully, searching out those skills that will be used most frequently—and balancing the self-development program so they prepare themselves to function in as many of the four T&D roles as possible.

If the T&D Specialists Will Do On-The-Job Training

Then initial training should make them able to	And later follow-up training can make them able to
Conduct structured on-the-job training	Develop performance standards
Comprehend the intent and structure of behaviorally stated learning objectives	Design visual aids for display and/or projection
Write behaviorally stated learning objectives for the skills in their own department	Lecture
	Lead discussions
Comprehend the structure and intent of performance standards	Create "real things" as visual aids (actual or facsimile objects for trainees to handle while learning)
Do task analysis	
Demonstrate proper performance of tasks in their department	Follow lesson plans that call for experience-based methods
Comprehend and apply stimulus-response theory	
Reinforce successive approximations of desired student behaviors	
Use effective listening skills	
Use questioning skills	
Test achievement of learners	
Provide feedback of learning achievements	
Respond appropriately to feelings	
Probe for feelings	

As we know, there are at least four major roles to be filled in the T&D department. Designers of learning systems need special skills.

If T&D Specialists Will Design Learning

Their initial training should make them able to	*And later follow-up training can make them able to*
Create logical outlines	Conduct task analysis
Develop performance standards	Develop structures for special discussion formats as brainstorms, fishbowls, polling, collages, force-field analysis
Write behaviorally stated learning objectives	
Apply learning theory (especially positive reinforcement) in lesson plans	Develop entire modules based on experiential methods
Include effective questions in lessons	Prepare scripts for multimedia presentations
Provide outlines and materials for job instruction training (JIT)	Design new formats for lesson plans
Produce lesson plans in formats approved or required by client organizations	
Select appropriate media	
Design visual aids for display, projection, or handling	
Locate case studies, role-plays, and exercises in standard sources	
Design case studies	
Design role-plays	
Create storyboards and scripts for presentations	
Design behavior-maintenance systems and routinely include them in all training designs	
Design programmed instruction	
Provide mechanisms to test learner accomplishments of each objective	

Not all T&D specialists are involved with learning, or administer its processes. Before the decision is made to do any training, a great deal of performance analysis occurs by T&D staff people serving as consultants to the organization. What does their expertise include?

When T&D Specialists Serve As Consultants Who Identify and Solve Performance Problems

Initial training should enable them to	*Follow-up training should add competencies so they can also*
Question clients	Conduct and design conferences
Conduct performance audits (analysis)	Conduct ongoing organization development, implying skill in process analysis, structured data gathering, and "hot" data gathering such as organization mirroring, T-shirting, the library
Do task analysis	
Do cost-analysis of performance problems	
Analyze cost-effectiveness of solutions	
Probe for facts and feelings	Lead discussions, using fishbowls, brainstorms, confrontation, case studies, valuing exercises, etc.
Empathize and respond appropriately to facts and feelings	
Verify perceptual data	Conduct research and present the results to client-management and/or professional societies
Help write performance standards	
Use rational systems for problem	Implement a changed-contingencies system
Speak before large groups within the organization	
Comprehend a job-reengineering project	Help install reengineered jobs
Assist in installing a job-reengineering project	
Help maintain behaviors acquired in any change program	
Do contingency analysis	
Write investigative reports with recommended solutions for performance problems	
Present oral proposals to small groups	
Create behaviorally oriented learning objectives	
Do statistical analysis of raw data	

When we consider the skills required of the T&D manager, we are, of course, examining a list that looks like the behaviors of any manager—plus some important special considerations. Our chart will examine just those special things; we will assume that all the other administrative and managerial skills are part of the inventory the T&D manager brings to the position—or acquires immediately after the first day on the job! (If that's a hasty assumption, then the typical Management Education curriculum must be added to the top of the chart!)

The Administrator of the T&D Function, in Addition to a Full Inventory of Standard Management Skills, Will Need to Be Able To

Initially	*As later growth*
Plan the T&D mission	Conduct process analysis and T-groups
Establish position descriptions	Lead organization development interventions, employing all the consultative, data-gathering, and problem-solving skills listed for T&D consultants
Write a T&D policy statement	
Select a T&D staff on specific criteria	
Organize T&D resources to meet the departmental goals	
Provide for ongoing growth for the T&D staff	Respond constructively to new directions required for the development and redirection of the T&D department as a responsive subsystem in the total organization
Control the ongoing T&D activities	
Budget for T&D activities	
Write effective (results-getting) proposals	Design, help install, and monitor job reengineering
Lead discussions	
Speak before classes, conferences, workshops, management, and professional gatherings	
Practice positive reinforcement	
Explain learning theory, including andragogy and facilitation	
Comprehend all skills employed by other, subordinate T&D staff members	
Use dynamic listening skills	
Use all forms of questioning	
Write behaviorally oriented learning objectives	
Assist in writing performance standards for all departments	
Determine actual performance standards for the T&D department	
Complete and install contingency changes	
Design and install feedback systems	

Then there's *control of the situation.* Perhaps this is nothing more than asking that candidates be themselves. A significant trend in adult education and training is the need for instructors to be real people, not actors impersonating plaster saints. This in no way implies that T&D specialists can be undisciplined, totally spontaneous creatures who lose their tempers or speak their minds whenever the spirit moves them to do so. But it does mean that they don't fall apart at the seams when their own humanity spills out. They are able to handle that; they are in control of the situation.

One might argue that the T&D manager who finds these behaviors or skills in candidates has really measured the personality traits of those candidates. If so, so be it. The important thing is that looking for demonstrated skill in listening, questioning, reinforcing, communicating, and being congruent assures the T&D manager that candidates can *do* something that they already have in their inventory, some of the things they will have to do when they become T&D specialists.

Granted, the nature of the initial T&D assignments makes a difference. T&D specialists who will analyze performance problems need somewhat different proficiencies from those who will instruct. Even within the instructor's role, we expect different skills from classroom instructors, conference leaders, and on-the-job trainers. But as already noted, the enriched T&D placement moves incumbents through more than one of the four T&D roles. Besides, there are some skills that are equally important to successful performance in every one of the roles.

The Care and Development of T&D Specialists

Now that you have them, how do you care for them?

Growth and change are the output of the T&D function. Strangely enough, they are also the processes by which that change is achieved. But rather than wrestle with the involutions of such thinking, let's just look at a plan for the development of the T&D staff.

The development plan for T&D staff amounts to meeting a series of individual training needs by using any or all of the methods that solve any individual training need: independent study, coaching, seminars and workshops, membership in professional associations. The list is long.

This growth for T&D specialists is a form of job training, so the "Tell, Show, Do, and Review" stages are important—with special emphasis on *doing* some work as soon as possible. Designing or presenting short modules of existing programs is effective; so is membership in professional societies. Young T&D staff members make introducers, moderators, chairpersons, and chapter managers—each an excellent way to develop several competencies.

In what role will the specialist perform? We need to offer different training to different people, depending upon what they will do while serving in the T&D department.

Rotation Policies

"We have two kinds of people on our training staff," said the training manager sadly. "Promotable young people and the professionals."

That's rather common. The instructor position is often used as an educational experience for employees who are "going someplace" in the management of the organization. These "promotables" rotate through a year or two in the T&D department.

There's much to be said for such a system. T&D experience, early in the rotation program, gives high-potential employees a wide and steadily growing perspective of the entire organization: T&D offers great opportunities to work with lots of people from lots of departments and with people who have sharply differing motivations, needs, viewpoints, and value systems. Furthermore, if the assignment in T&D includes instruction, design, consultation, and administration, the "cadets" gain experience in sharply contrasted skills.

Then why would that training manager feel such sadness when commenting on the promotable young people and the "professionals"? Let's listen a bit more: "It's policy around here to keep people in training three years, then to move them on to higher jobs in management. But some of our people have been here for ten or twelve years! They just don't seem to make it."

And that's what's to be said against the system of "rotating through" T&D as an education for major management assignments. Not everybody "makes it"—and unfortunately the ones who don't make it usually become the "professionals." It's a quintessential expression of George Bernard Shaw's acidic comment, "Those who can, do; those who can't, teach." Only in T&D, those who can't teach keep on doing so. Then as balm to the organizational conscience, they are informally referred to as "the professionals." The fact is that they are often lousy instructors who continue to inflict their amateur incompetence on helpless learners!

All apart from the organizational awkwardness such failures represent, there is the considerable pain for the individuals and T&D managers on whose "island" they tend to get stranded. Further conversation with the training manager we've been quoting revealed yet another dimension to the tragedy: "In fact I was supposed to rotate out of here myself. They brought me in here, and I didn't know anything about training. My three years were up last August—but I see no sign of getting out!"

This is a real situation—and not an unusual one. What does it teach us? That rotation through T&D assignments can be a good thing or a bad thing, depending upon how we manage such a system. If we use T&D as a spring-board to other management assignments, we need to take certain precautions:

1. The selection process needs to be precise, uncovering skills which will indicate probable success as a T&D specialist. Seat-of-the-pants hunches that prospective T&D staff members look bright, or that they "have a knack for training"—these are no longer adequate.

2. If service in T&D is indeed to provide education for its incumbents, the T&D manager must establish and maintain precise programs for their continued growth. Normal budget ratios may be inadequate; higher per-centages of staff time must be invested in staff training. T&D specialists need the continuous acquisition of new technology in analyzing perfor-mance problems, in designing and implementing learning designs, and in general management practices. Remember the shoemaker's children? They were barefoot! Thorough plans to put professional shoes on "cadets in the T&D department" are vital. As much as 10 percent of the total work time may go to professional upgrading for new T&D specialists.

3. Systematic, binding contracts for "reentry" to the line organization need to be executed from the very beginning. The contingencies for successful tours within the T&D department need to be positively re-warding for the "tourists."

4. "Escape routes" must be established for cadets who perform badly in their early T&D projects. It doesn't follow that these marginal perfor-mances should purge such cadets from the "promotables program"—but it does follow that frank career counseling is in order. (Such escape routes and frank counseling are imperative whenever T&D specialists do badly in early assignments. If coaching cannot correct the problems, then reassignment should be considered a useful action. Nothing will be gained for the individual, the T&D department, or the total organization by permissively letting marginal T&D specialists es-tablish reputations as second-raters.)

Many T&D departments regard themselves as professional, career place-ments. Thus rotation is not an established mechanism, and they have no "launching pad" responsibilities. Yet in actual practice, most departments turn out to have both temporary and permanent T&D specialists on the staff. Effec-tive T&D specialists are attractive (and attracted) to other managerial assign-ments. When they make such moves, the T&D manager should analyze the pattern of movement out of the department: Where do these ex-T&D special-ists go? Do they go to lateral placements? To demoted positions? To promo-tions? Unless the pattern is toward better positions, the T&D department is breeding "shoemakers' children." It is making a lie of the theory that training, education, and development enhances human resources. When placement within the T&D department does not lead to happy external placement, or expanded responsibilities within, the T&D manager needs to get busy with a solid plan for developing the T&D staff.

Let's stress one point that might—but shouldn't—get lost in that last paragraph. Unless the good T&D specialists assume increasing responsibility *within* the T&D department, then the good people don't become the "professionals." Even if there is no rotation policy—but particularly when there is such a system—the "old-timers" on the T&D staff should be the most professional as well as the most senior.

Summary

Those lists of requisite skills seem a long way from Shaw's judgment that those who can, do—and those who can't, teach! It is also a long way from those forgotten "professionals" who never successfully rotated through a T&D assignment or who performed marginally and became incompetent incumbents. Perhaps their lonely obsolescence came about because no one cared specifically for their continued professional development.

Why is that list of requisite skills so long? Well, it may be too long for some organizations, unrealistic as a picture of what technology most T&D staffs really master. But it is also a long list because we've come a long way since Shaw first deprecated the teacher. In fact, we've learned that the T&D department does a lot more than just teach.

It isn't just that the T&D department is no longer perceived as starting and ending with training. In addition, behaviorist psychology, facilitative learning theories, performance analysis technologies—all these have accounted for growth in our perception of the T&D function.

With that growth has come the concept of accountability. And one big accountability is for T&D specialists to serve as performance problem solvers. To do that, there is the inevitable added accountability of selecting and developing the right people to identify important problems and to solve them effectively.

The impact of that challenge is more apparent when we stop to think that every behavior by a T&D specialist or a T&D manager impacts geometrically upon the organization. A successful class changes the performance of everyone who attends; a wise decision about how to solve a performance problem produces changed working conditions for entire populations, for incumbents, and for employees yet to be hired.

All the more reason for the careful selection and relentless energy in the continued growth of people on the T&D staff.

Does Employee Development Pay Off?

The ultimate purpose of all development metrics is to answer the basic question, "Does employee development pay off?" Everywhere we go, human resource professionals and other managers are hungry for clear evidence that development resources are being effectively used. At a gut level, most believe in development, but cannot produce data when challenged to provide evidence that will defend development investments. We have proposed new metrics that we believe will enable organizations to install more effective accountability systems and thus be able to answer that question continuously during their development efforts. Unfortunately, we have not yet received data and results from organizations using our proposed metrics.

However, there is a growing body of compelling evidence from a variety of sources that clearly indicates development efforts work when properly designed and carried out. The purpose of this section is to provide an overview of studies and data and show that when resources are invested in development and retention, they do eventually pay off—and usually quite substantially. This is the document that human resource professionals can use when management asks, "Does development really work?" The data reported here is focused on the effectiveness of development interventions, not just on the effectiveness of people possessing certain skills. Thus, it speaks directly to whether it is cost-effective for organizations to undertake development programs and initiatives.

Results from development programs can be considered in three domains with two groups within each domain (Swanson and Holton 1999):

BOX 18.1. Domains of Results from Development Programs

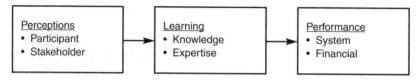

Traditionally, development results have been assessed on the basis of perceptions of participants, and, sometimes, knowledge-type learning (e.g., tests). However, the strategic value of development lies in performance results (system and financial) that are achieved only through developing expertise results (e.g., changing job behaviors). Unfortunately, surveys of results assessment practice over the last forty years show that very few development efforts assess performance results, and there has not been much increase in performance results assessment (Twitchell, Holton, and Trott 2000). Therefore, the question of whether development *really* pays off continues to linger. Thus, we will focus here on available data that provides evidence of a payoff for investments in development, either through change in performance or in financial returns.

Because there is not yet one authoritative source that documents such returns, we will draw on a variety of data sources to assemble a mosaic of evidence that collectively demonstrates that development does indeed pay off. These data sources are divided into the following sections:

- *American Society for Training and Development (ASTD) Learning Outcomes Report*—one of the largest samples of learning outcomes data available.
- *High Performance Work Practices Studies*—these show the relationship between high-performance work practices that have development as a core component.
- *Program Results Assessment Case Studies*—a large body of case study literature demonstrating that significant returns on investment are possible when development is done correctly.

American Society for Training and Development (ASTD) Learning Outcomes Report

ASTD's 2000 *Learning Outcomes Report* (Bassi and Ahlstrand 2000) is its second annual report of results from firms using its measurement kit. It covers only outcomes from formal training programs. The 2000 report includes outcome data obtained at two points—at the end of training and during follow-up after training. For end of training data, the outcomes represent 7,917 courses and 375,704 participants. Follow-up data represents 2,397 courses, 14,386 learner responses, supervisory responses on 1,695 courses, and 9,825 individual supervisor reports. The respondents represent a broad cross-section of countries, firm size, and training type.

Of most interest to us here are the post-training follow-up responses. These responses would be considered Learning-Expertise results using the results assessment framework discussed in the introduction. Two questions were asked of supervisors and training participants: What percent change occurred in participants' performance on the course objectives and in the participants' overall job performance? Because the supervisors' ratings tended to be lower than the participants', we will use them because they are the more conservative estimate.

For change in performance on the course objectives, the average improvement across all training types was 34 percent, ranging from 24 to 40 percent for training other than new employee orientation, which reported 67 percent improvement. This measure indicates how much change occurred in skill areas specifically targeted by the training. For change in overall job performance, the average improvement across all training types was 29 percent, ranging from 20 to 43 percent for training other than new employee orientation, which reported a 66 percent improvement. Participant ratings on improvement were close to supervisor ratings, though usually slightly higher. Reported improvement percentages for different training types are shown in Table 18.1.

TABLE 18.1. Supervisor Ratings of Performance Improvement

Training Type	% Performance Improvements on Course Objectives	% Improvement in Overall Job Performance
Technical processes and procedures	38	34
Product knowledge	38	42
New employee orientation	67	66
Professional skills	34	24
Information technology skills	34	27
Sales and dealer	40	42
Managerial/supervisory skills	34	30
Basic skills	32	26
Customer relations	38	34
Occupational safety	30	25
Executive development	31	28
Interpersonal communications	27	27
Quality, competition and business practices	24	20

SOURCE: Bassi & Ahlstrand, 2000.

These data clearly suggest strong performance improvement from training. Although there is no data here to indicate whether the changed performance resulted in financial returns, the strong improvements in overall job performance as reported by supervisors of participants (who are less likely to give biased results than the participants' responses) is compelling. Clearly, training makes a difference. The ASTD Learning Outcomes data points to this conclusion:

Core Conclusion #1
Training and Development can change job behaviors and overall job performance.

Studies in High-Performance Human Resource Practices

In recent years, researchers have focused on demonstrating the value of human resource practices in improving organizational performance. Various labels are attached to the set of practices, but "high-performance human resource (HR) practices" seems most appropriate. A core part of high-performance human resource practice is a strong commitment to employee development, particularly of skills critical to the success of the organization. Thus, these studies provide useful evidence of development's value, although they do not isolate the effect of development alone.

Because these studies appear in academic journals, many practitioners are not aware of them. This section will provide key findings from these studies that are useful to HR practitioners. The primary advantage of the findings in this section is that they are based on rigorous research methodologies that are usually generalizable to some extent. All represent organization, or plant-level, data, as opposed to traditional program-level results assessment and are considered key studies in justifying the value of HR development.

Studies of a Broad Cross-Section of Companies

Huselid (1997) surveyed 3,452 firms representing all major industries in the United States. The final sample was of 968 firms. The survey consisted of thirteen high-performance work practices that were clustered into two groups: Employee skills and organization structure (which contains development) and employee motivation. He then obtained financial data on each firm from publicly available sources to assess the impact of the high-performance practices on turnover, productivity (sales per employee) and financial performance (Tobin's Q and gross rate of return on capital) while controlling for a number of factors such as firm size and industry.

TABLE 18.2. Practical Results of Huselid

Measure	Change in Measure for Each 1 Standard Deviation Change in High-Performance
Turnover	1.3 raw percentage points 7.05% decrease from mean
Productivity	$24,044 sales increase per year
Financial performance	$18, 641 increase in market value $3,814 increase in cash flow

The results are encouraging. Clearly, development pays off in lower turnover, higher productivity, and improved financial performance.

Guzzo, Jette, and Katzell (1985) used a statistical technique called meta-analysis to aggregate the results from ninety-eight studies where what we now call high-performance work practices were introduced into organizations. The practices they examined included recruitment and selection, training and instruction, appraisal and feedback, management by objectives, goal setting, work redesign, financial compensation, decisionmaking techniques, sociotechnical interventions, supervisory methods, and work rescheduling. Three types of performance were examined: output, withdrawal from the organization, and disruptions in the organization (accidents, strikes, etc.). Thus, this is a very comprehensive analysis. The results are impressive:

- Over all the studies and intervention types, the average productivity of the worker receiving the interventions was 0.44 standard deviations above the average worker not receiving them. This is a very substantial difference.
- The effect was largest for disruption measures (effect = 0.82 std. dev.) and next largest for output (effect = 0.63 std. dev.).
- Training, goal setting, and sociotechnical systems design had the most powerful effects.
- For training alone, the average productivity for those receiving the interventions was 0.78 standard deviations above the average worker.
- The largest effect for training was 0.85 on the output measure, indicating that workers receiving training interventions performed 0.85 standard deviations above the worker not receiving training.

The National Organizations Study (NOS) is a special module of the General Social Survey that was conducted in 1991 with the support of the National

Science Foundation (Kalleberg, Knoke, Marsden, and Spaeth 1996). The NOS used a special procedure to obtain a sample of 727 firms representative of U.S. work establishments. A variety of questions were asked of organizations about their HR practices and their performances relative to their competitors. Five performance scales were developed to measure: Products (product quality and development); employees (attract and retain essential employees); customer satisfaction, relations, and market factors (marketing, growth in sales, profitability, and market share).

Results showed that training was significantly correlated with all performance measures except customer satisfaction. The specific correlations are illustrated in Table 18.3 below:

TABLE 18.3. Correlation of Training and Perceived Performance Measures

Performance Measure	Correlation with Training
Product	.181
Relations	.097
Employees	.149
Market factors	.221
Customer satisfaction	-.007

Delaney and Huselid (1996) also used the NOS data set but analyzed the data a little differently. They constructed measures of nine different HR practices from the NOS data and tested the ability of these measures to predict two performance measures: perceived organizational performance and perceived performance in the product marketplace. The correlation of training alone with performance in the product marketplace was 0.19 but only 0.06 with organizational performance. Training and the other HR practices together explained approximately 18.5 percent of the variance in organizational performance and 26.5 percent of the variance in product performance.

TABLE 18.4. Correlations of Regression Analysis of Training with Perceived Performance Measures

Perceived Performance Measure	Correlation with Training	Percent of Variance Explained by Training and Other HR Practices
Organizational performance	.06	18.5%
Performance in the product marketplace	.19	26.5%

Bartel (1994) examined a cross-section of companies that had below average productivity in 1983. Her analysis showed that these firms chose to implement training programs in about half of their employee groups as a result of the lower productivity instead of implementing other HR interventions. The result was an 18.86 percent productivity gain over a three-year period.

Studies of Manufacturing Plants

Youndt, Snell, Dean, and Lepak (1996) selected 512 manufacturing plants to study the effect of HR and manufacturing practices on plant performance. Data obtained from the final sample of 100 plants included measures of operational performance, human resource practices (two parts—human capital enhancing and administrative), and four dimensions of manufacturing strategy.

Two key results emerged:

- Only 15 percent of the variation in performance was explained by manufacturing strategy alone. When HR systems were added, 36 percent of the variation in performance was explained, and only the human capital enhancing dimension of HR practices was statistically significant.
- The effects of human capital enhancing HR practices actually occurred in combination with quality oriented manufacturing strategies.

Their results clearly indicate that development interventions that enhance human capital are very important in conjunction with high-quality initiatives. Furthermore, human capital enhancing HR practices explained more of the variation in performance than did manufacturing strategy.

Lam and White (1998) also studied manufacturing firms from fourteen different industries. Using a survey, they assessed the "HR orientation" of each company, which they defined as "a systematic organizational effort to attract, retain, and develop competent and committed employees" (357). Using an interesting methodology, they asked HR executives to provide information about two *competing firms* rather than their own company. This data was analyzed for the effect on three measures of financial performance: return on assets, growth in sales, and growth in stock values while controlling for various extraneous factors. The results showed that HR orientation was important over and above the influence of control variables. Together with controls, HR orientation

explained 26 percent of the variability in return on assets;
explained 25 percent of the growth in sales.

Arthur (1994, 1992) developed a technique that classified steel "mini-mills" in the United States in two groups: those with a control oriented culture, and those with a commitment culture. The commitment culture was defined to include high levels of employee development along with participation. Results showed that those with commitment cultures had higher productivity (lower labor hours per ton) and half the turnover rates of the control oriented cultures.

Survival of Firms with IPOs

Welbourne and Andrews (1996) examined the prospectuses of 136 nonfinancial IPO (initial public offering) firms to determine their emphasis on human capital/resources, including training. They then analyzed the data to determine the impact of emphasizing human capital on market value and five-year survival rates. After controlling for key extraneous variables, they found that the firms placing greater emphasis on human resources were more likely to survive for five years. In fact, valuing human resources along with rewards for performance correctly predicted 71 percent of the firms that survived for five years.

Retail Store Study

Russell, Terborg, and Powers (1985) examined a large international retail organization to assess the effects of training on store performance. In this organization, training programs for sales personnel were developed at the corporate level and distributed to each store. Store managers then made the decision about how many sales personnel to train. The average percent of sales personnel trained was 31.5 percent, but ranged as high as 80 percent. Store personnel were also asked to rate the degree of training emphasis in the store. Key results were:

- These two training variables explained 12 percent of the variability in store performance and 32 percent of the variability in store image, a key performance measure in retail.
- Each percentage point increase in people trained resulted in a sales gain of $37,258 for the average store.
- Improvement of one-half standard deviation in percentage trained (about 16 percentage points) increased store sales by $613,646.
- This was true even while controlling for the amount of support employees received.

Quality of Work-Life Companies

Lau and May (1998) conducted an interesting analysis to compare companies selected as the best companies to work for in the United States with the Standard and Poor's top one hundred companies (S&P 100). The first group they labeled "quality of work-life companies" because the selection criteria centered around employee satisfaction, retention, and growth opportunities. They selected four financial measures: sales growth, asset growth, return on assets, and return on equity.

The results are shown in Table 18.5 below:

TABLE 18.5. Comparison of Quality of Work Life and S&P Companies

Financial Measure	Mean for Quality of Work Life Companies	Mean for S&P 100
Sales growth	8.80%	2.53%
Asset growth	9.88%	4.62%
Return on assets	5.62%	3.58%
Return on equity	11.10%	10.20%

The difference between the two groups was statistically significant for all except return on equity. Thus, companies with higher quality of work life grew faster and had a higher return on assets. One must be very careful to not conclude that quality of work life causes higher returns because the cause and effect relationships cannot be determined from this data. Nonetheless, the association between quality of work life and financial returns is striking.

Leadership and Management Training

Burke and Day (1986) used meta-analysis to aggregate the results of seventy studies examining the effectiveness of leadership or managerial training. Their classic article shows the effectiveness of managerial development interventions. Their key results include:

- For studies using objective behavioral outcome measures (expertise):
  The average effect was to change behavior by 0.38 standard deviations, a very substantial change.
  Motivation training had the largest effect on behavior (effect = 0.81 std. dev.), human relations training having the next highest effect (effect = 0.41 std. dev.).

- For studies using objective performance results outcome measures:

    The average effect was to change results by 0.67 standard deviations, a very substantial change.

    Human relations had the largest effect (effect = 1.04 std. dev.) with general management having substantial effect as well (effect = 0.53 std. dev.).

Conclusion

The high-performance work practices studies generally bundle training or development with other related HR practices so that in one sense they are limited in their ability to speak to the value of development interventions alone. However, they also represent the most rigorous studies documenting the value of key HR strategies that have development as a core component. Thus, we suggest they provide important evidence that supports development as a key to strategic advantage and organizational performance. The correlations and percent of variance explained in the above studies are considered substantial from a practical viewpoint and collectively lead us to conclude that

Core Conclusion #2

Development should be a central part of HR strategy and HR strategy is a major determinant of organizational performance.

Program Results Assessment Case Studies

In addition to the Learning Outcomes Report and the high-performance work practices studies, numerous case studies have also documented the need for and the effectiveness of development programs. These case studies represent traditional program-level results assessments as opposed to the organization-level data reported in the previous section. The financial figures provided in these case studies provide a convincing argument that significant returns on investment can be achieved when developmental efforts are properly conducted. Included among the sources for these case studies are Swanson's article "Assessing the Financial Benefits of Human Resource Development" (Swanson 1998); and several books in ASTD's *In Action* series: specifically, *Measuring Return on Investment,* vol. 1 (Philips 1994); *Measuring Return on Investment,* vol. 2 (Philips 1997); *Measuring Return on Investment,* vol. 3 (Philips 2001); and *In Action: Measuring Learning and Performance* (Hodges 1999).

The table below illustrates the effectiveness of development by highlighting the financial payoff figures for some of the well-designed and well-executed development efforts. Note that not every case included in these texts appears in this table, nor is the table designed to be a statistical or representative sample of the cases. *What they clearly show is that development works when done properly and for the right reasons.* The basis of case selection included the following criteria:

- The development strategy was clearly described.
- The development initiative was properly executed.
- The financial benefits/value of the develop intervention was calculated and reported.

As you can see, these fifty-one cases (see Table 18.6 below) represent a variety of T&D initiatives (e.g., task/technical, sales, communication/soft skills, coaching, innovation, empowerment, computer/information technology, negotiation, process improvement, management and leadership development, and employee socialization). Some key findings from the cases include:

- The ROI (return on investment) for the sales training which ranged from 118 percent to 2,307 percent clearly presents compelling support for the effectiveness of properly executed sales training.
- The same can be said for task and technical training, which garnered ROI figures ranging from 7:1 to 159:1; and for literacy training, which resulted in an ROI of 741 percent.
- Similarly, the financial impact of supervisory, management and leadership development programs, with results including a $7 million savings, 77.2 percent sales increase, and ROI figures ranging from 160 percent to 1447 percent, provides significant returns by all definitions.
- In most of these cases, the actual ROI or other measured financial benefit greatly exceeded the forecasted benefits.

Core Conclusion #3
Development programs, when properly executed, can yield very high return on investments and improved performance.

Summary

This chapter provides ammunition to every HR professional who asks, "Does employee development pay off?" The data synthesized here provide compelling evidence that the answer is yes. More specifically, we conclude from the data that:

Collectively the data reported in this section provide clear and convincing evidence that development can be a key strategy for organizational improvement with substantial returns. Of course, it does not mean that all development is good, but that development done properly and for the right reasons will pay off.

TABLE 18.6. Program Results Assessment Case Summary: Swanson's Human Resource Development Article

Case Name	Industry Type	HRD Program	Target Audience	Results/ Expected Results
Optical lens grinding case	Optical	Technical training	Skilled workers in optical lens environment	$15 value to the quality completion of task
Mosham's cost-benefit analysis of industrial training	Manufacturing	Task training	Clothing machine operators	ROI of 8:1 for 4-year 30% increase in average performance level of new trainee/worker first year following training; performance level leveled off after 1st year
Swanson & Sawzin's industrial training research project	Manufacturing	Task training	Plastic mold operators	ROI of 10:1 in a 2-month period Greater training time required to reach competence through unstructured training, structured training workers produced significantly less waste and solved more production problems Break even point for development and delivery of structured training was 10 trainees
General Electric	Diversified	Soft skills training	Company managers	ROI of 8:1 for communication skills training, given the financial consequences of reduced turnover No significant difference in punctuality or number of grievances filed between experimental and control groups
G.D. Geroy & R. A. Swanson	Manufacturing	Technical training		Forecasted ROI: ROI estimates of 7:1; 11:1; 11:1; and 22:1 Actual ROI ROI of 27:1 for 1 of 2 trained workers and ROI of 159:1 for the second trained worker
Organization development program	Insurance	Not provided	Sales people	Forecasted ROI ROI estimates of 11:1 and 16.4:1 for OD performance value contribution resulting from $44,590 OD investment Actual ROI ROI ≥ 8:1

(continued on next page)

TABLE 18.6. *(continued)*

Case Name	Industry Type	HRD Program	Target Audience	Results/ Expected Results
Unstructured and structured on-the-job training case study	Manufac- turing	Task training	Assembly workers	Forecasted ROI ROI estimates of 411:1 for structured OJT for first task ROI estimates of 16:1 for second task ROI estimates of 63:1 for third task Actual ROI ROI ≥ 8:1

Assessing the Financial Benefits of Human Resource Development

Case Name	Industry Type	HRD Program	Target Audience	Results/ Expected Results
Universal healthcare	Health Services	Customer Service	All employees Targeted sale representatives	ROI = 11:1
Major insurance company	Insurance	General communica- tion training Coaching skills	Sales representa- tives Sales managers All employees directly connected with on-the-job appraisals	ROI = 7:1

ASTD In Action Series: Measuring Return on Investment: Volume 1

Case Name	Industry Type	HRD Program	Target Audience	Results/ Expected Results
Penske Truck Leasing Company	Truck leasing	Supervisory skills training	First-level supervisors	6.8% reduction in overtime 16.7% reduction in absenteeism
International Oil Co.	Petroleum	Customer service training	Dispatchers	ROI = 501%
Magnavox Electronic Systems Company	Literacy training	Electronics	Electrical and mechanical assemblers	ROI = 741%
North Country Electric and Gas	Electric and gas utility	Productivity and quality improvement	All supervisors and managers	ROI = 400%
Yellow Freight System	Trucking	Performance management system	Managers	ROI = 115%
Midwest Banking Co.	Banking	Sales training	Consumer loan officers	ROI = 1988%
U.S. Government	Federal government	Supervisory training	New supervisors	ROI = 150%

(continued on next page)

TABLE 18.6. *(continued)*

Case Name	Industry Type	HRD Program	Target Audience	Results/ Expected Results
Coca-Cola Bottling Company of America	Soft drink	Supervisory training	All supervisors	ROI = 1447%
Information Services Inc.	Information services	Interpersonal skills training	All employees	ROI = 336%
Multi-Marques Inc.	Bakery	Work process analysis and training	Administrative supervisors	ROI = 215%
Litton Guidance and Control Systems	Avionics	Self-directed work teams	All employees	ROI = 650%
Financial Services Inc.	Financial services	Selection and training	District Managers	ROI = 2140%
Midwest Automotive Plant	Automotive manufacturing	On-the-job training	Production employees	35% improvement in absenteeism rate 29% reduction in safety violations

ASTD In Action Series: Measuring Return on Investment: Volume 2

Case Name	Industry Type	HRD Program	Target Audience	Results/ Expected Results
Consortium of Companies	Varied	Innovative Training	Team leaders	Internal Rate of Return (IRR) = 35% The training lead to the initiation of team projects while increasing personal skills
Apex Corporation	Business products	Empowerment	Sales representatives	ROI = 2981%
Eastman Chemical Company	Specialty chemicals	Sales training	All employees in the division	ROI = 2307%; Participants exhibited greater teamwork than non-participants Level 2 — exhibited ability to comprehend various ideas and establish action plans Level 3 — giving feedback was most notable
Nortel	Telecommunication	Varied	Finance managers	Posting increased 300% Translation data increased 400% No exact ROI given Reproducible course design process resulted
Commonwealth Edison	Electric Utility	Machine operator training	Varied	ROI range = 57– 327%
Canadian Valve Company	Valve manufacturing	Information technology	Machine operators	ROI = 132%

(continued on next page)

TABLE 18.6. *(continued)*

Case Name	Industry Type	HRD Program	Target Audience	Results/ Expected Results
NYNEX Corporation	Telecom- munications	Telecom- munication managers	Three negotiation skills	ROI = 511%
Texas Instruments	Electronics	Public train- ing and jobs	Managers	ROI = 2827%
First Union National Bank	Banking	Skills	Relationship managers, support team members, and sales managers	ROI = 47.2%
Bell Atlantic	Telecom- munications	Computer- based maintenance training	Maintenance employees	ROI in year 1 = 319% ROI in year 2 = 366% 26% increase in ability to dispatch calls 22% increase in ability to reduce repeat calls assumed positive impact on customer service
Speedy Tele- communications Company	Telecom- munications	Performance management systems	Managers	ROI = 1500%
Global Technology Company	Technical products	Leadership training	New managers	ROI = 160%
Lenscrafters	Specialty retailing	Leadership training	Managers	Employee turnover decreased by 8% Customer satisfaction ratings rose Total and comparative store sales increase from 5–13.3% Earnings reached all time high: 77.2% increase

ASTD In Action Series: Measuring Return on Investment: Volume 3

Case Name	Industry Type	HRD Program	Target Audience	Results/ Expected Results
Cracker Box, Inc.	Restaurant	Performance management training	Managers Manager trainees	Benefits to Cost Ratio (BCR) = 3.98 ROI = 298%

(continued on next page)

TABLE 18.6. *(continued)*

Case Name	Industry Type	HRD Program	Target Audience	Results/ Expected Results
				300% ROI greatly exceeds the 25% target value Other benefits: stress reduction; increased job satisfaction; sense of achievement; improved teamwork; promotions; increased confidence levels
Apple Computer	Computer manufacturer	Process improvement	T&D consultants Executives Operations managers	ROI = 182% (1.82) 76% overall gain between pre and post learning objectives Unit per person per hour increased from 4.27 to 4.48 (5%) and labor efficiency increased from 1.14 to 1.2 (5%) from 60 prior to measurement period to 60 days after intervention implementation
Hewlett-Packard Company	Computer support services	Sales training	Inside sales management team Inside sales representatives	BCR = 2.95 ROI = 195% Intangible benefits: increase confidence; high retention rate of inside sales reps in comparison to industry average; improved teamwork; recognition by 2 leading analyst companies as #1 computing support service; increased sales capacity; reduced sales costs
First Union National Bank	Financial services	Sales training	Sales representatives	Forecasted ROI = 555% Actual ROI = 932%

(continued on next page)

TABLE 18.6. *(continued)*

Case Name	Industry Type	HRD Program	Target Audience	Results/ Expected Results
			Sales managers	Referrals increased from 12 to 25 in first 2 weeks after the program Income was 65% of annual forecast 160 days after the program Calls from relation managers and CMG product specialists increased 70%
Focus Corporation	Computer manufacturer	Process improvement	Production managers Production employees	Quality increased from 94 to 99.5% Productivity increased 28% Actual factory ROI was 310% (if state reimbursement excluded, ROI = 190%) Combined factory and field ROI = 570% when considering that the company had fewer service calls and returns for repair
Global Automotive Corporation	Automotive manufacturing	Sales launch training	Sales representatives all employees	BC Ratio = 1.923 Retail distributor ROI = 325%
Slick Manufacturing	Manufacturing	Computer training	Managers	ROI = 125% Elimination of overtime, customer loss and complaints
Nassau County Police Department	Police department	Interpersonal skill training	Office manager Police officers	Overall rating of group – 88% satisfaction vs. 96% satisfaction of all other Dale Carnegie training graduates (170,000) ROI = 144%
Miami VA Medical Center	Health care	Self-mastery training	All employees	ROI = 3%
Retail Merchandise Company	Retail stores	Interactive selling skill	Sales associates	BCR = 2.18 ROI = 118%

(continued on next page)

TABLE 18.6. *(continued)*

Case Name	Industry Type	HRD Program	Target Audience	Results/ Expected Results
		training	Sales managers	15% increase in sales Improved customer service and image as well as teamwork while increasing employee confidence and job satisfaction

In Action: Measuring Learning and Performance

Case Name	Industry Type	HRD Program	Target Audience	Results/ Expected Results
The Franklin Covey Company	Training provider	Management training	Manager Evaluation specialist	ROI of 809%
AT&T	Telecom- munication	Executive education	Evaluation specialist	Company sponsored internal and external executive education programs demonstrated significant behavior changes and ROI. External programs ROI = 998% Internal programs ROI = 1592%

ASTD In Action Series: Costing, Monitoring, and Managing Employee Turnover

Case Name	Industry Type	HRD Program	Target Audience	Results/ Expected Results
National Telemarketing Co.	Tele- marketing	Employee socialization	Newly hired HRD interviewers	Currently in implemen- tation stage: Company expects higher employee commitment and reduced turnover in position
Cellco	Telecom- munication	Management development plans	Long-term employees	20% decrease in turnover 10% increase in job satisfaction cost savings of $7 million
Capital One	Financial services	Employee benefits	All employees	.4% reduction in attrition increased performance and attendance

TABLE 18.7. Does Employee Development Pay Off?

Data Source	Core Conclusion from Data
ASTD industry reports	Training and Development can change job behaviors and overall job performance.
Academic studies	Development should be a central part of HR strategy and HR strategy is a major determinant of organizational performance.
Program results	Assessment case studies Development programs, when properly executed, can yield very high return on investments and improved performance.

Where Does It All End?

Where does it all end? It doesn't.

Training and development is by nature a cyclic thing: a problem requires solutions, which bring progress, which brings growth, which brings problems, which engender solutions, which bring growth, which brings . . . .

These inevitable phases of the T&D cycle are like the seasons: They cause each other, yet each in itself is an exciting, worthy experience.

If our look at the training and development function has seemed to be an endless succession of goals, standards, and problems; of objectives, learning, and feedback; of growth, stimulus, and response—well, that's correct! That's what T&D is all about. That's the relentlessness of it. That's the wonder of it!

If an organization has no mission, it has no reason for existing. If it has no standards, it has no way of knowing how to achieve its mission. But its standards won't always be met; there will be performance problems.

The job of T&D is to find solutions to performance problems. Now, solutions mean change, and change means new problems—just as new technology, new employees, new frontiers mean new problems. Perhaps it will all fit together into one concrete, constructive cycle if we "put it all together" this way:

- Organizations become established because someone finds a mission that cannot be achieved by one person working alone.
- Some output (product or service) is defined, but it is unattainable through the efforts of just one person.
- Distinct tasks are identified for the people needed to produce the product or service.
- Standards are set for each task. These standards involve units of work, time, and materials. These standards also involve levels of excellence—how the tasks must be performed to maintain an acceptable product or service.

So an organization is born, and it takes people, technology, time, and material. Let's summarize the process in pictorial form (Figure 19.1). That thin horizontal line at the center of the chart shows why training and development is a continuous activity. Remember how people have always said that a woman's work is never done? Well, in one sense, the T&D manager is like that—the behavioral housekeeper of the organization. And the work is never done!

That fact of life can be burdensome—the source of despair, of a sense of endlessness.

It can also be a joyous, encouraging thing—a security blanket. It means that there will always be full employment for T&D managers who stay aware of the goals of their organizations and sensitive to the performances of the people who make those organizations successful.

Adding zest and dimension to the business of being in the "change business" is that exciting volume of change that's going on within the "change business"! Growth is all about the T&D staff! Their mission involves producing growth in people and in organizations; their vitality and usefulness depend upon continuous growth in themselves.

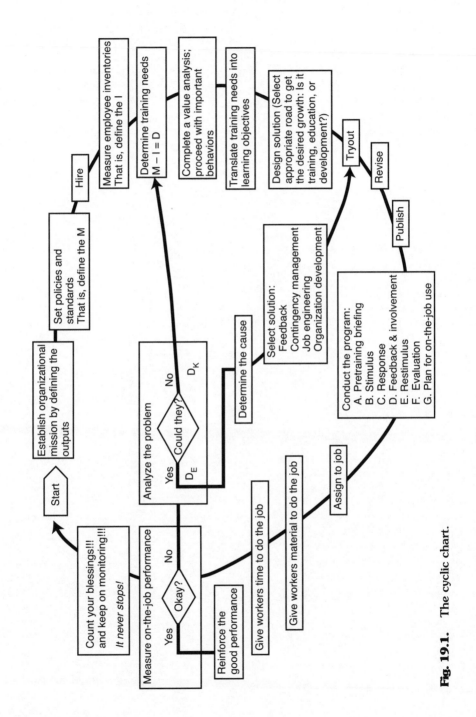

Fig. 19.1. The cyclic chart.

References

Alliger, G. M., and E. A. Janak. "Kirkpatricks's Levels of Training Criteria: Thirty Years Later." *Personnel Psychology* 42 (1989): 331–340.

Alliger, G. M., S. I. Tannenbaum, W. Bennet, H. Traver, and A. Shotland. "A Meta-Analysis of the Relations Among Training Criteria." *Personnel Psychology* 50 (1997): 341–358.

Argyris, C. *Reasoning, Learning and Action.* San Francisco: Jossey-Bass, 1982.

Arthur, J. B. "Effects of Human Resource Systems on Manufacturing Performance and Turnover." *Academy of Management Journal* 37 (1994): 670–687.

————. "The Link Between Business Strategy and Industrial Relations Systems in American Steel Mini-Mills." *Industrial and Labor Relations Review* 45 (1992): 488–506.

Baldwin, T., and J. K. Ford. "Transfer of Training: A Review and Directions for Future Research." *Personnel Psychology* 41 (1988): 63–105.

Bandura, Albert. *Social Learning Theory.* Englewood Cliffs, N.J.: Prentice-Hall, 1977.

Bartel, A. P. "Productivity Gains from the Implementation of Employee Training Programs." *Industrial Relations* (1994).

Bassi, L., and A. Ahlstrand. *The 2000 ASTD Learning Outcomes Report.* Alexandria, Va.: American Society for Training and Development, 2000.

Blake, Robert R., and J. S. Mouton. *The Managerial Grid.* Houston, Tex.: Gulf, 1964.

Bloom, Benjamin, ed. *Taxonomy of Educational Objectives: The Cognitive Domain.* New York: David McKay, 1956, 1964.

Boone, E. J. *Developing Programs in Adult Education.* Englewood Cliffs, N.J.: Prentice-Hall, 1985.

Broad, M. L. "Managing the Organizational Learning Transfer System: A Model and Case Study." In *Improving Learning Transfer in Organizations,* edited by E. F. Holton III and T. T. Baldwin. San Francisco: Jossey-Bass, in press.

Broad, M. L., and J. W. Newstrom. *Transfer of Training: Action-Packed Strategies to Ensure High Payoff from Training Investments.* New York: Addison-Wesley, 1992.

Brookfield, S. D. *Developing Critical Thinkers: Challenging Adults to Explore Alternative Ways of Thinking and Acting.* San Francisco: Jossey-Bass, 1987.

_____. *Understanding and Facilitating Adult Learning.* San Francisco: Jossey-Bass, 1986.

Bruner, J. *The Process of Education.* Cambridge, Mass.: Harvard University Press, 1960.

Buhler, C. "Basic Theoretical Concepts in Humanistic Psychology." *American Psychologist* 26 (1971): 378–386.

Burke, M. J., and R. R. Day. "A Cumulative Study of the Effectiveness of Managerial Training." *Personnel Psychology* 71 (1986): 232–245.

Delaney, J. T., and M. A. Huselid. "The Impact of Human Resource Management Practices on Perceptions of Organizational Performance." *Academy of Management Journal* 39 (1996): 949–969.

Dirkx, J. M., and S. M. Prenger. *A Guide for Planning and Implementing Instruction for Adults: A Theme-Based Approach.* San Francisco: Jossey-Bass, 1997.

Ford, J. K., and D. A. Weissbein. "Transfer of Training: An Update Review and Analysis." *Performance Improvement Quarterly* 10 (1997): 22–41.

Friere, P. *Pedagogy of the Oppressed.* New York: Herder & Herder, 1970.

Gagné, R. M., and W. W. Wager. *Principles of Instructional Design.* New York: Harcourt Brace Jovanovich, 1992.

Gronlund, Norman. *Assessment of Student Achievement.* 7th ed. Boston: Allyn and Bacon, 2002.

Guzzo, R. A., R. D. Jette, and R. A. Katzell. "The Effects of Psychologically Based Intervention Programs on Worker Productivity: A Meta-Analysis." *Personnel Psychology* 38 (1985): 275–291.

Hodges, T., ed. *In Action: Measuring Learning and Performance.* Alexandria, Va.: American Society for Training and Development, 1999.

Holton, E. F. III. "New Employee Development: A Review and Reconceptualization." *Human Resource Development Quarterly* 7 (1996): 233–252.

_____. "What's Really Wrong: Diagnosis for Learning Transfer System Change." In *Advances in Developing Human Resources,* edited by Elwood F. Holton III, T. T. Baldwin, and S. S. Naquin. Managing and Changing Learning Transfer Systems, vol. 2, no. 4. Thousand Oaks, Calif.: Sage Publications, 2000.

Holton, Elwood F. III, R. A. Bates, and W. E. A. Ruona. "Development of a Generalized Learning Transfer System Inventory." *Human Resource Development Quarterly* 11 (2000): 333–360.

Holton, E. F. III, and T. T. Baldwin. "Making Transfer Happen: An Action Perspective on Learning Transfer Systems." In *Improving Learning Transfer in Organizations,* edited by E. F. Holton III and T. T. Baldwin. San Francisco: Jossey-Bass, in press.

Houle, Cyril O. *The Design of Education.* San Francisco: Jossey-Bass, 1972.

Huselid, M. A., "The Impact of Human Resource Management Practices on Turnover, Productivity, and Corporate Financial Performance." *Academy of Management Journal* 38 (1997): 635–672.

Kalleberg, A. L., D. Knoke, P. V. Marsden, and J. L. Spaeth. *Organizations in America: Analyzing Their Structures and Human Resource Practices* (Thousand Oaks, Calif.: Sage Publications, 1996).

Kidd, J. R. *How Adults Learn.* Englewood Cliffs, N.J.: Prentice-Hall, 1978.

Kirkpatrick, D. L. "Techniques for Evaluating Training Programs: Part 1—Reactions." *Journal of the American Society for Training and Development* 13, no. 11 (1959a): 3–9.

_____. "Techniques for Evaluating Training Programs: Part 2—Learning." *Journal of the American Society for Training and Development* 13, no. 12 (1959b): 21–26.

_____. "Techniques for Evaluating Training Programs: Part 3—Behavior." *Journal of the American Society for Training and Development* 14, no. 1 (1960a): 13–18.

_____. "Techniques for Evaluating Training Programs: Part 4—Results." *Journal of the American Society for Training and Development* 14, no. 2 (1960b): 28–32.

_____. *Evaluating Training Programs: The Four Levels.* 2d ed. San Francisco: Berrett-Koehler, 1998.

Knowles, Malcolm. *Designs for Adult Learning.* Alexandria, Va.: American Society for Training and Development, 1995.

_____. *The Adult Education Movement in the United States.* 2d ed. Huntington, N.Y.: Krieger Publishing Co., 1973.

Knowles, M., E. F. Holton III, and R. A. Swanson. *The Adult Learner: The Definitive Classic for Adult Education and Human Resource Development.* Woburn, Mass.: Butterworth-Heineman, 1998.

Knox, A. B. *Helping Adults Learn.* San Francisco: Jossey-Bass, 1986.

Kolb, D. A. *Experiential Learning: Experience As the Source of Learning and Development.* Englewood Cliffs, N.J.: Prentice-Hall, 1984.

Laird, Dugan. *Approaches to Training and Development.* 2d ed. Reading, Mass.: Perseus Books, 1985.

Lam, L. W., and L. P. White. "Human Resource Orientation and Corporate Performance." *Human Resource Development Quarterly* 9 (1998): 351–364.

Lau, R., and B. May. "A Win-Win Paradigm for Quality of Work Life and Business Performance." *Human Resource Development Quarterly* 9 (1998): 211–226.

Lewin, K. *Field Theory in Social Science; Selected Theoretical Papers.* Edited by D. Cartwright. New York: Harper & Row, 1951.

Mager, Robert F., *Preparing Instructional Objectives.* 2d ed. Belmont, Calif.: Fearon, 1962, 1975, 1976, 1984.

McKeachie, Wilbert J. *Teaching Tips: A Guidebook for the Beginning College Teacher.* Lexington, Mass.: D. C. Health, 1969.

McLagan, Patricia A. 1978. *Helping Others Learn.* Reading, Mass.: Addison-Wesley.

_____. 1983. *Models for Excellence.* Washington, D.C.: American Society for Training and Development (ASTD).

Merriam, S. B., and R. S. Cafferella. *Learning in Adulthood: A Comprehensive Guide.* San Fransisco: Jossey-Bass, 1999.

Mezirow, J. *Transformative Dimensions of Adult Learning.* San Francisco: Jossey-Bass, 1991.

Nadler, Leonard. *Developing Human Resources.* Houston, Tex.: Gulf, 1970 (supported by the National Society for Training and Development).

Nadler, L., and Z. Nadler. *Developing Human Resources.* 3d ed. San Francisco: Jossey-Bass, 1989.

Noe, R. A., and N. Schmitt. "The Influence of Trainee Attitudes on Training Effectiveness: Test of a Model." *Personnel Psychology* 39 (1986): 497–523.

Ormond, J. E. *Human Learning.* 3d ed. Upper Saddle, N.J.: Merrill/Prentice-Hall, 1999.

Phillips, J. J. *In Action: Measuring Return on Investment.* Vol. 1. Alexandria, Va.: American Society for Training and Development, 1994.

_____. *In Action: Measuring Return on Investment.* Vol. 2. Alexandria, Va.: American Society for Training and Development, 1997.

_____. *In Action: Measuring Return on Investment.* Vol. 3. Alexandria, Va.: American Society for Training and Development, 2001.

Piaget, Jean. *Science of Education and the Psychology of the Child.* New York: Viking, 1970.

Rogers, Carl R. *Freedom to Learn.* Columbus, Ohio: Charles E. Merrill, 1969.

Rouillier, J. Z., and I. L. Goldstein. "The Relationship Between Organizational Transfer Climate and Positive Transfer of Training." *Human Resource Development Quarterly* 4 (1993): 377–390.

Rummerlhart, D. E., and D. A. Norman. "Accretion, Tuning, and Restructuring: Three Models of Learning." In *Semantic Factors of Cognition,* edited by J. W. Cotton and R. Klatzky. Hillside, N.J.: Erlbaum, 1978.

Rummler, G. A., and A. P. Brach. *Improving Performance: How to Manage the White Space on the Organization Chart.* 2d ed. San Francisco: Jossey-Bass, 1995.

Russell, J. S., J. R. Terborg, and M. L. Powers. "Organizational Performance and Organization Level Training and Support." *Personnel Psychology* 38 (1985): 849–863.

Schrock, S., Coscarelli, W. and Eyres, P., *Criterion-Referenced Test Development.* 2d ed. Alexandria, Va.: International Society for Performance Improvement, 2000.

Skinner, B. F. *About Behaviorism.* New York: Alfred A. Knopf, 1974.

_____. *The Technology of Teaching.* New York: Appleton-Century-Crofts, 1968.

Swanson, Richard A. "Demonstrating the Financial Benefit of Human Resource Development: Status and Update on the Theory and Practice." *Human Resource Development Quarterly* 9 (1998): 285–295.

_____. Assessing *the Financial Benefits of Human Resource Development,* Cambridge, Mass.: Perseus Publishing, 2001.

Swanson, Richard A. *Analysis for Improving Performance: Tools for Diagnosing Organizations & Documenting Workplace Expertise.* San Francisco: Berrett-Koehler, 1996.

Swanson, R. A., and E. F. Holton III. *Foundations of Human Resource Development.* San Francisco: Berrett-Koehler, 2001.

_____. *Results: How to Measure Performance, Learning, and Satisfaction and Satisfaction Outcomes in Organizations.* San Francisco: Berrett-Koehler, 1999.

Tiger, Lionel, and Robin Fox. *The Imperial Animal.* New York: Holt, Rinehart, and Winston, 1971.

Training Magazine (October 2002). Minneapolis, Minn.: Lakewood Research.

Twitchell, S., Elwood F. Holton III, and J. Trott. "Technical Training Evaluation Practices in the United States." *Performance Improvement Quarterly* (2000).

Wallace, S. R. Jr., and C. M. Twitchell. "Evaluation of a Training Course for Life Insurance Agents." *Personnel Psychology* 6, no. 1 (1953): 25–43.

Warren, Malcolm W. *Training for Results.* Reading, Mass.: Addison-Wesley, 1969.

Welbourne, T. M., and A. O. Andrews. "Predicting the Performance of Initial Public Offerings: Should Human Resource Management Be in the Equation?" *Academy of Management Journal* 39 (1996): 891–919.

Whetten, David A., and Kim S. Cameron. *Developing Management Skills.* 4th ed. Reading, Mass.: Addison-Wesley Longman, 1998.

Youndt, M. A., S. A. Snell, J. W. Dean Jr., and D. P. Lepak. "Human Resource Management, Manufacturing Strategy, and Firm Performance." *Academy of Management Journal* 39 (1996): 836–866.

Index